INDIA'S QUEST FOR SECURITY

DEFENCE POLICIES, 1947–1965

INDIA'S QUEST FOR SECURITY: Defence Policies, 1947–1965

LORNE J. KAVIC

Berkeley and Los Angeles 1967
UNIVERSITY OF CALIFORNIA PRESS

University of California Press
Berkeley and Los Angeles, California
Cambridge University Press
London, England
Copyright © 1967, by
The Regents of the University of California
Library of Congress Catalog Card Number: 67-16788

MAPS BY ADRIENNE MORGAN

To Eileen, Lurliene, Sandra, and Michael

ACKNOWLEDGMENTS

For this study, I am indebted to many organizations and individuals. The Australian Commonwealth Scholarship Committee and the Australian National University provided the opportunity for research during a period of three years in Australia and a visit of several months in India and Pakistan.

I wish to record my appreciation to the staffs of the R. G. Menzies Library at the Australian National University, the Australian National Library, the Australian War Memorial, and Sapru House, New Delhi, for their assistance in providing required materials.

I am thankful to those many individuals who interrupted their busy schedules to discuss various aspects of the subject with me, but whose identities I cannot disclose. I should also like to express my gratitude for the hospitality extended to me in New Delhi and Karachi by Bill and Julie Montgomery and Dick Seaborn.

To Dr. T. B. Millar of the Department of International Relations, Institute of Advanced Studies, at the Australian National University, I am indebted for his constructive suggestions throughout the preparation of this book and for his patience and encouragement.

CONTENTS

INTRODUCTION 1

One THE DEFENCE POLICY OF BRITISH INDIA, 1858–1947 8

Two THE ORIGINS, BASES, AND AIMS OF INDIAN DEFENCE POLICY 21

Three HIMALAYAN POLICY, 1947–1958 46

Four HIMALAYAN POLICY, 1959–1961 62

Five THE INDIAN ARMY, 1947–1962 82

Six THE INDIAN AIR FORCE, 1947–1962 102

Seven THE INDIAN NAVY, 1947–1962 116

Eight DEFENCE PRODUCTION, 1947–1962 126

Nine CIVILIAN–MILITARY RELATIONS, 1947–1962 141

Ten HIMALAYAN CONFLICT, 1962–1965 169

Eleven THE NEW INDIAN DEFENCE PROGRAMME 192

CONCLUSIONS 208

APPENDIXES 219

SELECTIVE BIBLIOGRAPHY 247

INDEX 253

MAPS 265

(Maps have not been included in copies distributed in India because of circumstances beyond the publisher's control.)

Negotiate from strength, not from weakness, else you will find yourself negotiating first at some one else's expense—which is dirty—and then at your own—which is disastrous.

                LORD VANSITTART

ABBREVIATIONS USED IN NOTES

CAD	Constituent Assembly Debates
ICWA	Indian Council of World Affairs
INC	Indian National Congress
LAD	Legislative Assembly Debates
LSD	Lok Sabha Debates
RUSI Journal	Royal United Services Institution Journal
USI Journal	United Services Institution Journal

INTRODUCTION

Two of the unshakeable realities of international politics are the primacy of national self-interest and the importance of military power as a factor in international relations. No government, however pacific-minded, has ever been able to rely solely upon the political ethics of other states or upon its own diplomacy to deter direct attack or interference with its external interests. Armies have, therefore, been a feature of every state in recorded history.

Total security has rarely been possible even for the most powerful of nations, and the basic dilemma of defence policy—how to achieve maximum security with minimum expenditure on the armed forces—has never allowed of a simple solution. Every contingency cannot be provided for, and strategy, like politics—to which it is closely bound—is always a choice between alternatives. A nation's quest for security can never be conducted heedless of the antagonisms which that search may provoke among other powers or among its own people. There must always be a considered relationship between commitments and power and between power and resources. There must also be a willingness to employ such forms of power as may be required to preserve vital interests, of which the most basic is usually considered to be the territorial integrity and political independence of the state. The essence of a sound national security policy is for government to define the nation's vital interests and to develop sufficient power, alone or in concert with others, to secure those interests.

How did the government of India approach the issues of national security during the first two decades of the country's existence as an independent state? What was its conception of the national interest? From what sources did it perceive of possible hostile action, and in what fashion? What precautions did it take against the various contingencies of conflict? Although some time has passed since the humiliation inflicted by Chinese military forces, the manner in which the Nehru administration sought to secure India against attack is still subject to extensive speculation, largely unsupported by factual evidence.

The public postures of the Indian government during the period are well known as a result of keen international interest in Indian affairs and the ambitious diplomacy which characterised Jawaharlal Nehru's tenure of office as Prime Minister of the Indian Union. His government professed to see no threat to India from the Communist bloc.[1] New Delhi fostered, with considerable success, the attitude that Indian policy represented a fresh approach to interstate relations, in which moral force was superior to physical force. Nehru claimed in 1960 that India's policy was rooted in a line of thinking which was wholly opposed to the purely military line of thinking.[2] Nonalignment, peaceful coexistence, disarmament, and the peaceful settlement of disputes were put forward as the 'Indian formula' for world peace.

In practice, however, was New Delhi immune from the very fears and neuroses it suspected and condemned in others? Did the Indian government pursue policies distinct from the traditional approach in which, though moral considerations or means are not ruled out, power is viewed as the principal means for achieving the nation's ends? Various statements made by Nehru and the more significant actions taken by his administration suggest that there was nothing particularly unique in the manner in which a sovereign India moved

---

[1] The Deputy Prime Minister and strong anti-Communist, Vallabhbhai Patel, declared in 1948 that no foreign country would dare attack India. *Hindustan Times*, 6 December 1948. Nehru informed Trygve Lie in Paris on 18 January 1951 that he 'was not concerned about the security of his country'. Trygve Lie, *In the Cause of Peace* (New York: Macmillan, 1954), pp. 360-362. In 1953, the Indian Prime Minister purported to see no threat to India from external Communism or any other source. Remark on a B.B.C. interview, 12 June 1953, cited in J. C. Kundra, *Indian Foreign Policy 1947-1954: A Study of Relations with the Western Bloc* (Groningen: J. B. Wolters, 1955), p. 69n. Writing under a pseudonym in 1954, Sir Narayana Raghavan Pillai, a high-ranking official of the External Affairs Ministry, expressed the view, with regard to Western warnings about the Communist threat, that 'We may be stupid or completely blind but where we do not see the menace we cannot pretend to do so, merely because we are so advised by no doubt wiser people'. 'P', 'Middle Ground Between Russia and America: An Indian view', *Foreign Affairs* (January 1954), p. 261.

[2] Speech to the Bangalore session of the Indian National Congress at Sadasivanagar, 17 January 1960. Jawaharlal Nehru, *Speeches, 1953-1957* (New Delhi: Publications Division, GOI, 1958), pp. 266-267.

among world realities to seek the achievement of the national interests.

While New Delhi fostered the attitude that India's approach to external issues was based upon higher ideals than those that motivated other governments, Nehru admitted that 'every country's foreign policy, first of all, is concerned with its own security'.[3] The Gandhian creed of nonviolence was eulogised but, as the Indian Prime Minister declared in the Lok Sabha (Lower House) on 15 February 1956: 'I am not aware of our government having ever said that they adopted the doctrine of Ahimsa [non-violence] to our activities. They may respect it, they may honour that doctrine, but as a government it is patent that we do not consider ourselves capable of adopting the doctrine of Ahimsa'.[4] Defending the virtues of a friendly approach to relations with other countries, Nehru nonetheless cautioned the Lok Sabha on 8 December 1959: 'To that friendly approach must necessarily be allied the watchful, the vigilant approach and a "preparations approach" '. Although consistently arguing the need for countries to approach one another with less distrust, Nehru conceded in the Rajya Sabha (Upper House) on the following day that 'no country finally puts its trust in any other country . . . in the ultimate analysis they have always to keep a loop-hole in their minds that the other party will not play up or that other things may happen or national interests may come into play'.

While urging other states to resolve disputes through negotiation, the Nehru administration resorted to force on a number of occasions to obtain its goals. The princely states of Junagadh and Hyderabad were coerced into the Union, army and police units were despatched to aid the legally constituted authorities in the strategic hill states of Sikkim and Nepal against disaffected elements, and military campaigns were waged against unruly tribesmen and Pakistani regulars in Kashmir, against the Portuguese in Goa, and ultimately against the Chinese in the North-East Frontier Agency and Ladakh. Naga demands for self-determination were rejected, and a force which eventually comprised some 30,000 troops and police was deployed in Nagaland to deal with the dissident tribesmen. India provided an infantry battalion for the United Nations peace-keeping force in the Gaza strip in 1956. Her infantry brigade in the former Belgian Congo in 1961 spearheaded a United Nations action aimed at

[3] *LSD*, pt. 2, vol. 23 (8 December 1958), col. 3959.
[4] *Ibid.*, pt. 2, vol. 1 (15 February 1956), cols. 814–815.

crushing the secessionist Katanga government of Moishe Tshombe.

While lecturing the great powers on the evils of the armaments race, the Indian government during the period from 1947 to 1962 expended on defence a sum exceeding Rs 3,000 crores (about $6,300 million),[5] or between 21 and 46 per cent of the current expenditure of the Indian government. Nehru claimed as late as 1963 that his government's preoccupation with internal problems of poverty and illiteracy had made it content to assign a relatively low priority to defence requirements in the conventional sense;[6] by 1962, however, India possessed the largest navy and air force of any country in the Indian Ocean region and one of the largest standing armies in the world.

The *raison d'être* of this defence programme was never made clear by the government, on the grounds that it was not considered to be in the national interest to reveal information about such matters. The Indian public and press were, in any case, generally apathetic, and Parliament consistently passed by unanimous vote whatever defence estimates were placed before it. The annual debate on the defence grants has aptly been described as the 'duet of the deaf'[7] and as 'an elegant or inelegant repetition . . . spiced with Opposition criticisms, interspersed with sallies and enlivened occasionally by an odd fresh incident, such as the buying of MIGs or appointment of the chief of staff'.[8] In the 1962 debate on the defence grants, held at a time of national concern with Himalayan developments, an opposition motion censuring the government 'for failure to effectively guard the land frontiers of India and preserve inviolate India's territorial integrity' was defeated by 185 votes to 35. The vote evidenced rather sharply that only slightly more than one-third of the members of the House were sufficiently interested in the disposition of over one-quarter of the budget to appear to record their judgement. Commenting on the vote, the military correspondent of a leading Indian newspaper concluded that 'after this one discovers not that defence is such a miserably dull topic, but that how few men in democracy [that is, the Indian Cabinet] could indeed have such tremendous power'.[9]

[5] For a partial breakdown of central revenues and expenditures for the 1950–60 period, and for a comparison between Indian defence expenditures and that of selected countries for the 1957–59 period, see Appendix I. For a breakdown of Indian defence expenditures, see Appendix II.

[6] 'Changing India', *Foreign Affairs*, 41:3 (April 1963), p. 459.

[7] *Hindu Weekly Review*, 23 March 1959.

[8] Military correspondent in the *Indian Express*, 9 June 1962.

[9] *Ibid.*

In the absence of any useful official explanation for the Indian military programme, the popular view was to attribute much of the expenditure (at least up to late 1959) to the existence of strained relations with Pakistan.[10] As the Indian weekly, *Thought*, stated in 1955, the Indian government and people both looked upon Pakistan as King Charles' head, and 'No amount of expense and effort is, therefore, regarded as too much if that helps maintain the superiority we have hitherto enjoyed and apparently still enjoy over Pakistan . . .'[11] Pakistan's receipt of United States military aid from 1954 onwards was thus widely viewed both inside and outside India as provoking significant increases in Indian defence expenditures.[12]

With the notable exception of V. K. Krishna Menon—whose political appeal in India was largely built upon an extreme anti-Pakistani stance—Indian government leaders did not openly encourage this viewpoint, but neither did they discourage it. In retrospect, however, Nehru claimed in the Rajya Sabha on 9 November 1962 that his government had, from the entry of the Chinese into Tibet in 1950–51, been engaged in developing a war machine for the 'inevitable' confrontation with China. Does the evidence bear out Nehru's contention of a considered and long-term response to the Chinese threat, faulty only in timing? What was the actual relative influence of Pakistani and Chinese postures on Indian defence planning? Was the contingency of an East–West conflict and India's possible involvement completely ignored? To what extent was the defence posture of an independent India—and particularly its Himalayan policy—merely a continuation of former British policy?

Any study of Indian defence and foreign policy must also include

---

[10] In 1951, Maurice Zinkin expressed the view that the prevailing level of defence expenditure might drop by £45 million (about $126 million) once the Kashmir issue was settled. *Asia and the West* (London: Chatto and Windus, 1951), p. 240. Lord Birdwood wrote in 1952 that 'at least half' the 'abnormal' defence outlay of both India and Pakistan could be related to the Kashmir issue. 'The Need for Agreement in the Indian Sub-Continent', *Asiatic Review*, 48:173 (January 1952), p. 7. Selig Harrison wrote in 1959 that responsible officials of both the Indian and Pakistani governments privately admitted that, if it were not for Indo-Pakistani tension, the two standing armies could be reduced by as much as one-third. *New Republic*, 7 September 1959, p. 13.

[11] 1 June 1955, p. 1.

[12] See, for example, the *Eastern Economist*, 30 December 1955 and 13 March 1959; the *Sydney Morning Herald*, 13 February 1956; M. A. Fitzsimons, 'British Foreign Policy and Southern and Far Eastern Asia', *Review of Politics*, 24 (1962), p. 133.

a discussion of the manner in which policy was formulated, particularly in view of Nehru's death in early 1964. Although no exhaustive examination has yet appeared of the process by which these policies were made during the 1947–62 period, the evidence would seem to bear out the opinion of Nehru's biographer, Michael Brecher, that the Indian Prime Minister was the 'philosopher, the architect, the engineer and the voice of his country's policy towards the outside world'.[18] To what extent did Indian defence and foreign policy reflect Nehru's personal hopes, fears, and predelictions —feelings not necessarily shared to the same degree, if at all, by those who now exercise power in India? What was the nature of the military contribution to policy, and of the relationship between the civil and military branches of government? A discussion of these and related questions will permit some assessment of the future trends of Indian defence policy.

Lastly, it is important to study the nature of India's reactions to the traumatic experience of the border conflict with China in October–November 1962 and the minor 'war' with Pakistan in late 1965. What recent official assessment has been made of the Chinese and Pakistani threats? Concern is being expressed in official Indian circles about Sino-Pakistani collusion against India, but is military policy being formulated on this premise? What is the significance of India's five-year defence programme, and how has it been affected by the 'war' with Pakistan and the cessation of Western 'lethal' military aid to both India and Pakistan pending some sort of Indo-Pakistani rapprochement? Has the policy-making process in India become unduly weighted in favour of extreme chauvinism, as Pakistan professes to fear, or in favour of a military establishment in excess of current needs and national capabilities, as many Western observers have suggested?

---

[18] Michael Brecher, *India's Foreign Policy: An Interpretation* (New York: Institute of Pacific Relations, 1957), p. 9. A former High Commissioner for Canada in India, Escott Reid, wrote in a despatch in 1957 that 'For the people of India, he [Nehru] is George Washington, Lincoln, Roosevelt and Eisenhower rolled into one . . . He is king as well as prophet and priest, for he is the symbol of the unity of India; he is the spokesman of India, the head of its government. Sometimes he behaves as if he were also the leader of the opposition'. 'Nehru: An Assessment in 1957', *International Journal* (Summer 1964), p. 279. For similar views, see 'Vivek', *India Without Illusions* (Bombay: New Book Company, 1953), pp. 95 and 116; Frank Moraes, *India Today* (New York: Macmillan, 1960), p. 217.

INTRODUCTION

The purpose of this study is to contribute at least partial answers to the many questions associated with Indian defence since 1947. A historical background is provided by a review of the defence policy of British India during the 1858–1947 period. Succeeding chapters deal with the bases and aims of the Nehru government's defence policy; the elaboration of policy as conditioned by the country's resources and the thinking of its leaders; the fate of policy as reflected by the response of China and other countries and by the Indian people; and the future.

The material used in this book has been collected from diverse sources, including the written works and published speeches of Nehru, Indian Parliamentary debates, the annual reports of the Ministries of Defence and External Affairs, and the White Papers on Sino-Indian relations for the period from 1954–62. Substantial reliance, however, has been placed upon press items, military and technical journals, and personal interviews with serving and retired officers and officials—both Indian and non-Indian—who have understandably insisted upon remaining anonymous.

Chapter One

THE DEFENCE POLICY OF BRITISH INDIA, 1858–1947

The period of Crown rule in India extended from Queen Victoria's Royal Proclamation on 1 November 1858 to the formal withdrawal of British authority from the subcontinent on 15 August 1947. During this era, the Indian peoples lived united under one paramount rule and in unexampled security from internal disorder and external aggression. The price of such security imposed a considerable burden on India's meagre financial resources [1] but must necessarily be viewed with reference to the chaotic state of pre-British India and the turmoil which afflicted other parts of the world during the 1858–1947 period.

BASIC PRINCIPLES

This noteworthy achievement was effected by a government headed by Englishmen and subordinate to the ultimate dictates of Britain in all spheres of administration. Despite the primacy of imperial considerations, however, the policies of the British rulers of India were based upon what were considered to be the best interests of the Indian peoples. The interdependence of India and Britain in defence was a basic premise of policy, and the British government was under a constant liability to reinforce India with troops in the event of an emergency; at the same time, India was responsible for reciprocal action in times of imperial need, conditional on the situation prevailing within India and on its frontiers. Where troops were drawn from India to protect British interests in other parts of the world (interests from which India could not

---

[1] Defence expenditure rose from Rs 16.7 crores (1857–58) to Rs 54.3 crores (1930–31) while dropping during the same period, as a percentage of net expenditure, from 47.7 to 23.5 per cent. See Appendix III for the outlay on defence for selected years from 1891 to 1950.

divorce itself), their transportation and maintenance was usually a charge on the Home Exchequer because of the limitations of Indian financial resources.

The foreign policy of the British rulers of India was directed towards securing the alliance, integrity, or neutralisation of the borderlands and minor states covering the land approaches to the Indian empire. The system which resulted from these efforts came to be known as the 'ring fence' and comprised two more or less concentric circles. The 'inner ring' consisted of the Himalayan kingdoms of Nepal, Bhutan, and Sikkim and the tribal areas in north and northeast Assam and on the northwest frontier. The 'outer ring' consisted of the Persian Gulf sheikhdoms and of Persia, Afghanistan, Tibet, and Siam. The 'inner ring' was gradually brought under varying forms of control,[2] while intensive diplomatic activity, backed by the threat or use of force, denied a foothold in any of the 'buffer' states in the 'outer ring' to a major power without compensatory advantage.

The success with which the 'ring fence' was maintained during a century of intense rivalries among the great powers, including two destructive global conflicts, was due to a number of factors. Great power rivalries, skilful British manipulation of the balance of power, and British naval domination of the Indian Ocean minimised the possibility of a serious major threat to India. The situation was enchanced by the major powers' internal preoccupations or more vital interests in other parts of the globe, and by the weakness of the small states immediately beyond India's frontiers. Nonetheless, those responsible for Indian defence could not ignore the possibility of external and internal threats to their authority and domains.

The diversity of the Indian peoples posed a constant threat to internal security. Half-civilised and militant tribes in the northwest and northeast were a serious and continuing danger to the settled areas and to the tranquillity of India generally. The tribal problem on the northwest frontier was closely bound up with the disposition of power in Afghanistan and the attitudes of that country's leaders towards British rule in India. Afghanistan itself occupied a position of great strategic significance astride the traditional invasion routes linking Central Asia with the northern plains of India, and its

[2] In view of its relevance to the post-1947 period, the policy pursued by the British Indian government in the Himalayan region has been briefly reviewed in Appendix IV.

existence as an independent state was a *sine qua non* of Indian security. Thus the major preoccupation of the defence planners of British India was the security of the northwest frontier against the recurring hostility of the fanatical tribals and possible hostile actions by Afghanistan and Russia.

At the time of the transfer of India to the direct control of the Crown in 1858, the Russian threat seemed distant beyond the intervening khanates of Central Asia, and the tribals and Afghanistan were quiescent. India's defences were thus reconstructed with drastic financial retrenchments that provided primarily for internal security and the local defence of the frontier. The armies bequeathed by the East India Company were reorganised into a force of 60,000 British and 120,000 Indian troops with adjustments that took into account the class-caste composition of the latter. The 64-vessel Indian Navy was abolished for reasons of economy, and the naval defence of India was entrusted to the Royal Navy.[3]

India's defence posture remained static until Russia's absorption of the khanates and her infringement upon the borders of Afghanistan and Persia in 1884–85. The Indian army was immediately strengthened, and defence works were pursued with urgency on the northwest frontier. The war scare passed and the conclusion of the Pamir Boundary Agreement in 1895 settled the question of the Russo-Afghan border, but the continuation of Anglo-Russian suspicions regarding the other's intentions in Central Asia led to a major reconstruction of India's defences between 1899 and 1907.

The new Viceroy, Lord Curzon, created a North-West Frontier Province in 1901 and substituted 'a policy of frontier garrisons drawn from the people themselves, for the costly experiment of large forts and isolated posts thrown forward into a turbulent and fanatical country . . . a policy of military concentration as against diffusion and of tribal conciliation in place of exasperation'.[4] After his appointment as Commander-in-Chief in 1902, Lord Kitchener reorganized the forces into two armies echelonned back from the North-West Frontier along the strategic railway lines, facilitating

---

[3] The Indian Navy was replaced by the noncombatant Bombay Marine which in 1877 was amalgamated with the other naval establishments in India to form Her Majesty's Indian Marine (renamed the Royal Indian Marine in 1892). In 1869, India commenced payment of a subvention towards the Royal Navy which, from 1896, totalled stg 100,000 per annum.

[4] Extract from Lord Curzon's budget speech, 27 March 1901. Cited, *Lord Curzon in India* (London: Macmillan, 1906), p. 408.

the despatch—in the event of a new Russian threat to Afghanistan—of one army to the banks of the Helmand River and the other to the heights beyond Kabul.[5] The Army's policy of maximum self-sufficiency was enhanced by concentrating harness and saddlery shops at Kanpur and constructing a gun carriage factory at Jubbulpore, a cordite factory at Aruvankadu, a lyditte-filling plant at Kirki, and rolling mills and a rifle factory at Ishapore—all in northern India.[6]

THE FIRST WORLD WAR

At the start of the First World War, India's defence outlay totalled Rs 29.8 crores (1913-14), or 24 per cent of the total expenditure of the central government. The armed forces consisted of 75,000 British and 160,000 Indian soldiers exclusive of noncombatants and reserves,[7] a small noncombatant Royal Indian Marine, and an ordnance establishment which, since Kitchener's reforms, had been augmented with a small arms ammunition plant at Dum Dum and a clothing factory at Shahjahanpur. A Royal Air Force unit was in the process of being set up.

Within the limitations imposed by India's meagre financial resources, the Army was prepared for war: for her internal security, for tribal control on the northwest and northeast frontiers, and for defence against a minor power like Afghanistan and against a major power like Russia, pending the arrival of imperial aid. India's limited military responsibilities had been reaffirmed by a majority report of the Army in India, prepared by the Nicholson Committee in 1913 and accepted by the Indian government in that same year.[8]

---

[5] For the resulting composition and distribution of the army, see the *Military Handbook of General Information on India*, compiled in the Division of the Chief of the Staff, Intelligence Branch (Simla: Government Press, 1908), pp. 337-338, 347-348. For changes in the communal and regional composition of the Indian army during the 1856-1930 period, see Dr. B. R. Ambedkar, *Pakistan, or Partition of India* (Bombay: Thacker, 3d edition, 1946), pp. 60 and 65.

[6] For a useful survey of earlier ordnance development under the Company, see Brig.-Gen. H. A. Young, *The East India Company's Arsenals and Manufactories* (Oxford: Clarendon Press, 1937).

[7] For the composition of the army in 1914, see *Whitaker's Almanac, 1915*, p. 585.

[8] The committee declared that: 'While India should provide for her own defence against local aggression and, if necessary, for an attack on the Indian Empire by a great Power until reinforcements can come from home, she is not

The degree of India's preparedness was thus based upon a principle of limitation, and its designers specifically excluded from their calculations the added, and external, role which the army was to undertake during a war.

The war effort of India was, nonetheless, noteworthy in terms of men, money, and materials. During the course of the conflict, India recruited 680,000 voluntary combatants and 400,000 noncombatants, despatched 1,215,000 men overseas, and incurred 101,000 casualties in numerous theatres of war. India supplied equipment and stores for the various theatres to the value of £80 million and, in 1917–18, made Britain a free gift of £113,500,000, which was equivalent to an entire year's revenue and which added 30 percent to the national debt.[9]

POSTWAR DEFENCE PLANS

India's postwar military establishment aimed at sharp reductions in both civil and military expenditures. The Army was reduced to 200,000, but its wartime potential was augmented by the organisation of a more efficient Reserve and the establishment, in 1920, of an Anglo-Indian Auxiliary Force and an Indian Territorial Force composed of urban and rural units and a university training corps. The Royal Air Force was re-established in India with a front-line strength of six squadrons, and an Indian Air Force was created in 1932. The Royal Indian Marine was restored as a combatant service in 1928 and was slowly built up towards a sanctioned strength of four sloops, two patrol vessels, and two surveying vessels.

The creation of an Indian officer cadre was undertaken in 1917, at which time Indians were made eligible for the King's commission and ten vacancies per annum were reserved for Indian officer cadets at the Royal Military College at Sandhurst. In March 1922 the Prince of Wales Royal Indian Military College was opened at Dehra Dun with a capacity of 70 cadets to prepare Indians for Sandhurst

called upon to maintain troops for the specific purpose of placing them at the disposal of the Home Government for wars outside the Indian Sphere'. Cited, H. H. Dodwell, ed., *The Cambridge History of the British Empire*, vol. 5, *The Indian Empire, 1858–1918* (London: Cambridge University Press, 1932), p. 476.

[9] It must be noted, however, that India bore only the expense of her peacetime army, the additional troops being maintained at British expense. These figures are quoted in pounds sterling because of the difficulty of ascertaining the official exchange rate of the time.

and thus reduce the high rate of failures among Indian cadets sent to England.[10] The government commenced the complete Indianisation of eight infantry and cavalry units in 1923 and, following the proposals of the India Sandhurst Committee, established its own Indian Military Academy at Dehra Dun in October 1932 with a capacity of 60 cadets. In 1935, Kitchener College was inaugurated at Nowgong to train promising cadets from the ranks and, in 1936, an Army class was started at Government College, Lahore.

India's limited military liabilities were reaffirmed by Section 22 of the Government of India Act of 1919 and by the Imperial Defence Committee in 1920. Military planning proceeded on the basis of meeting the 'minor danger' of internal security and frontier defence, but its problems became more onerous because of the nationalist noncooperation movement, increasing Hindu–Muslim animosity, and renewed turbulence on the North-West Frontier.

Concern with Soviet Russian intentions led the War Office in November 1927 to formulate the Defence of India Plan to counter any Russian attack on Afghanistan.[11] The outline of the plan was largely prepared in 1928–29, but official interest quickly waned because of Russia's internal preoccupations and her involvement in border conflict with Japan in the Far East and Britain's growing concern with the rising power of Nazi Germany. By 1937, the plan was of only academic significance and had been shelved for all practical purposes.

The authorities immediately responsible for Indian defence were, however, mainly concerned with the traditional contingency of waging limited war with Afghanistan using India's own resources, that is, with a plan to meet possible Afghan and tribal hostility which could, if necessary, be expanded to include operations against an invading Russian army. The result was the Blue Plan of 1927, designed to take the offensive against Afghanistan on two lines of advance toward Kabul and Kandahar with the aim of compelling the Afghan government to sue for peace at an early date.

---

[10] The first Indian cadet was appointed to Sandhurst in 1918 but, of the first 83 entrants (of whom 35 were from the Punjab and 12 from the Bombay Presidency), approximately 30 per cent failed to graduate—as against 3 per cent of the British cadets. William Gutteridge, 'The Indianisation of the Indian Army 1918–45', *Race*, 4 (May 1963), p. 41.

[11] For details of this and subsequent plans, see Bisheshwar Prasad, *Defence of India: Policy and Plans*, Combined Inter-Services Historical Section, India and Pakistan (London: Orient Longmans, 1963), pp. 22–54.

The Blue Plan was jettisoned in 1931 for the Pink Plan, which was more limited in scope and aimed at a restraining action in the event that Afghanistan showed symptoms of hostility or seemed inclined to ally herself with Russia. The Indian operations would consist of an advance by the Northern and Southern armies to occupy Dacca and Wat Thana respectively, and thence continue onwards to Jalalabad and Kandahar. There was no provision for any advance beyond these last two points.

Both the Defence of India Plan and the Pink Plan were framed upon the assumption of Soviet antagonism with or without the collaboration of Afghanistan. They provided protection only to the North-West Frontier and did not safeguard the security of the coastline or the interior of the country. This complacency was dispelled by German rearmament, the Rome-Berlin Axis agreement, the Anti-Comintern Pact between Germany, Italy, and Japan in 1936, and Italian activities in Abyssinia and Afghanistan. German and Italian policies posed an increasing threat to Britain in the West, while Japan's ambitions for a 'co-prosperity sphere' in the south-western Pacific, her successes in China, and her growing influence in Siam were a potential threat to Indian security from the East. British authorities continued to view Russia as a threat to the North-West Frontier, but the changes in the international situation were considered to 'have materially increased India's vulnerabilities and her potential commitments'.[12]

These new circumstances, coupled with certain conditional external army commitments accepted by the government of India,[13] compelled reconsideration of the Pink Plan. A revision of the plan, which had been contemplated as early as 1936, was taken up in earnest in 1938, when an Outline Plan of Operations was drafted. The Outline Plan envisaged the possibility of war with Afghanistan and included within its scope the control of the cis-frontier tribes, the internal security of India, and the provision of a striking force at the frontier railheads. The estimate of Afghan military strength

---

[12] Defence Policy in India 1936-37, 'Change in the International Situation Affecting India's Defence Policy and Commitments', p. 5. Cited in *ibid.*, p. 35.

[13] By 1937, the GOI had accepted conditional military commitments in Iran, Singapore, Hong Kong, Egypt, and Burma amounting to over a division. Because certain schemes were being held in abeyance and because it was unclear whether these schemes were alternative ones, the British War Office in early 1937 endorsed a classification of the schemes according to priority. See memo from India Office dated 23 March 1937, cited in *ibid.*, Appendix I, pp. 241-242.

was based on possible active support to Kabul by the cis- and trans-frontier tribes. Assistance to Afghanistan from a foreign country was not taken into account, as in that event the war would become an imperial responsibility.

The plan also had the limited objective of ensuring that the Afghan government would seek an early peace so as to avoid disintegration of her government or prolonged occupation. Economic pressure on Afghanistan in the event of a war was viewed as impracticable, as that country's trade routes to the north and west did not permit of a blockade; hence resort was to be made to preventing war materials or foreign loans from reaching Kabul. The Outline Plan also took into account the possibility that sympathy in India for the Afghans might result in widespread disaffection against the government.

The plan of operations was based on the hypothesis that the Afghans would have the initiative in launching any attack and that the war would commence with air raids and strong anti-British propaganda in the frontier districts and Waziristan. Such a situation would be countered by a rapid Indian advance into Afghanistan by the field army, with the covering troops engaging the tribal forces. The hostile forces would be met as near to the frontiers as possible, most likely on the Khyber-Jalalabad-Kabul line of advance. The British campaign would commence with air action aimed at destroying the Afghan air force and various military objectives, concurrently with army occupation of Jalalabad; it was hoped that this latter action, combined with air attacks and minor diversionary actions on the Kandahar line of advance, would compel Kabul to sue for peace. If necessary, a further advance towards Kabul was contemplated, mainly by the Khyber route, using the Chaman-Kandahar approach as a diversion and thereby preventing Afghanistan from concentrating its forces against the main advance. However, the Outline Plan was made obsolete by a change in policy whereby Afghanistan came to be considered a sovereign independent power and thus a British, rather than a local Indian, concern. Subsequent planning was based on a purely defensive policy which included defence of the frontiers and coastline; any idea of a large-scale offensive into Afghanistan was excluded from the calculations, although small localised counteractions were not ruled out.

The altered basis of policy led to the issuance of an interim Plan of Operations in August 1938, this scheme being replaced later in the year by the Plan of Operations (India) 1938, though without any substantial change. This latter plan governed Indian defence policy until 1941.

The underlying note of these two plans was that an isolated attack against India by Afghanistan was most unlikely and that Afghanistan would launch such an attack only if compelled to do so by circumstances beyond its immediate control. If such an attack were launched, it was expected to involve regular Afghan land and air forces with foreign assistance and support by tribals from both sides of the Durand Line (the frontier drawn in 1893 to determine the respective sovereignty of the British and the Amir of Afghanistan). The army in India would then defend its vital areas and maintain its existing positions against the tribes. As the plan was eminently defensive in character, it was comprehensive enough to provide simultaneously for the defence of the North-West Frontier, internal security, coastal defence, and overseas commitments.

In the meantime, fluctuating revenues and the opposition of Indian nationalists to increased defence expenditures was forcing the government of India towards increasing reliance upon the British Exchequer. In 1933, Britain commenced payment of an annual subsidy of £1.5 million (approximately $7.2 million) towards the modernisation of Indian defences. In January 1938 Britain agreed to the cessation of India's annual naval subvention of £100,000 ($480,000) on the condition that India maintain an ocean-going squadron of not less than six modern escort vessels to co-operate with the Royal Navy. In subsequent negotiations, the British government indicated its willingness to increase the annual grant towards Indian defence by £500,000 ($2.4 million) from 1 April 1939, to absorb the cost of four of the British battalions stationed in India, and to request Parliament to authorise a capital grant of up to £5 million ($24 million) for re-equipment programmes in India. The offers were, however, conditional upon the actual assignment of the Imperial Reserve and a clear and precise definition of its role. The government of India agreed to these conditions.[14]

The problems of Indian defence were reassessed in 1939 by an expert committee appointed by Britain at the request of the government of India and presided over by Admiral of the Fleet Lord Chatfield. The report of the committee was published on

---

[14] For the principle underlying the agreement, see telegram from Viceroy to Secretary of State, XX No. 1265-S, dated 24 September 1938, para 4. Cited in ibid., p. 7.

4 September 1939 with the announcement that Britain had accepted it with minor modifications.[15] In the meantime, India had anticipated acceptance of the report and had commenced the modernisation and mechanisation of the army, the improvement of port defences, and the raising of the first Indian Air Force squadron and of some flights for coastal defence. Although the Imperial Reserve as such had not been formed up to the outbreak of the Second World War, elements assigned to it were despatched overseas in August.

THE SECOND WORLD WAR

The defence expenditure of India for the last year of general peace (1938–39) totalled Rs 46.68 crores, or about 23 per cent of the total revenues of the central government. This outlay provided for the maintenance of a Regular Army of 260,000 organised in a field force of four divisions plus covering and internal security formations;[16] a Navy of eight minor vessels;[17] an Air Force consisting of one incomplete IAF squadron and six RAF squadrons,[18] and a modest ordnance establishment of eight factories.[19] The armed forces had limited responsibilities[20] and were dependent upon external (mainly British) sources of supply for all major items of weaponry and technical equipment. Military vehicles were provided by Canadian and American suppliers, shipbuilding was limited to minor vessels, and there was no aircraft industry or even aircraft repair facilities in India.

---

[15] For a summary of the Committee's report, see Appendix V below.

[16] For the composition of the Indian army on the eve of the war, see Appendix VI. This force was augmented by 60,000 British troops and a Reserve of 40,000, an Auxiliary Force of 24,000, the Territorial Force of 20,000, and the States Forces, totalling 40,000 personnel. There were also tribal levies on the North-West Frontier and five battalions of the Assam Rifles stationed in the northeast frontier areas.

[17] See Appendix VI.

[18] See Appendix VI.

[19] These comprised the Metal and Steel Factory (Ishapore), the Rifle Factory (Ishapore), the Gun and Shell Factory (Cossipore), the Gun Carriage Factory (Jubbulpore), the Ammunition Factory (Kirki), the Cordite Factory (Aruvankadu), the Harness and Boot Factory (Kanpur), and the Clothing Factory at Shahjahanpur.

[20] For details of the specific responsibilities of the armed forces in 1939, see Nandan Prasad, *Expansion of the Armed Forces and Defence Organisation,*

War Effort

The war provoked another noteworthy military effort by India, although India's financial liabilities in the defence sphere were strictly limited in accordance with the provisions of a financial settlement between the British and Indian governments in November 1939.[21] The Army was expanded to a force of over two million men, the Navy to 126 vessels of all types, and the Air Force to nine squadrons.[22] Shipyards in Bombay, Calcutta, and Karachi constructed merchant vessels and small naval craft, and aircraft repair and maintenance facilities were established at Bangalore under the registered name of Hindustan Aircraft Limited. The ordnance establishment was expanded to a total of thirty production units, comprised of seventeen 'ordnance', nine clothing, two parachute, and two harness and saddlery.[23] India became a staging and supply base for the Southeast Asian theatre. Indian forces served with distinction in East and North Africa, the Middle East, Sicily, and Italy and throughout Southeast Asia, their major effort being in the last theatre.[24] Some 50,000 Indian servicemen lost their lives in the conflict.

Lessons of the Second World War

The Second World War provided many useful lessons for the planners of Indian defence. It confirmed the conclusion of the Chatfield Committee regarding India's need to associate itself, for its very survival, with the Allied defence of the Middle East and

---

1939–45, Combined Inter-Services Historical Section, India and Pakistan (London: Orient Longmans, 1956), pp. 393, 398–399.

[21] For details, see R. N. Bhargava, *The Theory and Working of Union Finance in India* (London: Allen & Unwin, 1956), pp. 281–282.

[22] For the composition of these services at the conclusion of the European conflict, see Appendix VII. Details regarding the provincial, state, communal, and class compositions of the services are given in Nandan Prasad, Appendix 9, p. 456; Appendix 13, p. 460; and Appendix 14, p. 461.

[23] See Lt.-Gen. Sir Wilfred Lindsell, 'The Development of India as a Base for Military Operations', *RUSI Journal* (May 1947), p. 223. The labour force in the ordnance factories rose from 15,000 in 1939 to 100,000 in 1944. See letter from Sir Gerald Butler published in the *Daily Telegraph* on 17 November 1962.

[24] Indian personnel comprised 80 per cent of the British Commonwealth and Empire forces in Malaya, China, Indochina, and Indonesia on V-J Day, totalling about 700,000 men. Brig. J. N. Chaudhuri, 'The Indian Army', *Asiatic Review* (October 1947), p. 306.

Southeast Asia. The war exposed the excessive reliance that had been placed upon distance, physical geography, and the deterrent of potential, as opposed to actual, Allied military power to discourage a would-be aggressor and prevent him from advancing to India's land and maritime frontiers.[25] The Japanese incursions into eastern Assam and the Bay of Bengal had demonstrated Britain's inability to secure India against attack by a major Asiatic foe while simultaneously waging a desperate struggle for her own existence west of Suez. The war attested to the relatively limited military capabilities of India without major external help The famine in Bengal in 1942-43 and the mass panic which had gripped eastern India at the appearance of Japanese naval units and aircraft in the Bay of Bengal in 1942 were pointed reminders of certain problems of resources and national morale which could have far-reaching consequences for Indian defence in times of acute national danger. Also, as the government of India noted in a statement on industrial policy released in 1945: 'The experience of two wars has demonstrated the dangers, both to India and to the rest of the Commonwealth, inherent in India's dependence on overseas supplies for vital commodities required for defence'.[26]

With the successful completion of the war, the question of India's postwar defence requirements was the subject of a number of articles by various British and Indian military writers. Most of these observers argued the need for a regional approach to Indian security, the most popular proposal being for a regional Commonwealth strategy in which India would play a focal role.[27] The most comprehensive argumentation for such a scheme was advanced by

[25] As the official British war historian has written: 'An invasion of India's north-eastern frontier across the grain of the country had never been visualised because of the distance of any possible enemy, the difficulties of the terrain and the fact that such communications as there were in Burma ran north and south. The traditional threat had always been from the north-west and India's defences had been planned to meet it'. S. Woodburn Kirby, *The War Against Japan*, vol. 2 (London: HMSO, 1958), p. xvi.

[26] Cited in C. H. Philips (general ed.), *Select Documents on the History of India and Pakistan*, vol. IV, *The Evolution of India and Pakistan, 1858-1947* (London: Oxford University Press, 1962), p. 700.

[27] See, for example, Lt.-Col. G. L. W. Armstrong, 'The Defence of the Indian Ocean and the Far East', *USI Journal*, 77:326 (January 1947), pp. 71-73; Lt.-Col. S. G. Chaphekar, 'A Frank Survey of India's Defence Problems', *ibid.*, 78:327 (April 1947), pp. 240-245; Lt.-Col. G. N. Molesworth, 'Some Aspects of Future Security in the Indian Ocean Area', *Asiatic Review* (January 1946), pp. 28-29.

K. M. Panikkar,[28] a man later described by Alan Campbell-Johnson as 'one of about half a dozen men who may well have a great influence in the shaping of Indian policy at home and abroad'.[29]

In the meantime, the British authorities had made their own assessment of India's postwar military needs [30] and, as of October 1946, planning appears to have aimed at the creation of an army comprised of a 'few' infantry divisions, an armoured division, an airborne division, and 'some' frontier brigade groups; the development of a balanced fleet with a nucleus of three cruisers; and the expansion of the existing ten RIAF squadrons into a balanced force of twenty fighter, bomber and transport squadrons.[31] Because of the political situation, however, such planning was necessarily tentative; the ultimate decisions about the postwar defence policy of India were left to the political leadership of emerging nationalist India, which had assumed the responsibilities of de facto power with the formation of the interim government, headed by Jawaharlal Nehru, in September 1946.

[28] Panikkar's views were put forward in various articles and monographs: 'Defence and National Efficiency', *Asiatic Review* (July 1945); *India and the Indian Ocean* (London: Allen & Unwin, 1945); *The Future of South-East Asia* (London: Allen & Unwin, 1943); and *The Basis of an Indo-British Treaty* (London: ICWA, 1946).

[29] *Mission with Mountbatten* (London: Robert Hale, 1951), p. 269.

[30] See Appendix VIII.

[31] See Field Marshal Sir Claude Auchinleck, 'Planning India's Post-War Armed Forces', *USI Journal*, 76:325 (October 1946), pp. 321–322.

Chapter Two

THE ORIGINS, BASES, AND AIMS OF INDIAN DEFENCE POLICY

The nationalist leaders of independent India brought with them into responsible office a long tradition of opposition to the defence policy of the British Raj.

THE NATIONALIST LEGACY

Up until 1919, Indian nationalist opinion, as expressed through the Indian National Congress (INC), reflected prevailing opinion in influential British circles. In the context of India's pressing poverty, Congress argued the need to lessen the military burden on Indian revenues by limiting her military liability to internal security and the defence of the actual frontiers. There developed a general disbelief in the possibility of any Russian invasion and a marked tendency to minimize the threats posed by Afghanistan and the militant tribals on the North-West Frontier, and to attribute much of the problem to the imperialist urges of British authorities. A natural corollary of these premises was strong opposition to the 'forward policy' of projecting defence strategy beyond India's natural frontiers.

The general identification of Indian and British interests was, however, attested by the wholehearted support advanced by the Congress for the imperial war effort throughout the First World War. In 1919, the militant nationalist and orthodox Hindu, B. G. Tilak, even envisaged India as a powerful steward of the League of Nations, maintaining the peace of the world and the stability of the British empire against all aggressors and disturbers of the peace, whether in Asia or elsewhere.[1]

This identification vanished in 1920–21, however, with the

---

[1] Cited in Bimla Prasad, *The Origins of Indian Foreign Policy* (Calcutta: Bookland Private, 1960), p. 64.

emergence of a more independent and militant Congress under the leadership of Mohandas K. Gandhi. In September 1920, Congress adopted Gandhi's plan to cease co-operating with British authority and, in May 1921, Gandhi threatened to preach nonsupport for the government in the event of hostilities between Britain and Afghanistan. The following month, the Congress Working Committee advised Indian soldiers not to co-operate with the British government in the event of hostilities with the Turkish Nationalist government. In November of the same year, the All India Congress Committee adopted its first formal declaration of independence from British foreign policy and its first statement of the foreign policy which a free India would like to pursue.[2] In accordance with its hardening attitude towards colonialism, Congress in 1927 demanded the withdrawal of all Indian troops from China, Mesopotamia, Persia, and all British colonies and foreign countries. The following year, Congress charged that the policy of the government had been 'traditionally guided by considerations of holding India under subjection and not of protecting her frontiers'.

The Congress was particularly emphatic in its condemnation of the reversion, after the First World War, to a 'forward policy' on the North-West Frontier. In 1931 it recorded the opinion that 'the military and financial resources of India should not be employed in furtherance of this policy and that the military occupation of the tribesmen's territory should be terminated'. In 1936 Congress condemned the policy as a 'total failure', rejected the charge that the frontier Pathan tribes were truculent, and announced: 'This policy has been pursued in the interests of imperialism and mostly with the object of justifying the heavy military expenditure in India and of providing training under semi-war conditions for otherwise idle troops maintained for imperial purposes'. There was a marked tendency to envisage a free India relatively secure against attack. While this was based to a considerable degree upon emotion and the fact that nationalist leaders did not have the responsibilities of office, it was supported by pragmatic reasoning on the part of the influential Jawaharlal Nehru.

NEHRU'S VIEWS ON DEFENCE

In his presidential address to the Kerala Provincial Conference of the INC at Payyanur on 28 May 1928, Nehru declared that India

[2] For the wording of the declaration, see Dr. N.V. Rajkumar (ed.), *The Background of India's Foreign Policy* (Delhi: Navin Press, 1952), pp. 44-45.

was protected by the balance of power. He dismissed the specific threats which might face a free India: France, Germany, and Italy were 'too much involved in their mutual hatred and jealousies and are too afraid of each other to trouble us at all'. The United States was 'too far away for effective action'. Japan had to face the hostility of the United States and the Western European powers and 'cannot dare embark on a new adventure, which would be fraught with the greatest risks for her'. Afghanistan 'may at most carry out a number of successful raids before we can defeat it and hold it in check'. Nehru felt that the danger from Russia was 'largely imaginary, as every one knows or ought to know, that no country is in greater need of peace than Russia'.

> The great War, the civil war, the famine and the blockade have shaken her foundations and done her tremendous injury . . . she desires peace to build up the new social order she has established . . . Her whole government is based on the good-will of the peasantry and she cannot count on this good-will in an oppressive campaign. She has so many enemies that she dare not of her own accord start an invasion of India and leave her Western flanks exposed to attack. Nor has she any economic reason to covet India . . . She wants capital and machinery and India can supply neither.

Thus, he concluded, 'no danger threatens India from any direction and even if there is any danger we shall be able to cope with it'.[3]

In his most comprehensive statement on Indian defence, contained in two articles published in 1931, Nehru expanded on his balance-of-power thesis as it related to India:

> It may be that some will covet her, but the master desire will be to prevent any other nation from possessing India. No country will tolerate the idea of another acquiring the commanding position which England occupied for so long. If any power was covetous enough to make the attempt, all the others would combine to trounce the intruder. This mutual rivalry would in itself be the surest guarantee against an attack on India.

He therefore felt that an independent India would occupy a favourable position in the world, largely free from the danger of external invasion and more secure than if she continued to be involved in British imperial policy.[4]

Speaking in London on 4 February 1936 under the auspices of the Indian Conciliation Group and in the context of a deteriorating

---

[3] Cited, Jagat S. Bright (ed.), *Important Speeches of Jawaharlal Nehru* (Lahore: Indian Printing Works, n.d.), pp. 138 and 153.

[4] Cited, Prasad, *Origins*, pp. 281–283.

international situation, Nehru once again advanced the view that a free India would enjoy relative security against external aggression. He felt that the frontier problem could be solved by a 'friendly approach' along economic lines, as the restlessness of the tribes was due to their harsh environment. Afghanistan was dismissed as a threat on the grounds that it possessed no offensive strength. Nehru felt that there was no power in the contemporary world which was more peaceful and less inclined to aggression than the Soviet Union. He considered that Japanese aggression against India was virtually precluded by her fear of exposing her flanks to America and Russia, her need to absorb China before descending upon India, and the fact that she would first have to traverse Southeast Asian waters and overcome the Western naval forces there.[5]

Nehru's last pre-war pronouncement on defence was contained in an article entitled 'The Unity of India', written in January 1938. He again dismissed the possibility of an attack by a European power on the grounds that each was too fearful of its neighbours:

Soviet Russia is definitely out of the picture so far as aggression goes; she seeks a policy of international peace, and the question of Indian territory would fulfill no want of hers. Afghanistan and the border tribes also need not be considered in this connection. Our policy towards them will be one of close friendship and co-operation, utterly unlike the 'Forward Policy' of the British which relies on bombing combatants and non-combatants alike.

'But even if these people were hostile and aggressive', Nehru concluded 'they are too backward industrially to meet a modern army outside their own mountains'.[6]

Nehru professed to have no fear of any attack by Japan, which, in his view, would first have to absorb China—a 'monumental task'—and would have to engage in conflict with other great powers at some stage. The overland route was blocked by deserts, and the Himalayas offered 'an effective barrier, and not even air fleets can come that way'; the maritime approach was long, intricate, and dangerous. 'A Japanese invasion of India could become a practical proposition only if China has been completely crushed, and if the United States, the Soviet Union and England have all been effectively humbled. That is a large undertaking'.

[5] Jawaharlal Nehru, *India and the World* (London: Allen and Unwin, 1936), pp. 251–253.
[6] Nehru, *The Unity of India: Collected Writings, 1937–1940* (London: Lindsay Drummond, 1942), pp. 24–25, 252.

Thus we see that, normally speaking, there is no great or obvious danger of the invasion of India from without. Still, we live in an abnormal world, full of wars and aggression. International law has ceased to be, treaties and undertakings have no value, gangsterism prevails unabashed among the nations. We realise that anything may happen in this epoch of revolution and wars and that the only thing to be done to protect ourselves is to rely on our own strength at the same time that we pursue consciously a policy of peace. Risks have to be taken whatever the path we follow. These we are prepared to take, for we must.[7]

By the eve of the Second World War therefore, the framework of Indian defence policy had been defined by the man whose predispositions were to be mirrored in the defence posture ultimately adopted by the Indian Union. Nehru envisaged a free India secure against attack either by its geo-strategic position, its size, or the balance of power. He did not dismiss the possibility of aggressive actions against India by Afghanistan or the tribes on the North-West Frontier, but he was inclined to minimise these threats as mostly of nuisance value and containable by relatively small but efficient armed forces. He contemplated the speedy development of an effective defence force to maintain the country's territorial integrity—primarily, it would seem, in accordance with the Curzon scheme for the North-West Frontier from 1904 to 1919.[8] He wished to see the speedy withdrawal of British forces from a sovereign India, and his strong suspicion of, and aversion to, great power politics clearly weighed heavily against India's involvement in external military entanglements.

Notwithstanding the attempt by Congress to utilise the Japanese threat to force an immediate transfer of power in India to itself—resulting in the brief, violent but abortive rising in August-September 1942—the Indian peoples made a significant contribu-

[7] *Ibid.*, p. 252.
[8] The All-India Congress Committee, meeting in Faizpur in 1936, had stated that a solution to the frontier problem would be an enquiry into the economic, political, and military situation aimed at a final and peaceful settlement in co-operation with the border tribes. Resolution VIII, cited in Rajkumar, *Background*, p. 53. In an interview with Sir C. Sankaran Nair sometime in the late 1920's, Gandhi had expressed the view that Afghan (that is, tribal) attacks on the territory of a free India could be deterred by providing the tribes with a little subsidy and by introducing the spinning wheel (that is, cottage industries) among them. Cited in Patricia Kendall, *India and the British* (London: Charles Scribner, 1931), p. 402. Congress leaders had thus conceived of no real alternative to the existing British approach, and a popular Indian government intended to be equally as firm with these peoples.

tion to the Allied victory, which stimulated the nationalist view that a free India would exert a major influence in world affairs. Sir Mohammad Zafrullah Khan, chairman of the Indian delegation to the Third Unofficial Commonwealth Relations Conference in London in 1945 and subsequently Foreign Minister of Pakistan, declared in his opening speech that 'The war has brought to India a forcible and vivid realisation of her own strategic importance and indeed of her own potential strategic domination in all the vast area of oceans and lands that lie between Australia and the west coast of Africa'.[9] A similar view was expressed by another prominent Indian, Penderal Noon, in a book published at about this same time.[10]

These views were also reflected at the highest levels of the Congress party. The deputy leader of the party, Asaf Ali, envisaged in early 1946 an independent India capable of functioning as the 'policeman and arsenal of the East'.[11] While in prison in 1944, Nehru recorded the view that both India and China were potentially capable of joining America, the Soviet Union, and Britain (if the resources of the empire were added to her own) as great powers, and he estimated that India's potential resources were probably more varied and extensive than China's. Though he recognised that, geographically, India was not a Pacific power, he felt that she would inevitably exercise great influence there while developing as the centre of political and economic activity in the Indian Ocean area, in Southeast Asia, and up to the Middle East.[12] The All India Congress Committee declared in September 1945 that a free India would 'especially seek to develop common policies for defence, trade and economic and cultural development with China, Burma, Malaya, Indonesia and Ceylon as well as the countries of the Middle East'.[13]

Nehru made a number of subsequent references to the strategic indivisibility of the Indian Ocean region. In a message to the youth of Ceylon delivered from Bombay on 9 October 1945, he declared that India 'is likely to become the centre for defence purposes and

---

[9] Cited in Richard Frost, *The British Commonwealth and World Society* (London: Oxford University Press, 1947), p. 155.
[10] Noon, *The Future of India* (London: Pilot Press, 1945), p. 57.
[11] *LAD*, vol. 3 (4 March 1946), p. 1818.
[12] Nehru, *The Discovery of India* (London: Meridian Books, 1945), pp. 547-548.
[13] Cited in Rajkumar, *Background*, p. 90.

trade for Southern and South-East Asia. It is my hope that regional arrangements within the four corners of a world agreement will bind together all these countries of South and South-East Asia'.[14] In a speech in Karachi on 9 January 1946, Nehru claimed that the defence of the Indian Ocean region could not be organised without India's co-operation and that in the natural course of events these neighbouring countries and India should come together for mutual protection as well as mutual trade.[15] Speaking in Bombay on 15 March 1946, he stated that 'the Indian Ocean region depends for its defence greatly on India, which is strategically situated in the centre. Thus both South-East Asia and the Middle East defence arrangements will partly depend on India'.[16] On 22 August of the same year, he declared that the Middle East, Middle West, Southeast Asia, and China 'all impinge on India; all depend on India, economically, politically or for defence purposes . . . India is also the centre viewed in terms of the defence of the countries of Western Asia. It is obvious that India has to be some kind of base for defence'.[17]

Though clearly cognizant that Indian security was closely bound up with that of countries contiguous by land, Nehru expressed the view in Bombay on 15 March 1946 that 'the whole question of defence in future warfare is so much in a fluid state, owing to scientific developments, that it is difficult to prophesy about the future'. He declared that 'it is quite impossible for me to say what military or other alliances a free India may give approval of. Generally speaking, she would not like to entangle herself with other peoples' feuds and imperialist rivalries'.[18] In any case, as Nehru informed a Bombay audience on 6 June 1946, if India was threatened she would 'inevitably' try to defend herself by all means at her disposal—with the clear implication that such means did not exclude atomic bombs.[19]

[14] Cited in Bright, *Important Speeches*, p. 71.
[15] *Ibid.*, p. 262.
[16] *Ibid.*, p. 359.
[17] Cited, M. Venkatarangaiya, 'Indo-American Political Relations', in *Aspects of India's Foreign Relations*, paper no. 2 (London: ICWA, August 1949), p. 2. Nehru had predicted India's membership in a regional federation in 1936, 1940, and as late as August 1946. See, respectively, Jawaharlal Nehru, *Towards Freedom* (New York: John Day, 1941), p. 367; *The Unity of India*, p. 327; and 'Inter-Asian Relations', *India Quarterly* (October–December 1946), p. 327.
[18] Cited in Bright, *Important Speeches*, p. 360.
[19] *The Unity of India*, pp. 353–354. The view was expressed in reply to a

In a broadcast from New Delhi on 7 September 1946, Nehru reaffirmed the intention of a free India 'as far as possible, to keep away from the power politics of groups aligned against one another . . .'[20] and expressed the hope that India would develop close and friendly contacts with other nations. In accordance with its anticolonial stance—but also reflecting the desire to divest India of external military commitments—the interim government (which held office from 2 September 1946 to 14 August 1947) ordered the return of Indian forces outside the subcontinent.[21] Significantly enough, Nehru, while stressing India's geo-strategic importance in his inaugural address to the Asian Relations Conference in Delhi on 23 March 1947, denied any Indian pretensions to formal 'leadership' of Asia and made no reference whatever to any scheme for an Asian federation.[22]

INTERIM DEFENCE PLANS

Demobilization continued, apparently towards the provisional targets set earlier by the British authorities, but within the limitations imposed by the serious communal rioting and the more general problems associated with demobilization.[23] On the recommendation of an Expert Committee on Ordnance Factories, the interim government decided to retain fifteen of the existing ordnance plants as the peacetime ordnance establishment and to dispose of the other

query as to whether the future GOI would have atomic bombs in its arsenal. Nehru stated his hope that India would develop atomic power for peaceful uses but warned that, so long as the world was constituted as it was, every country would have to develop and use the latest scientific devices for its protection.

[20] Nehru, *Independence and After: A Collection of Speeches, 1946–1949* (New York: John Day, 1950), p. 341.
[21] The last undivided contingent of the Indian Army to return from abroad left Japan on 25 October 1947.
[22] Nehru, *Speeches, 1946–1949* (New Delhi: Publications Division, GOI, 1958), p. 302.
[23] For the progress of demobilization, see Nandan Prasad, *Expansion of the Armed Forces and Defence Organisation, 1939–45*, Combined Inter-Services Historical Section, India and Pakistan (London: Orient Longmans, 1956), p. 215. The original plans had a provisional target of a reduction to 449,000 (including British personnel) by 1 April 1947 but were later revised to 500,000 by the same date and to 300,000 by 1 December 1947. See statements by Defense Secretary G. S. Bhalja, LAD, vol. 2 (4 March 1947), p. 1496; *ibid.*, vol. 3 (14 March 1947), p. 1953. Provisional planning thus involved a reduction to the approximate pre-war strength of British and Indian troops combined.

twenty-one units as part of the government's policy to divert capacity from war to peacetime production.[24] The interim government accepted the view adopted in Britain and other Western countries at the conclusion of World War II that there would probably be ten years before another general war and thus there was 'no question' that the Indian arms industry would have to be developed on a crash basis; existing sources of armaments could continue to be utilised for the time being.[25] Committees were established to investigate speedy nationalisation of the armed forces, the creation of a military academy along the lines of West Point, and the establishment of a cadet corps programme embracing schools and universities.

The interim government gave its early attention to the problem of the strength and composition of India's peacetime armed forces. Its basic approach was described by the Defence Secretary, G. S. Bhalja, during the debate on defence grants on 14 March 1947. He did not propose to go into the ethics of maintaining armed forces; 'I would only say', he stated, 'that whatever our ideology may be . . . as practical men, as wise men, as men on whom the responsibility for the defence of the country lies, it would be foolish, it would be imprudent on our part to wildly cut down the forces to a figure which would put us at the mercy of any invader'.[26]

The Indian Armed Forces have been built up as a whole for the defence of India as a whole, and so far at least as defence is concerned, planning can only proceed on the basis of an undivided India. By reason of her geographical position, natural resources and great potentialities for future development, India occupies a key position in Asia. It is clear that in a major war no one power, however great, will be able to stand alone except for a short initial period. In present world conditions security can only be guaranteed by the maintenance of sufficient armed forces to encourage friends and deter possible aggressors, thus ensuring from all a healthy and friendly respect.

[24] As the peacetime demands on the plants earmarked for retention were considered 'negligible', the interim government decided that spare capacity in these remaining factories should be utilized for civilian production as a temporary measure to narrow the gap between supply and demand. See statement by Finance Minister Liaquat Ali Khan, *LAD*, vol. 2 (February 1947), p. 1320.
[25] See Nehru's statement in the Rajya Sabha, 9 November 1962. Cited in *Hindu*, 11 November 1962.
[26] *LAD*, vol. 3, p. 1953.

The minimum requirement to ensure this, he continued, was a highly efficient field army, a balanced air force, and a sufficient naval force to guard India's long coastline and her seaborne trade.[27]

Although the interim government was unable to make firm decisions regarding either the size of the peacetime defence budget or the strength and composition of the armed forces (notwithstanding the ten expected years of peace), it appears to have reached certain tentative conclusions. It estimated that the annual outlay on defence might be fixed at about Rs 110 crores [28] for a military programme involving a well-equipped and mobile army of about 200,000 men backed by a reserve and a large territorial army, an air force of twenty squadrons of all types, and a small naval task force built around three light cruisers and including two aircraft carriers.[29] The plans, in effect, were a very slight modification in the 'lowest limit' prepared by British planners before the end of the Second World War and apparently referred to by Field Marshal Auchinleck in his article on postwar defence planning for India's armed forces published in October 1946.[30]

The problems of internal security and the North-West Frontier had undergone no radical change and still required the maintenance of strong military forces.[31] In accordance with India's weak finances and her pressing problems of internal development, her military liability was restricted to the maintenance of law and order in India, defence against Afghanistan (neither side having allies), and protection of India's coasts, coastal merchant shipping

[27] *Ibid.*, vol. 2 (14 March 1947), p. 1496.
[28] See statement by Dr. John Matthai, a former Finance Minister, to the local Rotary Club at Kottayam in October 1952. Cited in Bhargava, *The Theory and Working of Union Finance in India* (London: Allen and Unwin, 1956), p. 284.
[29] Information obtained from informed Indian civil and military authorities and deduced from such data as is available.
[30] As this article appeared the month following the formation of the interim government, it may have reflected early tentative conclusions by that authority, but this cannot be confirmed.
[31] Pre- and post-partition communal and communist-inspired disorder must have removed any illusion in official quarters that internal harmony would automatically follow the removal of alien rule. Nehru also made it clear at a press conference in New Delhi on 26 September 1946 that the government meant to maintain order among the tribes on the North-West Frontier for reasons involving both internal tranquility and external defence. Statement cited in D. R. Bose (ed.), *New India Speaks* (Calcutta: A. Mukerjee, 1949), p. 33.

and fisheries, and assistance in the protection of ocean shipping. In the event of an attack by a major power like the Soviet Union or China, Indian planning clearly expected the intervention of friendly major powers including Britain to provide the necessary succour. It is probable that operational planning for the North-West Frontier reverted to some form of the Interim Plan of 1938.

IMPACT OF PARTITION

The defence planning of the interim government was undercut by the formation of the Muslim state of Pakistan simultaneous with the formal withdrawal of British power from the subcontinent at midnight on 14/15 August 1947. There was some recognition, however, of the need for 'some kind of permanent joint defence council of the two states, since the defence of India as a whole must be of supreme concern to both dominions'.[32] The matter was discussed by Indian and Pakistani representatives on the Joint Defence Council [33] in 1947, but, as Defence Minister Sardar Baldev Singh explained to the Indian Parliament in early 1949, 'after careful consideration of the matter we came to the conclusion that the time was not ripe then to have an organisation of this kind. Both Pakistan and we were reluctant due to the intense feelings then prevailing'.[34]

The 'intense feeling' arose from the communal bloodbath which both preceded and accompanied partition, related differences involving the division of the cash balances and military stores of an undivided India between the two new dominions, and a feeling of mutual suspicion and animosity provoked by the manner in which the princely states of Junagadh, Hyderabad and Kashmir were integrated into the Indian Union.

[32] *Times of India*, 7 July 1947. That the possibility was not dismissed out of hand is apparently substantiated by a report in the *Hindustan Times* in early 1947 which outlined plans for the defence of India allegedly passed by the interim government with the concurrence of both its Congress and Muslim League members. The plans envisaged a relatively small aggregate expenditure on defence, based on the assumption of a co-ordinated external defence of the subcontinent—whether a state of Pakistan existed or not—and of a defence agreement with the British Commonwealth. See reference to the report in *The Economist*, 17 May 1947, p. 748.
[33] The Joint Defence Council was set up to co-ordinate the division of the armed forces between India and Pakistan.
[34] *CAD*, pt. 2, vol. 2 (19 March, 1949), p. 1220.

The forced accession of Junagadh was a small affair: when the Muslim ruler tried to cede the state to Pakistan on 15 August, an agitation was fomented and Indian troops proceeded to occupy the small states of Babariawad and Mongrol (both tribute states of Junagadh) on 1 November and Junagadh itself on 9 November. When the ruler (Nizam) of land-locked Hyderabad resisted Indian pressures (including a total blockade of the state) to accede to the Union, the Indian government used the excuse of internal disorders to initiate a 'police action'. On 13 September 1948 units of the 1st Armoured Division, supported by the Royal Indian Air Force, struck eastwards from Sholapur, westwards from Bezwada, southwards from the Central Provinces, southeast from Bombay Province, and north across the Tungabhadra River. Despite some spirited resistance by the Nizam's forces, the Hyderabad authorities formally surrendered on 17 September.

CONFLICT IN KASHMIR, 1947-48

The dispute over Kashmir, which has been well-documented,[35] grew out of a Muslim revolt in Poonch against the despotic Dogra Hindu regime which escalated into an invasion by Pathan tribals on 22 October 1947. Desperate for military aid to stem the rapid tribal advance on his capital, Srinagar, the Maharaja acceded to the Union on 26 October as the essential prerequisite of Indian aid. In the early hours of 27 October, over one hundred Indian civil and military aircraft were hastily mobilised to fly troops, equipment, and supplies to Srinagar. The only unit immediately available, a Sikh battalion, was flown to Srinagar and succeeded in braking the tribal advance though forced back to within 17 miles of the capital. Reinforced to brigade strength and organised into the Jammu and Kashmir Division under Major-General Kalwant Singh, Indian troops counterattacked on 3 November and broke through tribal defences astride the Baramula road on 7 November, recap-

---

[35] See, for example, Michael Brecher, *The Struggle for Kashmir* (Toronto: Ryerson Press, 1953); Josef Korbel, *Danger in Kashmir* (Princeton: Princeton University Press, 1954); Lord Birdwood, *A Continent Decides* (London: Robert Hale, 1956); V.P. Menon, *The Integration of the Indian States* (Calcutta: Orient Longmans, 1956), chap. XX. Details of the military operations have been collated from press reports for the period, from published official and unofficial reports, and observations, and from interviews with informed individuals.

turing Baramula (30 miles northwest of Srinagar) the following day. Advancing westwards along the Srinagar–Rawalpindi road against extensive demolitions and roadblocks, the steadily increasing Indian forces occupied Mahura and Uri on 12 and 14 November, respectively. With the Vale cleared of hostile forces save for isolated pockets, the Indian units proceeded in the direction of Pakistan's frontiers and took Poonch (40 miles southwest of Srinagar) on 23 November. They took Kotli (15 miles southwest of Poonch) three days later, only to evacuate it on 1 December because of logistics problems.

The initiative thereupon passed to the tribal and Azad (Free) Kashmir forces, who commenced, on 23 December, an offensive in southern Kashmir along a 90-mile front extending from Jammu to the Jhangar–Naoshera area. In severe fighting, Indian troops were driven from the important road junction of Jhangar on 31 December but managed to hold Naoshera against heavy attacks in early February 1948.

With the return of better weather in the early spring, the Indian forces, which had meanwhile been reorganised into Srinagar and Kashmir divisional commands, resumed their offensive and recaptured Jhangar on 18 March. Localised activities continued through the summer while Indian forces were built up to the equivalent of three divisions, plus state forces and a newly organised militia. In November, the Indian army launched twin offensives in the southwest and northeast, supported by tanks, artillery, and aircraft. The Srinagar Division (under Major-General K. S. Thimayya) forced Zoji La Pass and recaptured Dras on 16 November, entered Khalatse, the gateway to the Ladakh Valley, on 23 November and recaptured the communications centre of Kargil on 24 November. The Jammu Division (under Major-General Atma Singh) retook Poonch on 22 November.

From the outset of hostilities, the buildup of Indian forces in Kashmir had increasingly alarmed Pakistan, which feared that her own defences in the Punjab would be hopelessly compromised by Indian control of the contiguous areas in Kashmir. The immediate despatch of Pakistani troops into Kashmir was prevented only by the knowledge that such an act would lead to the immediate resignation of all British military personnel serving with the Pakistan armed forces, whose services were essential to the development of an efficient military establishment. The result was that the involvement of the Pakistan Army was set back by at least several months and ultimately came about in an unobstrusive fashion. 'Leave' was liberally granted to regular Pakistan Army personnel, who proceeded to take it with the Azad Kashmir forces. Early in 1948 the Pakistan 7th Division was deployed behind Azad Kashmir forces to forestall any sudden collapse which might enable Indian troops to drive through to the frontiers of Pakistan. On 17 March 1948 a battery of mountain guns with an infantry escort went into action near Poonch, and on 10 May the 10th Brigade of the 9th Division advanced from Muzaffarabad towards Tithwal and drove Indian troops back some distance. In the latter part of June, Pakistan shifted its 9th Division to Abbottabad and into positions extending from Bagh to Tithwal. In response to rapid Indian advances in November, the Pakistani government pulled troops away from the vulnerable Lahore front—where India had deployed two armoured brigades—and concentrated the 10th Brigade, a parachute brigade, two field regiments of artillery, and a medium artillery battery west of Jammu town. From this position they could threaten the tenuous communications of the Indian forces in Kashmir which extended from Amritsar through Pathankot and Jammu to Poonch.

It had early become apparent to the Indian government that Kashmir could ultimately be secured only if Pakistan denied aid and refuge to the tribal and Azad Kashmir forces. India accordingly had taken the matter to the Security Council of the United Nations on 1 January 1948, with the request that it intervene to prevent further Pakistani interference in Kashmir. The efforts of that body to find a basis for negotiations acceptable to both India and Pakistan proved unavailing until the progress of the conflict forced both parties into a more accommodating mood in December 1948. RIAF aircraft attacked a Pakistani arms dump at Palak on 13 December and, on the following day, Pakistani artillery commenced a 36-hour barrage of Indian lines of communications near Akhnur which shattered Indian ammunition dumps and communications and successfully searched out Indian divisional headquarters at Naoshera. The threat of general war loomed—a war which would have spelt disaster for both countries in the prevailing context of pressing internal problems, communal strife, and military weakness. It appears to have been just such a conclusion, arrived at independently by both governments with the strong encouragement of high-ranking British officers serving with both armies, that led to the ceasefire effected on 1 January 1949 under United Nations' auspices and both sides' subsequent acceptance of a ceasefire line defined by U.N. observers.

The ceasefire coincided with the return of some degree of normalcy to the Indian internal scene and provoked fresh interest in the question of eventual Indo-Pakistani co-operation in defence and other spheres.[36] The Governor-General of India, C. Rajagopalachari, called in early January for an end to the hatred and distrust which affected the relations of the two dominions,[37] and Pakistan's Foreign Minister, Sir Zafrullah Khan, emphasised the need for friendly relations due to the strategic, political, and economic interdependence of the two countries.[38] In the Constituent Assembly on 19 March, Indian Defence Minister Singh said that he felt confident that the proposal for joint defence would be examined when relations between the two countries improved. In April the Governor-General of Pakistan, Khwaja Nazimuddin, declared that 'a joint defence plan is a possibility when relations between India and Pakistan improve, or it may develop as necessity may compel', and 'high officials of the Indian Defence Ministry' were reported as having stated that, while the present moment was 'premature', they envisaged joint Indo-Pakistani defence arrangements in the 'near future'.[39] Even after a crisis in March–April 1950, in which Indian forces were concentrated near Pakistan's borders in the Punjab—seemingly as a deterrent to any hasty actions contemplated by Pakistani politicians—Nehru expressed the hope to an American correspondent that 'ultimately we [India and Pakistan] should surmount the difficulties. Ultimately we should develop a common economic and defence policy. Forces may well be gradually driving us in that direction—joint policies for transportation, irrigation, communications and national defence'.[40]

It must have been clear to Indian leaders almost from the outset, however, that there was little likelihood of quickly overcoming the deep suspicions with which the two dominions viewed each other. In the prevailing context, prudence and the anti-Pakistani mood of the Indian public—from which India's political leadership

---

[36] Even while the conflict was raging, Prime Minister M. A. Jinnah of Pakistan had informally proposed joint defence in early 1948. While Nehru claimed to have received no such offer either officially or unofficially, he declared in Parliament on 30 March 1948: 'The question of joint defence, however, is important from the point of view of both India and Pakistan, and Government will gladly consider this when the time is ripe for it'. *CAD*, vol. 4, p. 2722.

[37] Cited in *Hindu*, 10 January 1949.

[38] *Ibid.*, 17 January 1949.

[39] Cited by Robert Trumbull in *New York Times*, 22 April 1949.

[40] Cited by C. L. Sulzberger in *ibid.*, 26 April 1950.

was by no means aloof—required that certain precautions be taken against a renewal of hostilities arising from the Kashmir dispute.

Defence Plans Against Pakistan

In a 1949 assessment of Pakistan as a military threat, Indian military planners are understood to have regarded the possibility of Pakistani attacks across the Punjab plains, the Rajasthan desert, or from East Pakistan as extremely unlikely. Border incidents were viewed as inevitable, but the only probable military contingency was believed to be a 'tribal' invasion of the Indian-occupied portion of Kashmir more elaborate in scale and conception than that of 1947–48 and built around a sizeable core of Pakistani regulars.

It was evident to the planners that, in any renewed conflict limited to Kashmir, Pakistan would have a geographical advantage. Pakistan could easily provide arms and supplies to the tribals and thus tie down a considerable Indian force at slight cost to itself, easing the imbalance between Indian and Pakistani military forces elsewhere along the frontiers. In the event that Pakistan chose to undertake direct action in Kashmir, its forces would enjoy relative ease of access to the operational theatre and at a time and place of its own choosing. India, on the other hand, would be forced to deploy large forces for an essentially police function to counter a tribal–Azad Kashmir threat along the lengthy ceasefire line in times of general Indo-Pakistan 'peace' or, if regular Pakistani forces intervened in Kashmir, to engage these units in a manner in which India's greater military power could be brought to bear only at disproportionate expense and inconvenience. Even then, India would not have the assurance of winning a decisive victory if Pakistani regulars, tribals, and Azad Kashmir forces could retire to sanctuary in the territory of West Pakistan.

The only practicable alternative was to make no distinction between tribal–Azad Kashmir and official Pakistani actions or to concede the possibility of another limited war in Kashmir at a time and on a scale determined by Karachi. Such a policy would place the onus on the Pakistan government to deter large-scale tribal depredations against the Indian sector of Kashmir and to exercise similar restraint upon the Azad Kashmir forces [41] on the

---

[41] These forces have totalled about 32 battalions since 1948 and are recruited from some of the finest military manpower in the sub-continent, the Poonch Muslims.

penalty of general war. In the event of general hostilities, it was clear that India would enjoy marked superiority in military resources, both in being capable of mobilisation over an extended period, and in having greater material resources. Strategically, also, India had great advantages. Indian territory surrounded East Pakistan, whose nearest point was a thousand miles from West Pakistan; West Pakistan was long and narrow with few trunk roads, only one trunk railway, and a single port (Karachi); and every centre of importance in Pakistan save Quetta was within 150 miles of Indian territory. Furthermore, Pakistan had no domestic source of modern arms and military stores and her ability to wage war could be severely restricted by an Indian blockade of Karachi and diplomatic efforts aimed at preventing, or at least minimising, the possibility of Pakistan's acquiring military aid from any other country.

The Indian Cabinet accepted the thesis advanced by its military advisers, and contingency planning proceeded on the basis of possible operations in Kashmir, Punjab, and Rajasthan with precautionary measures on the borders of East Pakistan. The plan was based on the hypothesis that Pakistan would have the initiative in launching an attack in Kashmir with possible diversionary attacks in other sectors. In the event of such actions, Indian troops in Kashmir would seek to contain the opposing forces while the main Indian field army made a determined and rapid advance towards Lahore and Sialkot, with a possible diversionary action towards Rawalpindi or Karachi to prevent a concentration of Pakistani forces in the major operational theatre in the West Punjab. The primary aim of this strategy was to inflict a decisive defeat on Pakistan's field army at the earliest possible time and, along with the possible occupation of Lahore, to compel the Pakistan government to seek peace. The role of the army would be decisive, with the other two services providing support.[42] Simultaneous efforts would be made in the diplomatic sphere to prevent Pakistan from receiving foreign war material or credits. If Pakistan did not seek an early peace, the Indian government expected that the major powers would provide the necessary pressure on Karachi leading to a cessation of hostilities and some sort of political settle-

[42] Neither side would be likely to strike at major population centres for fear of reciprocal action not commensurate with any short-term gain. The Indian government would also have to avoid a sharp deterioration in communal relationships within the Union.

ment. India's strategy was punitive, there being no intention either to overrun large areas of Pakistan or to occupy Pakistani territory for any period following a ceasefire, either policy being clearly in excess of Indian military capabilities. This basic strategy remained unchanged right up to October 1962, as, despite Pakistan's membership in CENTO (Central Treaty Organization) and SEATO (Southeast Asia Treaty Organization), it was assumed that Pakistan's Western allies would not provide her with support for an 'aggressive' policy toward India but would direct their efforts at effecting an early cessation of hostilities.

IMPACT OF THE COLD WAR

This strategy was conceived at a time when the Indian government could regard the cold war—restricted to Europe until late 1949—with a certain detachment. With the establishment of the People's Republic of China in October 1949, however, India could no longer be a distant onlooker, particularly after October 1950, when Chinese Communist troops entered Tibet to reassert Chinese control.

India's vital interests were basically unchanged by the withdrawal of British power from the subcontinent and the formation of Pakistan. While Pakistan had inherited responsibility for the historical problem of the North-West Frontier, India could not remain unaffected by Pakistan's involvement in this quarter or elsewhere. India's location at the head of the Indian Ocean gave her a strategic stake in the power-political rivalries affecting all states in the Indian Ocean region. The fulfillment of the country's ambitious social and economic goals required continued and unrestricted access to the raw materials and food surpluses of Southeast Asia, the oil of Burma and the Persian Gulf, the markets of the world for her manufactures and products, and the financial and technical aid of the developed countries. The government could not ignore India's dependence upon foreign (largely British) shipping, British military stores and equipment, and friendly naval and air forces pending India's development of adequate air and naval services. Indian politicians could not remain unmindful to the fate of Indian minorities in the various countries on the Indian Ocean littoral and of the effect of Indian policies upon the treatment accorded them in these countries.

There is little doubt that responsible Indian leaders were aware of their country's stake in the containment of communist expansionism by either covert or overt means. There seems to have been a genuine consensus among Nehru and his associates—many of whom were far more outspoken about communism than was the Prime Minister—that formal alignment with the Western bloc would not be to India's advantage in the prevailing geopolitics.

BASES AND AIMS OF NONALIGNMENT

The foremost aim of the Nehru administration was to pursue rapid economic development and thereby provide the impoverished Indian masses with at least the basic requirements of life on a scale above the traditional one of bare subsistence. For purely practical reasons, therefore, India had to minimise military expenditure within the limitations imposed by prudence. The Indian government publicly professed its intention to seek social and economic progress with due regard for individual rights, and it early dealt severely with the Indian Communist party's challenge to public peace and the foundations of democratic government. It was not prepared, however, to pick quarrels with the Communist states or to embark in company with the colonialist-tainted Western powers upon any moral crusade against the adherents of a doctrine that had certain features of considerable attraction for many educated Indians. Proud of their independent nationhood, convinced that India was a potential great power and was destined to play a major role in international affairs, Indians were zealous to exercise this independence to the maximum—and free of the suspected inhibitions imposed by membership in a bloc dominated by powers of far superior industrial and military resources.

Acutely aware of the country's economic and military weakness, Nehru viewed alignment as beyond India's means and felt, moreover, that 'it would not be in consonance with dignity . . . to interfere without any effect being produced'.[48] In an article published in 1952, the influential G. S. Bajpai, the first Secretary-General of the Indian Ministry of External Affairs, expressed the view that no immediate Indian interest would be served by the country's implicating herself 'by artificial ties . . . in the ordinary combinations or coalitions of the friendships or enmities of the two camps in which the major part of the world is to-day unfor-

[48] Statement in Parliament, 8 March 1948, cited in *Independence and After*, p. 215.

tunately divided'. He declared that in a world of power politics armed power constituted the only safeguard against a threat to a country's independence—a fact which India could no more ignore than Switzerland and Sweden. He felt that India must develop her strength as a sanction for her foreign policy, to safeguard her independence and so to maintain an equilibrium in Asia. Expanding on the last contention, Bajpai argued that power developed by India in the defence of neutrality could help create an enduring balance of power for the reason that

> a certain equipose between political combatants can introduce a certain element of caution regarding the attitude of neutrals into their calculations and thus prevent an outbreak of hostilities. But this can be true only of a potentially great Power like India . . . In Asia she alone can help to create and maintain a political equilibrium which no potential aggressor would lightly dare to disturb.

'Thus viewed', he concluded, 'the idea of a balance of power is nothing evil nor incompatible with India's highest ideals'.[44]

A posture of nonalignment between the two power blocs was thus primarily conceived as a means of achieving a *modus vivendi* with the two Communist land powers, thereby affording neither China nor Russia sufficient provocation to invade India alone or as part of a general attack against the non-Communist world.[45] *Panch sheel* (peaceful coexistence) and the concept of a peace area were natural corollaries to such a position, all of them being attempts, first and foremost, to buffer India against East–West (that is, great power) rivalries.[46]

Nonalignment did not appear to involve unnecessary risks, in the opinion of India's leaders. Pakistan had inherited the troublesome problem of the North-West Frontier with probably a better chance of resolving the vexatious issue posed by her co-religionists among the tribes and Afghanistan. Pakistan itself was more a serious

[44] G. S. Bajpai, 'India and the Balance of Power', *Indian Year Book of International Affairs*, vol. 1 (Madras, 1952), p. 4.

[45] Nonalignment was believed to render the possibility of an attack on India from a major power as 'negligible, if not nil'. H. M. Patel, *The Defence of India*, R. R. Kale Memorial Lecture 1963, Gorkhale Institute of Politics and Economics (Bombay: Asia Publishing House, 1963), p. 3.

[46] Panikkar described the main aims of Indian foreign policy as 'the creation of an area of primary and strategic importance around her; creation of a secondary area of strategic importance; and lastly, development of a policy conducive to world peace and progress'. Cited in J. C. Kundra, *Indian Foreign Policy, 1947–1954* (Groningen: J. B. Wolters, 1955), p. 71n.

nuisance than a mortal threat to Indian security and could be handled without external assistance; in any event, the contingency of conflict with Pakistan was regarded in high military circles as remote. The Western nuclear deterrent secured the countries lying on the peripheries of the Russian and Chinese states against overt aggression. Russia's severe losses in the Second World War appeared to necessitate her lengthy preoccupation with internal reconstruction. In the event of a general war, the subcontinent would offer few if any economic enticements to an aggressor and would generally enjoy a low priority in Soviet war plans.[47] In the event that India were attacked in strength by a major power like Russia or China, her leaders probably felt confident that the requisite aid would be speedily forthcoming, if for no other reason than to prevent its vast resources from falling to the enemy. On the assumption that Moscow and Peking appreciated this fact, New Delhi virtually dismissed the possibility of an attack by either or both of the Communist powers. China nevertheless posed a problem requiring close attention.

RESPONSE TO THE PEOPLE'S REPUBLIC OF CHINA

Before the establishment of the People's Republic of China on 1 October 1949, the Kuomintang had given notice that it meant to restore China to its former primacy in Asia and to regard an independent India with a certain condescension.[48] Of immediate concern to Indian leaders, was the fact that no Chinese government recognized the validity of India's treaty rights with Tibet or of the McMahon Line, a line laid down by Sir A. H. McMahon in 1912-13 and recognised as the joint frontier by the governments of India and Tibet after negotiations at Simla in 1913-14. Also, the Kuomintang leaders made it clear that they intended to give both

[47] Nehru told Brecher in 1956 that he could not conceive of any kind of attack or invasion of India, not because of every country's love for India but for the reason that, given India's poverty, an aggressor would probably acquire further problems instead of profits. Michael Brecher, *The New States of Asia* (London: Oxford University Press, 1963), p. 205. Nehru told Norman Cousins in 1951 that a major conflict would not affect Indian territory directly because 'India does not come into the picture at all as an important theatre'. Norman Cousins, *Talks with Nehru*, recorded interview (New York: John Day, 1951), p. 51.

[48] See, for example, Panikkar's observation in his book, *In Two Chinas* (London: Allen & Unwin, 1955).

issues their attention.⁴⁹ Even as the Communists swept to victory over the Chinese mainland, however, New Delhi 'did not consider that it need apprehend any hostile activity' from the north for the reason that the vast Tibetan plateau and the Himalayas were a formidable barrier to aggression from that direction.⁵⁰ This view was undoubtedly reinforced by the assumption that any Chinese government that emerged from the civil war would have to devote its entire energies to the massive task of reconstruction.

The actual emergence of a People's Republic in China, however, appears to have dispelled some of this complacency in the context of communist insurrection in India, Burma, Malaya, and the Philippines and the 'hard line' pursued by Russia towards the West. The Communist leadership of China was at least as dedicated to the restoration of China's historical power and influence as the Kuomintang had been, and it had the added motivation of communist ideology and the sense of purpose associated with a revolutionary movement. Its attitude towards India was anything but friendly; Mao Tse-tung, in his book, *The Chinese Revolution and the Chinese Communist Party,* published in 1939, had listed Burma, Nepal, and Bhutan, among other areas, as Chinese territory, and, even before its actual triumph in China, the Communist leadership had depicted India as a 'semi-colonialist country' requiring liberation through the establishment of a communist regime.⁵¹ On 1 January 1950 Peking declared its intention to 'liberate' Tibet. In a written ultimatum to the Khampa leader, Topgay Pangdatshang, in the same month, the Chinese Communist government allegedly declared its intention to 'liberate' Tibet and after that Nepal, Sikkim, and Bhutan and warned the Kham Tibetans, who occupied southeastern Tibet, to co-operate in this scheme or be annihilated.⁵²

The emergence of a Communist regime in China caused con-

---

⁴⁹ Official Chinese maps issued in 1943 had embodied territorial claims down to the pre-1914 'Outer Line', and the Kuomintang had protested against the activities of Indian government officials in the Assam tribal areas south of the McMahon Line in notes to the British Embassy in July, September, and November 1946 and in January 1947, and to the Indian Embassy in February 1947. See note from the Chinese Foreign Affairs Ministry to the Indian Embassy dated 26 December 1959 in *White Paper,* III, pp. 64–65.

⁵⁰ H. M. Patel, *Defence of India,* p. 3.

⁵¹ See reply from Mao Tse-tung to a message of greeting from the Indian Communist party, cited in P. C. Chakravarti, *India's China Policy* (Bloomington: Indiana University Press, 1962), p. 4.

⁵² George N. Patterson, *Tragic Destiny* (London: Faber, 1959), p. 31.

siderable alarm in certain quarters in India.[53] The implications of this development were not lost upon the Indian government,[54] and Panikkar claims to have expressed the view to Nehru in early 1950, before his departure as India's first ambassador to Communist China, that 'with a communist China cordial and intimate relations were out of the question'—a view with which Nehru allegedly agreed.[55] India's response, however, had necessarily to take note of geography and China's superior power. The national Indian government accepted the Tibetan policy of the British Indian government to the extent that, though it recognised Tibetan autonomy it also recognised China's suzerainty (as distinct from sovereignty). Thus, when an observer from the Chinese (Kuomintang) Foreign Ministry protested to Nehru at the Asian Relations Conference in New Delhi in March 1947 regarding a map displayed in the conference hall on which Tibet was shown as a political entity separate from China, the map was removed.[56] Following Peking's announced intention to 'liberate' Tibet, a 'high official of the External Affairs Ministry' informed an American correspondent in February that India would not commit troops to defend the regime of the Dalai Lama but would employ only diplomatic means in defence of Tibetan autonomy.[57] India defended the legality of the Chinese action at the United Nations, opposing any debate on the grounds that it was an internal affair of China, restricting her own response to criticisms of the Chinese resort to force—the method, not the right. Having conceded the Tibetan 'buffer' of the Raj, the Indian government moved to seek a *modus vivendi* with the new China.

The desire for close relations with China was a natural manifestation of the anticolonialism and 'Asian-ness' resulting from Indian colonial subjection, but the strategic motivation was per-

[53] See, for example, statement by the Premier of Assam, Gopinath Bardolai, as cited in the *Hindustan Times*, 5 December 1949; Frank Anthony in Parliament on 17 March 1950, *CAD*, pt. 2, vol. 2, p. 1720; M. R. Masani in Parliament on 4 August 1950, *ibid.*, pt. 2, vol. 5, p. 301; Basil Gould, a former British Political Representative in Tibet, in the *Hindustan Times*, 15 November 1950.

[54] See Nehru's statement in Parliament on 27 November 1959 as cited in *Prime Minister on Sino-Indian Relations*, vol. I, *In Parliament* (New Delhi: Ministry of External Affairs, 1961) p. 213.

[55] *In Two Chinas*, p. 87.

[56] Chakravarti, *India's China Policy*, p. 8.

[57] Robert Trumbull in *New York Times*, 15 February 1950. He correctly concluded that 'Tibet appears to be written off by New Delhi'.

haps an even stronger factor in determining the subsequent efforts of the Indian government to assiduously cultivate Chinese friendship. As the Deputy Minister for External Affairs, B. V. Keskar, explained in the Lok Sabha on 28 March 1951:

> The Government is not unmindful of the protection of our frontiers adjoining Tibet. I may go further and say that the Government feels that the best way of protecting that frontier is to have a friendly Tibet and a friendly China. It is obvious that such a complicated and big frontier cannot be well protected if we have a border country which becomes hostile to us. Therefore, we feel that in tackling the question of Tibet and China, we should always keep in mind that a friendly China and a friendly Tibet are the best guarantee of the defence of our country.

India's speedy recognition of the People's Republic (30 December 1949), her passive acquiescence to China's forceful re-entry into Tibet in October 1950, her defence of China's legal right to assert control of Tibet, and her support for Peking's claim to the Chinese seat at the United Nations were manifestations of this conclusion—if not solely provoked by it. A further corollary was the 'normalisation' of relations with China regarding Tibet in the much-publicized agreement concluded, after lengthy negotiations initiated by India, in Peking on 29 April 1954, in which India relinquished her inherited treaty rights.[58] Significantly enough, Nehru regarded the preamble, containing the five principles of panch sheel or peaceful coexistence,[59] as the most important part of the agreement, for it was felt to be an agreement not to commit aggression against each other.[60]

Certain sections of the press nonetheless sounded words of caution regarding Peking's bona fides. *Pioneer* expressed the view on 1st May 1954 that 'nothing has been secured to rule out further penetration of Chinese Communists into regions bordering on India', and the *Times of India* declared on 4 November that, while Nehru was justified in believing China to be too preoccupied with internal problems to undertake aggression, 'that it is an

---

[58] Text in *Foreign Policy of India: Texts of Documents, 1947-59* (New Delhi: Lok Sabha Secretariat, 2d edition, December 1959), pp. 101-09.

[59] The principles, as enunciated in the preamble, are: mutual respect for each other's territorial integrity and sovereignty, mutual nonaggression, mutual noninterference in each other's internal affairs, equality and mutual benefit, and peaceful coexistence.

[60] See *Times of India*, 1 May 1954; 'INSAF' in *Hindustan Times*, 1 May 1954; *Indian Express*, 4 May 1954.

assumption is something of which Mr Nehru himself is very much aware'. That the Prime Minister himself had doubts about the value of China's professed friendship was evidenced by a circular on foreign policy addressed to the presidents of the Congress party's provincial units shortly after the conclusion of the Sino-Indian agreement on Tibet. In this he stated: 'Surely it is better, with nations as well as individuals, to hope for and expect the best, but at the same time to be prepared for any eventuality'.[61]

[61] Extract from Congress Bulletin, June–July 1954, cited in M. W. Fisher and J. V. Bondurant, *Indian Views of Sino-Indian Relations*, Berkeley, Calif.: Indian Press Digests, Monograph Series, no. 1 (1956).

Chapter Three

HIMALAYAN POLICY, 1947-1958

OFFICIAL ASSESSMENT

The long-term apects of Himalayan security were investigated by the high-level North and North-Eastern Border Defence Committee, established in February 1951 at the request of the Defence Ministry. The report of the committee, submitted to the ministry in early 1953, included a large number of recommendations. Among the major proposals were 'the reorganisation and expansion of the Assam Rifles, the extension of administration in the NEFA, development of intelligence network along the border, development of civil armed police, development of communications and check posts'.[1]

The recommendations were examined by an *ad hoc* committee of secretaries from the ministries concerned and finally by the Defence Committee of the Cabinet. The recommendations, with several exceptions, were accepted and implemented. The Ministry of Home Affairs undertook the development of the border areas with the relevant state governments, which received substantial help from the Union government under the Five Year Plans. The construction of a number of roads was entrusted to Army engineers, while other road construction was undertaken by the Ministry of Transport. A few of the roads proposed by the Committee, however, 'were not accepted or proceeded with, either for tactical reasons or because expenditure on the construction of such roads was colossal and out of proportion to the good that they may do'.[2]

NORTH-EASTERN FRONTIER AGENCY

The Indian government appears to have viewed the immediate danger from Chinese activities as coming from the direction of the North-Eastern Frontier Agency (NEFA), as the area was now

[1] Prime Minister Nehru, replying to the debate on India-China relations in the Rajya Sabha on 9 December 1959. Cited, *Prime Minister on Sino-Indian Relations*, vol. I: *In Parliament* (Ministry of External Affairs, undated), p. 251.
[2] *Ibid.*, pp. 251-252.

called. The Nehru administration had unobstrusively continued British policy towards the tribals in north and northeast Assam. The NEFA and the remote tribal areas continued to be treated for administrative purposes as a responsibility of the Ministry of External Affairs, consistent with British practice and the special attention required by these areas for reasons of strategy and tribal welfare.[3] Regular administration was extended to the Subansiri Division in 1949, to the Abor and Mishmi Hills districts in 1949–50, and to Tawang in February 1951.[4] In 1953 the Indian Frontier Administrative Service (IFAS) was established in the External Affairs Ministry to administer the NEFA.

Although these measures were undoubtedly influenced in the later stages by Tibetan developments, their basic motivation was seemingly in accord with the explanation Nehru later made in a letter to the Premier of the People's Republic of China, Chou En-lai, dated 26 September 1959: 'Shortly after India attained independence in 1947 the Government of India decided, as a matter of policy, to bring these frontier areas under more direct administrative control to enable them to share in the benefits of a welfare state, subject to the protection of their distinct social and cultural patterns'.[5] After the Chinese entry into Tibet in October 1950, however, strategic factors became paramount, as the government publicly declared. Speaking in Parliament on 20 November 1950, Nehru stated that, notwithstanding Chinese pretensions to sovereignty over areas in Assam south of the [McMahon] line fixed by the 1914 Simla treaty, 'The McMahon Line is our boundary, map or no map. We will not allow anybody to come across that boundary'. The same day, the Indian Defence Ministry declared that it was continuing to reinforce the northern border. On 23 November, Nehru assured Parliament that northern border defences were being kept 'constantly under review' and that no invader would be permitted to cross that border.

In response to reports received by the government late in 1950 of Chinese troops in some strength near the McMahon Line, about one hundred Army paratroops were dropped into unreconnoitred frontier areas to deter surreptitious Chinese intrusions.[6] The Assam

---

[3] The NEFA was constitutionally a part of Assam administered by External Affairs, with the Governor of Assam acting as the agent of the President of India.
[4] Ministry of External Affairs, *Report*, 1949–50, p. 9.
[5] *White Paper*, II, p. 42.
[6] Information obtained in an interview with a high-ranking Indian army

Rifles were reorganised in 1953, albeit without any apparent increase in strength. In 1954 the government approved a considerable expansion of the Security Intelligence Services for the eastern and northern frontiers, with particular emphasis on the NEFA; the Director of the Intelligence Bureau [7] invited applications to the Security Services from candidates from the fourteen different tribes who fulfilled the necessary educational qualifications.[8] Young tribesmen were also encouraged to enter the Army as a career.

Immediate steps were taken to improve communications throughout the mountainous tribal areas. The NEFA contained only about one hundred miles of road as of 1950, much of this being badly damaged by the earthquake which shook Assam in that year. Road construction was emphasised in a special five-year development plan for NEFA sanctioned in 1953, and the allocation for roads rose in a subsequent revised plan. The committees set up for NEFA communications—which included representatives from the ministries of Defence, External Affairs, and Transport and from the Army and Air Force—worked out an integrated and economical plan of airfields, motor and jeep roads, and trails for porters, mules, and horses. Included in the programme was the construction of fair-weather airstrips at Along and Ziro and of roads to link Dirrang Dzong with Foothills and Kimin with Ziro.[9] By 1957, Army engi-

---

officer. Nehru claimed in Parliament on 23 February 1961 that within a year of the Chinese invasion of Tibet, his government had increased the number of checkposts in NEFA from three to 25, covering 'most' of the important routes, that a 'little later this number was further increased all along the NEFA border and the middle sector', and that in 1954 these checkposts were moved closer to the actual border. *Prime Minister on Sino-Indian Relations*, vol. I, p 386. According to one observer, the number of border checkposts was increased in NEFA from the three in existence in 1950 to 18 major posts and 15 outposts in 1951 and to 44 major posts and 56 outposts by 1954. P. C. Chakravarti, *India's China Policy* (Bloomington: Indiana University Press, 1962), p. 165n.

[7] The mainstay of government intelligence is the Intelligence Bureau, which functions under the control of the Home Ministry and is responsible for all intelligence activity, including that beyond India's frontiers. The armed forces have a smaller and subordinate military intelligence service, but its scope is limited to internal military security and to intelligence within operational areas.

[8] Colin Reid, *Daily Telegraph*, 8 June 1954. Reid stated that 'attempts by political groups and other organizations to cause estrangement between the India Government and tribesmen are said to be the reason for the measures'.

[9] See statement by the Parliamentary Secretary to the Minister of External Affairs, J. N. Hazarika, in Parliament on 16 March 1956, *LSD*, pt. 1, vol. 2, cols. 1097–1098. See also his statement in *ibid.*, pt. 1, vol. 2 (6 April 1955), cols. 1911–1912.

neers had pushed through a road from Tezpur half-way to Bomdila and were almost all the way to Ziro. They were relieved in that year by the NEFA Public Works Development Organisation (PWDO), which completed the construction in late 1959.

Related to the security of the McMahon Line, though the areas involved did not lie immediately contiguous to it, was the unresolved question of the Naga tribes, who inhabited the area astride the Indo-Burmese border. Many Nagas had been reluctant—some had adamantly refused—to accept their automatic transfer from British to Indian rule in 1947 and had boycotted the 1952 Indian elections. Their growing discontent erupted into open insurrection in early 1956. The policy of the Nehru administration towards the Nagas had, up to this point, been basically a continuation of the former British policy of the minimum possible interference with the traditional society consistent with the maintenance of law and order and loose political control. The Indian government would not tolerate any Naga demands for independence, however, and it replied to the insurrection by rejecting any possible negotiations and moving to crush the revolt by force. A thick curtain of secrecy descended over the area, which was declared closed to all persons save those sanctioned by the Defence Ministry.

The strength of the security forces in the Naga areas was steadily built up in early 1956, and major counteractions were begun on 15 April 1956 by army units, elements of the Assam Rifles, and armed police units from various states. The hard core of perhaps 1,500 or 2,500 Naga 'effectives', however, managed to elude their pursuers while continuing their activities. The mounting burden of the 'pacification' campaign led the government to attempt to compromise with Naga demands by forming, on 1 December 1957, the Naga Hills–Tuensang Frontier Area embracing some 400,000 Nagas. When this did not appreciably diminish hostile activity the Indian authorities made an effort, in 1959, to associate 'loyal' Nagas with the pacification campaign by creating a force of Naga Home (Village) Guards as a military-cum-police force to be posted near 'troubled' villages, that is, those of suspect loyalty.

MIDDLE SECTOR

In 1950 there were in the middle sector (Punjab, Himachal Pradesh, and Uttar Pradesh) only two checkposts, both on the Himachal Pradesh–Tibet border.[10] The number of checkposts in

[10] See Nehru's statement in Parliament on 23 February 1961, cited in n. 6 above.

this sector, however, was increased in 1951, and the posts were moved closer to the Tibetan border in 1954.[11] At the beginning of 1954, the Uttar Pradesh state government voted a supplementary grant of over Rs 170,000 for expenses incurred for special police guarding the border with Tibet. It was announced in Lucknow in mid-October that the strength of the state's armed frontier constabulary was to be doubled and the force reorganised with a stronger headquarters. In September, the Ministry of External Affairs created a new section to co-ordinate much of the administration in the frontier areas of Kashmir, Punjab, Uttar Pradesh, and Himachal Pradesh.

Improvements were also made in the communications in these areas. Work commenced in 1951 on the Hindustan-Tibet road, which was eventually to extend from Simla to the Tibetan border.[12] In June 1954, the Uttar Pradesh authorities announced that a $5.6 million road-building programme financed by the Centre was shortly to be launched to link places of strategic importance in the Kumaon Hills adjoining the borders with Nepal and Tibet. The first air link with the Kulu Valley was opened on 18 January 1956, and on 25 May 1956 a seven-mile jeep road linking Sainwala to Kandaiwala (Himachal Pradesh) was officially inaugurated, with plans to extend the road to the Tibetan border via Chini within three years. The opening of the Rohin bridge on 5 November 1958 provided an all-weather route between Gorakhpur (Uttar Pradesh) and eastern Nepal. During the Second Plan period (1956-61) the Punjab state government constructed a nine-mile connecting Grampjoo and Keylong.

LADAKH

Indian attention had initially been drawn to Ladakh by the advances of Pakistani forces early in the Kashmir conflict. Their capture of Kargil had temporarily cut the 200-mile mule track

---

[11] *Ibid.* Robert Trumbull reported in the *New York Times* on 4 August 1951 that eight new police checkposts had been established on the Uttar Pradesh–Tibet border, all reinforced with more than the usual complement of police and two of them equipped with wireless.

[12] A Hindustan–Tibet road was first suggested in 1841 by an official of the East India Company, J. D. Cunningham, as an inducement to merchants from Amritsar to Delhi to undertake the journey to Gartok in search of shawl wool. For details on subsequent progress, see Alistair Lamb, *Britain and Chinese Central Asia* (London: Routledge and Kegan Paul, 1960), p. 83.

linking Srinagar and Leh via the 11,500-foot Zoji La Pass, forcing the Indian Army to improvise an airstrip at Leh and hastily construct an alternate and less vulnerable land route to Leh from Manali in the East Punjab via the 16,200-foot Bara Lacha Pass. With the recapture of Kargil by Indian forces in November 1948, Ladakh returned to Indian control. An infantry battalion and supporting arms were thereupon permanently sited at Leh against the contingency of renewed conflict with Pakistan.

The Chinese entry into western Tibet late in 1950 does not appear to have greatly alarmed New Delhi about the security of adjacent Indian territory, perhaps because of a belief that the barren Ladakhi landscape was a physical deterrent. Certain precautions were nonetheless taken. In 1950 posts were established at Chushul and Demchok,[13] and in 1951 'army' units were purportedly stationed in various checkposts and 'expeditions' were sent by the Army and the police to the farthest points of Indian territory.[14] In mid-1954 the Ministry of External Affairs assumed control of the 300-mile Ladakh–Tibet border and reorganised the system of checkposts, which had hitherto been manned somewhat haphazardly by the state police. In response to successive Chinese intrusions after 1954, additional posts were established, except in Aksai Chin because it was a very difficult area of access and because the government was 'busy elsewhere'.[15]

Construction of a motor road from Srinagar to Leh commenced in 1954, and in early 1956 it was reported that work was being speeded up on the road, which was designed 'to provide a closer link with Kashmir's northernmost strategic areas of Ladakh whose 37,000 square miles border with Tibet on the east and Chinese Sinkiang on the north'.[16] Work on this project was halted in 1958, however, after the discovery of financial irregularities; the engineers were suspended and an enquiry was initiated.

Himalayan Kingdoms

In accordance with the dictates of national security—but in contradiction of his avowed policy of anti-imperialism and non-intervention in the internal affairs of other states—Nehru pursued

[13] *The Round Table*, 211 (June 1963), p. 215.
[14] See Nehru's statement in Parliament on 23 February 1961, cited in n. 6 above.
[15] *Ibid*.
[16] Delhi correspondent in *The Times*, 29 May 1956.

the former British policy of direct or indirect control over the Himalayan states of Sikkim, Bhutan, and Nepal.

Sikkim

On 15 August 1947 India inherited Sikkim as a protectorate, with the right to send a political officer to assist the Maharaja in the administration of the country, relations being temporarily governed by a standstill arrangement. In early 1949, considerable unrest and occasional rioting occurred throughout the state as a result of dissatisfaction with the feudal system. Acting on the request of the Maharaja and ostensibly 'in the interests of law and order' [17], the Indian government intervened on 7 June by despatching a company of troops, who functioned under the general direction of the political officer resident in Gangtok, the capital. Indo-Sikkimese relations were regularised in a treaty signed on 5 December 1950, which reaffirmed the relationship in existence on 15 August 1947. Sikkim was therein designated a 'Protectorate of India', with India retaining responsibility for the defence and territorial integrity of the tiny state with the right to construct and maintain communications for strategic purposes and to take such measures as it considered necessary for the defence of Sikkim and the security of India, preparatory or otherwise and whether inside or outside the kingdom.[18]

In 1951, the Indian government seconded an experienced political officer, J. S. Lall, to serve as *dewan* or chief minister of Sikkim. Under his guidance extensive administrative, land, and tax reforms were subsequently introduced. The Indian subsidy totalled $168,000 in each of 1951, 1952, and 1953 and rose to $478,000 in 1954 and $1,120,000 in 1955.[19] That year marked the commencement of a Rs 3 crore seven-year development plan underwritten by India in which the emphasis was placed upon communications; included was a

---

[17] *Hindustan Times*, 8 June 1949.

[18] For the text of the treaty, see *Foreign Policy of India: Texts of Documents, 1947-59* (New Delhi: Lok Sabha Secretariat, 2d edition, December 1959), pp. 37-40. The preface to the treaty as reprinted in an official publication is a comment by the *Hindustan Times* dated 7 December 1950 which states: 'This treaty will be hailed as a big step in strengthening frontier defences. Now that the Himalayas are no longer insuperable barriers as of old, it is a matter of vital import to ensure adequate safeguards along the frontiers'. *Foreign Policy of India*, p. 35.

[19] Rosemary Brissendon, 'India and the Northern Frontier', *Australian Outlook* (April 1960), p. 21.

road from Gangtok to Natu Pass on the Tibetan border, which Nehru formally opened in September 1958 while en route to Bhutan.[20] Consistent with the practice followed by the British Indian government, a permit from Indian authorities continued to be necessary for any foreigner wishing to visit Sikkim—and such permits were granted sparingly.

Bhutan

India also inherited the Anglo-Bhutanese treaties of 1865 and 1910 and a standstill agreement was concluded, in effect from 15 August 1947, to govern Indo-Bhutanese relations pending further discussions. In 1946, after the British government had declared its intention to withdraw its authority from the subcontinent, Bhutan had sought clarification from the Congress leadership concerning Bhutan's status with Britain and a sovereign India. On 23 April 1948 a Bhutanese delegation visited Delhi and handed the Ministry of External Affairs a request for revision of the 1865 treaty. Bhutan asked for return of 800 square miles of territory ceded to British India in the 1865 treaty and promised to forego claims to a subsidy; as an alternative, Bhutan requested the return of 300 square miles of adjoining forest land in West Bengal and Assam and an increase in the existing subsidy from Rs 200,000 to Rs 800,000. Desirous of retaining a special position in the strategic kingdom, New Delhi was able to effect a compromise arrangement in a treaty of friendship concluded at Darjeeling on 8 August 1949.[21]

Under the provisions of the treaty, the Indian government guaranteed Bhutan's internal autonomy and increased the annual subsidy to Rs 500,000 while obtaining the right of consultation on matters involving Bhutan's external relations [22] and supervisory privileges over the importation into Bhutan of ordnance materials or stores which might be required or desired for the strength and welfare of

---

[20] In the absence of either railroads or airstrips, Sikkim's direct surface contact with the external world remained a rather primitive road linking Gangtok with the Indian railhead at Siliguri, seven miles to the south via Rangpo. The Rangpo–Gangtok link via Singtam was, however, closed to heavy traffic during the monsoon season.

[21] For the text, see *Foreign Policy of India*, 2d edition, pp. 17–19.

[22] This clause has been described, in a rather paternal fashion, by one Indian daily as 'designated as a shield for Bhutan inasmuch as it secures her against the danger of being sucked into the vortex of the cold war'. *Times of India* leader, 3 February 1961.

Bhutan. India also agreed to return to Bhutan 32 square miles of territory in the Dewangiri district of Assam, a cession sanctioned by Parliament on 8 August 1951.

Following the Chinese occupation of Tibet in 1950–51, the Reserve Bank of India undertook to meet all of Bhutan's foreign exchange needs for development purposes on request and with no fixed ceiling. Bhutan continued, however, to regulate the entry of outsiders, including Indians, and India's official representative continued, as in the past, to reside in Gangtok. The isolation of the kingdom was a cause of increasing concern to New Delhi in view of Chinese activities in Tibet and the appearance of Chinese cartographic claims to portions of Bhutan. In September 1958 Nehru accordingy undertook an arduous five-day journey to Bhutan by pony, mule, and yak via Sikkim and Yatung (Tibet), a visit 'intended to remind its feudal authorities that their lawful overlord is in Delhi and not Peking.' [23] A direct outcome of the visit was the announcement, in New Delhi on 7 October 1958, that steps were being taken to construct direct road links between Jayanti and Sentula and between Garubhada and Hatisar. By the end of the 1958 fiscal year, the Indian government had begun work on these roads and had also agreed to make available Rs 150,000 for road development within Bhutan.[24]

Nepal

Nepal covers 600 miles of India's northern frontier, and its stability and integrity are, therefore, of vital concern to any Indian government. On 15 August 1947 the Indian Union inherited the relationship laid down in the Anglo-Nepalese treaty of 1923, by which the complete independence of Nepal was recognised. Shortly after partition, New Delhi concluded a tripartite agreement with Britain and Nepal whereby India obtained the right to recruit Gurkhas for her army—a right previously restricted to Britain alone. During the troubled 1947–49 period, India was also able to obtain the services of a Nepalese force of about one brigade for internal security duties. Unlike Britain in the past, however, the Indian Union could not hope to monopolise Nepal's external relations.

The Union government approached the issue of relations with Nepal with circumspection, and not until it became clear that a Communist victory in China was imminent did it state publicly,

[23] *The Economist*, 26 September 1958.
[24] Ministry of External Affairs, *Report*, 1958–59, p. 12.

and in categorical terms, its deep interest in Nepalese affairs. In early 1950, as soon as the newly established Chinese Communist regime announced its intention to 'liberate' Tibet, the Indian and Nepalese governments undertook bilateral discussions relating to defence.[25] In a strongly worded statement in Parliament on 17 March 1950, Nehru noted the 'identical interests' of the two countries and declared: 'It is not necessary for us to have a military alliance with Nepal . . . [but] the fact remains that we cannot tolerate any foreign invasion from any foreign country in any part of the sub-continent. Any possible invasion of Nepal would inevitably involve the safety of India'. He added, however, 'I have not the slightest apprehension of any invasion of Nepal. I do not think any such invasion of Nepal is easy or possible, nor do I think it is at all likely'; he only wished, he said, to make it clear to Parliament the official policy in such matters.

Nehru visited Nepal in June. The interdependence of the two countries was reaffirmed in a treaty of peace and friendship signed in Kathmandu on 31 July 1950.[26] In letters exchanged between the two governments on the same occasion, it was stipulated that 'neither Government shall tolerate any threat to the security of the other by a foreign aggressor. To deal with any such threat the two Governments shall consult together with each other and devise effective counter-measures'. In apparent accordance with the provisions of the treaty, Nepal, in response to Tibetan developments, tightened the system of frontier guards on its northern border with the aid of Indian personnel. The extent of these precautionary measures is reflected in the rise in the cost of these defence posts from $42,000 (1952) to $280,000 (1954).[27]

India's deep interest in developments affecting Nepal was restated by Nehru after the outbreak (in late 1950) of a revolt against the feudal regime of the Rana family by armed supporters of the Nepali Congress party operating from bases in India. Speaking in the Constituent Assembly on December 6, the Indian Prime Minister declared:

[25] The initiative reportedly came from Nepal. See Robert Trumbull in the *New York Times*, 16 February 1950. Trumbull also cited an External Affairs Ministry spokesman as stating that, while India would not commit troops in defence of the Dalai Lama's regime, she would regard an attack on Nepal as an attack on India.

[26] For the text, see *Foreign Policy of India*, 2d edition, pp. 31–33.

[27] L. G. Pine (ed.), *The International Year Book and Statesman's Who's Who 1959* (London: Burke's Peerage, Ltd.), p. 449.

So far as the Himalayas are concerned, they lie on the other side of Nepal, not on this side. Therefore, the principal barrier to India lies on the other side of Nepal. We are not going to tolerate any person coming over that barrier. Therefore, much as we can appreciate the independence of Nepal, we cannot risk our own security by anything not done in Nepal which permits either that barrier to be crossed or otherwise leads to the weakening of our frontiers.

This declaration was incompatible with the noninterventionist pledge entered into by the Indian government in the July treaty, and the preparation and launching of the attacks into Nepal from Indian soil—with the complicity of at least the Bihar state government—were also scarcely consistent with the same solemn undertaking. The Union government continued to profess its neutrality, but its actions were unmistakably anti-Rana.

The reform-minded King Tribhuvan and his family were granted refuge in the Indian embassy in Kathmandu on 6 November and were flown to Delhi in an Indian Air Force plane on 11 November. Deposed by an emergency session of the Rana-controlled Nepalese Parliament on 7 November in favour of the three-year-old Crown Prince, the King was nevertheless received by the President of India on 13 November and the Indian government continued to recognise him as the Nepalese head of state, and apparently influenced Britain and the United States to adopt a similar policy. Indian authorities gave constant advice to both parties to the dispute during the period of change-over in Nepal, Nehru acting as mediator in discussions held between the representatives of the Ranas and of the King Tribhuvan–Nepali Congress alliance in New Delhi in January–February 1951. These discussions culminated in an agreement which ended the lengthy (1846–1951) tenure of the Rana oligarchy.

India's involvement in Nepal steadily deepened. In response to Dr. K. I. Singh's abortive coup on 22 January 1952, Indian troops were despatched to Nepal to assist in suppressing this ostensibly communist-inspired peasant uprising and were instrumental in Singh's capture. Alarmed at Singh's relationship with elements of the poorly armed, organised, and equipped Royal Army of some 25,000, the Nepalese government requested the assistance of Indian army officers to reorganise the force. An Indian military mission was accordingly established on 7 April 1952 [28] and proceeded with a

---

[28] According to a high-ranking Indian military informant interviewed by the writer, the Indian government had initially proposed to bring Nepalese army personnel to India for training but were persuaded by their military advisers

sweeping reorganisation of the Royal Nepal Army into a light division of 6,000 men with better quarters, rations, pay, and equipment and dispersed from Kathmandu to garrisons in the provinces. Selected personnel were also sent to the Indian National Defence Academy for training as officers. In July 1953 the Indian government provided transportation for Nepalese troops assigned to recapture Bellauri, a town near the Indian border, from Communist rebels and also placed a strong force of armed police at the disposal of the Nepalese government.

The Indian aid programme to Nepal steadily increased in scope, involving the despatch of experts to improve the civil service, the undertaking of irrigation projects and aerial geological surveys, the construction of schools and hospitals, the development of communications, and the provision of training facilities for Nepalese in India. In 1952 India pledged an annual subsidy of about Rs 800,000 and extended a loan of about Rs 1.35 crores. After political and economic talks in New Delhi during the period 18-22 July 1953 between Prime Minister M. P. Koirala and Nehru, the Indian government agreed not to levy excise duty on Indian goods exported to Nepal and to provide Rs 1 million a year over a five-year period for seven or eight small irrigation projects. India pledged further aid totalling Rs 7 crores in 1954 and made available Rs 10 crores towards Nepal's first Five-Year Plan, which was announced on 21 September 1956. When Nepal was struck by widespread drought in 1957, India rushed food from its own lean stocks. New Delhi continued to provide all of Nepal's oil and petroleum needs for rupee payment although itself forced to expend scarce foreign exchange to acquire these items.

Indian Army engineers, with Nepalese labourers, constructed a temporary fair-weather airstrip at Gauchar in 1951-52, and improvements to this airfield culminated in the inauguration of the country's first all-weather airport on 13 June 1955. In 1953, Indian Army engineers began construction of the 80-mile Tribhuvan Rajpath to link Thankot (near Kathmandu) with Bhainse Dhoban (near Amlekganj, the railhead close to the Indian frontier) and, despite delays caused by severe floods in 1954, the Rs 3 crore road was formally opened on 30 June 1957. India also joined in a tripartite agreement with the governments of Nepal and the United States,

that a mission inside Nepal would permit its members to familiarise themselves with the country against future contingencies. The mission never numbered more than about two dozen instructors plus cooks and servants.

signed on 2 January 1958, by which they planned to construct 900 miles of roads in Nepal over a five-year period at an estimated cost of $7.5 million, towards which the United States pledged $5 million, India $1,875,000, and Nepal $525,000.*[29]

These various activities indicated that New Delhi appreciated Nepal's crucial role in Indian security. As one American observer aptly commented: 'Once a hermit, then a buffer, she has now become the meat of the sandwich'.[30]

The Indo-Nepalese relationship, however, was subject to constant crises directly or indirectly attributable to the pervasive Indian influence in the country. The Nepalese were sensitive to their country's total dependence upon India for markets and imports, and the restrictions placed upon Nepal's imports and exports by the October 1950 trade agreement merely made Indian intentions even more suspect. The many men demobilised from the Royal Nepal Army after it was reorganized by the Indian military mission, as well as civil servants affected by the presence of Indian administrators, Communists whose party was banned on 25 January 1952 probably with Indian encouragement, opposition politicians who viewed New Delhi as the main bulwark of any incumbent authority in Kathmandu—all possessed grievances which could readily be fanned into open demonstrations of ill will towards India.

When King Tribhuvan passed over the strong man of the Nepalese Congress, B. P. Koirala, and chose instead M. P. Koirala as the first commoner Prime Minister, the followers of the former blamed the move on the aggressive Indian ambassador, C. P. N. Singh, and B. P. Koirala himself charged Singh with taking an 'undue interest' in Nepal's internal affairs. Anti-Indian feeling in the Kathmandu Valley was aggravated by a chronic budgetary and trade deficit. When Nehru visited Kathmandu in the summer of 1951, he was met with a black flag demonstration organised by Tanka Prasad's Praja Pareshad party. An Indian parliamentary delegation on a goodwill visit to the Nepalese capital in May 1954 met with a hostile public reception organised by the Nepali Congress and protesting against the activities of the military mission.

---

*The agreement was subsequently terminated by mutual decision of the three parties for unexplained reasons after only 300 miles of road had been completed.

[30] A. M. Rosenthal, 'Grim Shadows over the Cobra Throne', *New York Times Magazine*, 27 May 1956, p. 47.

The situation caused the Indian ambassador to issue a formal statement in June, denying any Indian desire to interfere in Nepali affairs and explaining the co-operative nature of the Indian military mission and aid programme.[31]

With the conclusion of the Sino-Indian agreement on Tibet in April 1954, the Indian government encouraged Nepal to 'regularize' its relationship with Tibet.[32] In May the King of Nepal and two of his ministers held talks with Indian officials in New Delhi, after which Nepalese Foreign Minister D. R. Regmi announced that his government would take up the question of Nepal-Tibetan talks 'very soon'.[33] Prime Minister Koirala talked with Nehru before and after the latter's visit to China in October and, at a press conference in New Delhi on 13 November 1954, the Indian Prime Minister stated that the question of diplomatic relations between Nepal and China was a matter for the Nepalese government. On 1 August 1955, a joint communiqué issued in Kathmandu by representatives of the Nepalese and Chinese governments declared that an agreement had been reached which affirmed panch sheel as the basis of Sino-Nepalese relations and provided for the establishment of diplomatic relations.

New Delhi's apparently passive acquiescence in the establishment of Sino-Nepalese diplomatic relations was, in the view of a leading Indian weekly, 'opening the sluice gate to a veritable flood and unknowingly heading for tragic consequences in her mistaken belief that such crumbs of friendship will keep Peking in good humour'.[34] The Nehru government could hardly have been unmindful of the dangers of formal relations between Kathmandu and Peking, but it probably regarded them as inevitable, and opposition as futile. It appeared to take the same attitude towards the Nepalese-Soviet agreement in July 1956 regarding the exchange of diplomatic representatives.

Any hopes that India may have had that Chinese (and Soviet) penetration of Nepal could be restricted to a diplomatic presence were quickly dashed when both China and Russia offered economic aid for Nepal's first Five-Year Plan. The alarm with which the Indian government viewed the Sino-Nepalese aid agreement of October

---

[31] See *Times of India*, 18 June 1954.
[32] For some comments, see *The Statesman*, 16 April 1954.
[33] Cited, *Hindu*, 7 May 1954.
[34] *Thought*, 13 August 1955, p. 3.

1956 [35] was revealed in several ways. The former Nepalese rebel, Dr. K. I. Singh, on his return from exile in China had professed to hold the same views concerning his country's future as did the Indian government.[36] He visited New Delhi in the second week of October and was received by Nehru, the President of India, and the Indian Home Minister. Voicing beliefs which he evidently considered would enhance his attractiveness to Indian officialdom, Singh declared that he opposed Nepal's accepting Chinese aid, disapproved of Nepal's receipt of foreign aid from any country other than India, and opposed the presence of other than an Indian embassy in Kathmandu.[37] In the same month, Indian President Rajendra Prasad visited Nepal and declared in Kathmandu on 22 October 1956 that 'any threat to the peace and security of Nepal is as much a threat to the peace and security of India. Your friends are our friends and our friends yours'.[38] The resignation of Nepalese Prime Minister Archarya on 9 July 1957 and his replacement by Singh could, therefore, be regarded as somewhat of a pro-Indian shift in Kathmandu, which was not perceptibly affected by the King's imposition of direct rule later in the year, on 14 November.

Significance of Himalayan Activities

The significance of India's activities in the Himalayan region during this 1947–59 period, though generally unnoticed by observers preoccupied with studying Nehru's global diplomacy in all its peculiar manifestations, did not pass without comment in the Western press. In late 1954 one observer declared that 'all along the frontier from Kashmir to Assam doors are being guarded more closely than before. India's small but efficient Army is watching the Himalayan passes'.[39] An American political columnist wrote in June 1956:

The dominantly realistic side of Mr Nehru's foreign policy is Himalayan. Tibet's great plateau with a southern border of no less than 2500 miles overshadows the Indian plain. India has taken care to put the intervening Himalayan countries of Sikkim, Bhutan and Nepal under its protection. Included in the category of prudent diplomacy of course is exchange of

---

[35] Text in Girilal Jain, *India Meets China in Nepal* (New York: Asia Publishing House, 1959), pp. 166–70.
[36] See *The Statesman*, 19 November 1955.
[37] See *Times of India*, 12 October 1955.
[38] *Ibid.*
[39] Ferdinand Kuhn, *Washington Post*, 27 December 1954.

words about co-existence with Peiping. But roads and airfield construction which has marked Red China's transformation of Tibet offsets all these assurances. Security rises superior to fine sounding phrases even in India.[40]

Or, as the English weekly, *Time and Tide*, commented on 10 October 1958: 'Mr Nehru becomes more of a realist every day about the relationship between India and China. A large part of India's growing military budget is being quietly spent on building strategic roads and strengthening patrols on the Tibetan border and not as is commonly supposed on the border of Pakistan'.

While fully aware of the strategic implications of China's occupation of Tibet, the Indian government had responded to the altered Himalayan situation in a manner that must be described as politically discreet, diplomatically cautious, economical of financial and material resources, and projected over a long term. The overriding determinant of its policy was to avoid giving provocation to Peking at almost all costs and to continue the tranquillity of the Himalayan region primarily by astute diplomacy. Prudence dictated that certain precautionary measures be taken to deter surreptitious Chinese intrusions of the long and difficult Himalayan frontiers, subversion of the frontier tribes, and inroads into India's dominant position in the Himalayan kingdoms—but these measures were modest in scope. In the absence of a clearly recognizable challenge from China, priority had for understandable reasons to be given to national economic development in the allocation of very limited resources and certain risks had to be taken. A vigorous and publicised programme of Himalayan security measures was also virtually precluded by the fear that such activities would compromise the government's professions of friendship and goodwill towards China and provoke the very response which Indian diplomacy sought to prevent—an overt challenge along the long Himalayan frontier. The measures actually undertaken by India in the Himalayan region, therefore, were diplomatic, administrative, and police measures; anything which could be construed by Peking as concerted defence preparations was studiously avoided.

[40] Herbert Elliston, *ibid.*, 10 June 1956.

Chapter Four

HIMALAYAN POLICY, 1959–1961

POLICY WEAKNESSES

The inadequacy of a cautious and limited response to Chinese policy should have become progressively more apparent to the Indian government. Only a few short weeks after the conclusion of the much-publicized 1954 agreement, Chinese patrols began a series of intrusions into territory claimed by Peking as *terra irredenta*. Chinese maps continued to appear showing large areas of the Himalayan region as within the international boundaries of the People's Republic of China. Perhaps most ominous was China's speedy road-building along the entire Himalayan frontier, and particularly the Aksai Chin road; surveys for the road commenced in 1955, actual construction was carried out in 1956–57, and completion of the project was announced in the Peking press on 5 October 1957, its location being noted on a map appended to the announcement.

The Indian government was well-informed on Chinese border activities and could scarcely have regarded the new roads and airstrips throughout southern Tibet as having only an internal significance. Nor could India view Peking's actions elsewhere with equanimity. The New Delhi correspondent of a leading English weekly wrote in early 1957 that China's support of the Soviet suppression of the Hungarian revolt and its attitude towards the Burmese frontier and Nepalese internal affairs 'has dimmed the faith of the External Affairs Ministry in neutralism—at any rate as far as south-east Asia is concerned'; he claimed that 'senior officials in New Delhi have now reached a point at which they have written off the Panch Sheela as scraps of paper'.[1] The 'discovery' of the Aksai Chin road later that year . . . served to confirm earlier suspicions.

In an *aide memoire* dated 24 September 1956 regarding the exchange of gunfire between Indian and Chinese 'police' in Shipki

---

[1] *The Economist*, 16 March 1957, p. 920.

Pass, the Indian government informed the Chinese government that the border Security Force had been directed 'on no account to retire from their position or to permit Chinese personnel to go beyond where they are even if this involves a clash' and warned that if China did not take immediate action to desist from such activities 'there might be an unfortunate clash on our borders'.[2] New Delhi was apparently more fearful of such an eventuality than was Peking, however, and her response to subsequent intrusions of her northern frontiers remained restricted to diplomatic notes and the continuation of certain road projects in threatened areas. According to an informed Indian military source, persistent reports by traders, airplane pilots, and police officials regarding Chinese activity along the Aksai Chin route were either dismissed as unimportant by Nehru and his Cabinet colleagues or totally ignored. Excessive caution characterized the Indian government's response to China's public revelation of the road's existence (itself a blatant challenge from Peking); two patrols (one of which was captured by Chinese 'frontier guards') were sent to check the co-ordinates of the road in the spring of 1958, and not until 18 October 1958 did India submit a formal protest about the road.[3]

The road was a clear indication of Peking's intention to assert her authority over *terra irredenta* in total disregard of the Nehru administration. It also focused closer attention on other territorial claims which had been appearing periodically in a succession of Chinese (and Russian) maps. In October 1954 Nehru had raised the issue of such maps with Chou En-lai and claimed to have been told that they were merely 'reproductions of the old pre-liberation maps' which the Chinese government had not had time to revise.[4] Nehru appears to have accepted this as implying that corrections would be made in due course to accord with his own interpretation of the Sino-Indian frontier[5] and to have chosen to regard subse-

[2] *White Paper*, I, p. 19.
[3] Text in *ibid.*, pp. 26-27.
[4] See letter from Nehru to Chou En-lai dated 14 December 1958 in *ibid.*, p. 49.
[5] See *ibid.* In a statement in the Rajya Sabha on 9 December 1959, Nehru admitted, however, to having had doubts about whether Peking really recognized the McMahon Line. Rather than raise the issue with China and ascertain the actual Chinese attitude—which might have revealed a Chinese claim 'which would pose a serious policy challenge to India with far-reaching consequences'— his government had decided to make it clear in every possible way that there was, from the Indian viewpoint, no doubt as to the alignment of the border, in the hope that 'the lapse of time and events will confirm it'. Writing in April

quent intrusions as minor issues initiated by local Chinese authorities and resolvable by secret negotiations. The Aksai Chin road, however, could not be rationalized in this fashion, and the appearance of further maps challenging India's conception of her Himalayan frontier, which appeared in both the *China Pictorial* and Moscow's *New Times* in July 1958, added to New Delhi's alarm and provoked yet another protest note to Peking.[6] In a lengthy letter to Chou En-lai dated 14 December 1958, Nehru protested at the 'incorrect' Sino-Indian boundary shown in an official Chinese journal and clearly sought a definitive reply from China on the entire frontier question.[7]

The reply of the Chinese Premier dated 23 January 1959 could have left no illusions in Nehru's mind now that he was faced with an unequivocal Chinese refusal to recognize the Indian conception of the Sino-Indian frontier almost in its entirety. Chou declared that his government had never recognized the McMahon Line; that the Sino-Indian boundary had never been formally delimited; that the boundaries shown on Chinese maps were consistent with those on earlier maps; and that the issue had not been raised previously because the 'time was not yet ripe'.[8] The Chinese government thereby laid claim to over 40,000 square miles to territory which India regarded as within its own frontiers—over 15,000 square miles in Ladakh, about 200 square miles in the middle sector, and some 32,000 square miles in NEFA.

Scarcely had New Delhi absorbed the full import of Chou's momentous letter than the border question was aggravated by the eruption of the long-simmering Tibetan revolt. Sporadic fighting had been in progress between Chinese troops and Tibetan guerillas, particularly in Kham, since about 1955, and Peking's cancellation of Nehru's proposed visit to Tibet in July 1958 was a direct result of such activity. Desirous of avoiding provocation to China, Nehru persisted in playing down the developments in Tibet. He told a Delhi press conference on 7 March 1959 that press reports of events in Tibet were often 'grossly exaggerated'[9] and, on 17 March, even as the Dalai Lama was fleeing from Lhasa toward asylum in India,

---

1963, however, Nehru stated that in 1954 there 'was no reason even to suspect that there was any major question about the frontiers with China'. 'Changing India', *Foreign Affairs*, 41:3 (April 1963), p. 459.

[6] See Indian note dated 21 August 1958, cited in *White Paper*, I, p. 46.
[7] Text in *ibid.*, pp. 48–51.
[8] Text in *ibid.*, pp. 52–54.
[9] Cited, *The Times*, 7 March 1959.

the Prime Minister referred to events in Tibet as 'more of a clash of wills at present than a clash of arms or physical bodies'.[10] Such a posture in the face of credible evidence to the contrary was subject to a rising tide of domestic and foreign criticism and, in defence of his policy, Nehru was forced to argue the primacy of the 'honour and dignity and the interest of India' over 'the honour and dignity of the causes for which we stand'.[11] At a press conference on 6 April, he admitted that his Tibetan policy had to take note, first and foremost, of Indian security: '. . . we have to keep the various factors in view, the major factor being, of course, our own security. After all, every Government's first duty is to protect its country in every way. The second factor, our desire to have and continue to have friendly relations with China. The third factor, our strong feeling about developments in Tibet. Now, sometimes there is certain contradictions in these. That is inevitable'. He concluded nebulously that 'one has, therefore, in so far as one can to make difficult choices'.[12]

He was faced with a situation from which the repercussions would be incalculable whatever course of action was followed. But, as an English journal warned prophetically: 'Mr. Nehru must choose. There can be honour in neutrality, but people who truckle to bullies cannot hope to lead their fellow men. On the contrary, it is all too likely that those who today ignore the cries of the oppressed will tomorrow themselves be the victims of the evil forces which they sought to ignore'.[13] Mr. Nehru could not ignore Indian public opinion, whose sympathy for the Tibetans was unmistakably clear. Nor could he ignore India's 'image' in the world, based—as his government had persistently claimed—on a higher moral plane than other governments were. Lastly, he could not overlook the symbolic importance of the Dalai Lama and the effect of India's treatment of him on Asia's large Buddhist population.

The result was that India granted political asylum to the Dalai Lama and to thousands of other refugees from the Tibetan fighting —an act which Peking could hardly be expected to regard as other than an unfriendly one. The contingency of a flight by the Dalai Lama had been foreseen.[14] According to one usually well-informed

[10] Cited, *Prime Minister on Sino-Indian Relations*, vol. I. *In Parliament* (Ministry of External Affairs, n.d.), p. 1.
[11] Statement in the Lok Sabha, 2 April 1959. *LSD*, 2d Sess., vol. 28, col. 9269.
[12] Cited, *Prime Minister on Sino-Indian Relations*, vol. II, *Press Conferences* (Ministry of External Affairs, n.d.), p. 16.
[13] *Time and Tide*, 3 April 1959.
[14] See Nehru's statement in the Lok Sabha on 27 April 1959, *LSD*, 2d Sess., vol. 30, col. 13498.

source, 'Mr Nehru was sounded, very discreetly, on the possibility of the Dalai Lama's finding refuge in one of the border states: Bhutan, Sikkim or even Nepal. These possibilities were all dismissed in favour of India itself as the lesser evil, presumably because of the possibility that China might over-run these countries in pursuit of the Dalai Lama'.[15] Such fears were not groundless. Chinese forces pursued the Dalai Lama and Khampa refugees right up to the Indian border, Chinese aircraft strafing and bombing up to the border in NEFA and Chinese troops at times crossing into Indian and Nepalese territory. The Dalai Lama and his party of eight crossed into NEFA on the evening of 31 March and were received by the Assistant Political Officer of the Tawang subdivision of the Kameng Frontier Division.

The Indian government stepped up its watchfulness on the NEFA frontier; patrols of the Assam Rifles became more active, checkposts were strengthened, and security was tightened to include even the re-routing of messages leaving Tawang from the military network to a special frequency.[16] But Nehru remained hopeful that if sufficient restraint were shown by his government, Peking would reciprocate after the initial resentment at India's grant of asylum to the Dalai Lama eased. Nehru ordered the Khampas to be disarmed as they entered Indian territory and made it clear that there was no question of a Tibetan government-in-exile on Indian soil and that Tibetans in India should refrain from political activities while 'guests' of India. He also reaffirmed his belief in panch sheel and rudely rebuffed informal suggestions from Ayub Khan for a joint Indo-Pakistan defence of the subcontinent, on the grounds that such an arrangement was tantamount to a military alliance and contrary to nonalignment; he even asked, ingenuously, defence arrangements 'against whom?'[17]

CHINESE AGGRESSIVENESS

The Chinese government was not prepared, however, to ease the tension and extricate Nehru from the painful dilemma into which he had manœuvred himself. Chinese officers in Tibet talked of 'liberating' Sikkim, Bhutan, Ladakh, and NEFA. Every conceiva-

[15] *Foreign Report*, 9 April 1959, p. 8.
[16] John Osman, *Daily Telegraph*, 8 April 1959.
[17] See his statement in the Rajya Sabha, 4 May 1959. Cited in *Prime Minister on Sino-Indian Relations*, vol. I, p. 42.

ble obstacle was placed in the way of the proper functioning of the Indian consulate-general, trade agencies, traders, and pilgrims in Tibet. New currency regulations suddenly introduced in Tibet in July made Indian currency illegal, with consequent heavy losses to Indian traders and an immediate plummeting of Indo-Tibetan trade. China also commenced a new series of border intrusions. On 28 July, a Chinese party appeared in the eastern Pangong Lake region of Ladakh, arrested six Indian policemen, and established a camp at Spanggur. On 7 August, another party ejected soldiers of the Assam Rifles from the border post at Khinzemane in NEFA, provoking an Indian note dated 11 August which stated that 'our security forces have instructions to resist trespassers and to use minimum force necessary for this purpose if warning given by them remains unheeded'.[18] The contempt in which Peking held the warning was reflected on 26 August, when a Chinese force ejected twelve soldiers of the Assam Rifles from the border post at Longju, located 3 or 4 miles south of the McMahon Line, and the Indian detachment fell back to Gallen, about two days' march distant.

Nehru was no longer able to maintain the secrecy of the previous five years relating to the Chinese border intrusions and, in reply to a series of questions and adjournment motions in the Lok Sabha on 28 August, he gave a full acount of the Longju incident and revealed the years of Chinese perfidy which his government had deliberately concealed from the public view in the hopes of a negotiated settlement free from public emotions. He declared, 'While I do not wish to take an alarmist view of the situation, we should naturally be prepared for any eventuality and without fuss or shouting keep vigilant'.[19] In a note to China of the same date, his government again warned that its frontier posts had been directed to use force to maintain the integrity of Indian soil,[20] and, to lend substance to this determination, the Army was assigned responsibility for the NEFA–Tibet border.

Nehru was prepared for minor adjustments on the border, but he stood firm on the principle that the borders should follow the line of the watershed. Unwilling to accept the Chinese challenge in all its reality, he persisted in the belief that somehow Peking would become more reasonable. For a brief period from late September to early November 1959, there were some indications of just such

[18] Cited, *White Paper*, I, p. 41.
[19] *LSD*, 2d Sess., vol. 33, nos. 16–20, cols. 4866–4870.
[20] Cited, *White Paper*, I, pp. 44–45.

a shift by China; after weeks of frustration, the Indian ambassador in Peking was received cordially by the Foreign Ministry and Chou replied with a warm telegram to Nehru's congratulations on the tenth anniversary of the People's Republic. Elated, the Indian government made every attempt to play down the dispute with China, but its hopes were quickly proven illusory. On 20 October, Chinese forces ambushed a patrol from the Indian Tibet Boundary Force in the Kongka Pass area of Ladakh, killing a number of men in the patrol and capturing the remainder.

The incident inflamed Indian public opinion and caused an emergency meeting of the Cabinet, which assigned the Army responsibility for the borders with Tibet of Jammu and Kashmir (Ladakh), Punjab, Himachal Pradesh, and Uttar Pradesh. The security of the Sikkim–Tibet border was entrusted to the Army in November. Nehru gave assurances that chances would no longer be taken with the northern borders, that past mistakes would not be repeated, and that his government would not hesitate to employ force in defence of the country's territorial integrity.[21] Speaking in the Rajya Sabha on 22 December 1959 during the debate on the correspondence exchange in the past between himself and Chou En-lai, he declared:

> We are committed from every point of view to defend our country, to preserve its integrity, to preserve its honour and self-respect. That is not a matter for argument . . . Opinions may differ as to how to do it . . . But the basic thing is clear, and in doing that, in the ultimate analysis, almost any price has to be paid. One cannot proceed on the basis of barter, haggling and the tactics of the market-place where a nation's honour and self-respect are concerned.

Unlike the past, substance had to be lent to such determination, and a reassessment was made of the defence preparations of the country, which had, up to this point, been conceived to meet a military threat, however remote, from Pakistan.

Ayub Khan's Joint Defence Proposal

The undisguised territorial designs of China had provoked renewed public discussion of a possible defence arrangement between India and Pakistan to accord with the strategic indivisibility of the subcontinent. Ayub Khan had referred to the matter in May and June 1959 and, despite Nehru's public rebuff, had repeated his offer to Nehru during his visit to Delhi on 1 September, arguing that the

[21] See his statement as reported in the *Hindustan Times*, 29 October 1959.

subcontinent's internal strife had always invited invasion from the north and that to avert such a recurrence India and Pakistan should compose their differences on a lasting basis 'to defend themselves against the common enemy'.[22] He referred to the proposal again at a press conference in Peshawar on 6 November and repeated the offer during a tour of East Pakistan in January 1960.

Strong support for such a rapprochement came, significantly, from a respected former Commander-in-Chief of the Indian Army, General K. M. Cariappa. In a New Delhi interview on 1 November 1959, he declared that, if immediate steps were not taken to dislodge the Chinese from Ladakh and NEFA, 'it certainly will become a hundredfold more difficult and costly in all respects to do so later', as 'delay and hesitation on our part to act will encourage the Chinese to take more liberties, to keep on making more claims on our territory and to send forward more troops across the frontiers'. He did not see how the political and military implications of the Chinese moves could be separated, and favoured Indian initiative to bring about defence co-operation with Pakistan.[23]

He argued even more forcefully for such a rapprochement in an article published later in the same month. The solution of the Kashmir issue would, General Cariappa claimed, release large numbers of troops from both sides for use along the external borders and would help India to honour her promises to protect the security of Bhutan, Sikkim, and Nepal. He cautioned, 'The defence problems of India and Pakistan are indivisible . . . Pride and prestige factors must be subordinated to achieving the actual need of the hour—which is the security and economic prosperity of the millions in our two countries'.[24] Support for a common defence pact with Pakistan was also expressed by Balraj Madhok, President of the Delhi state branch of the Jan Sangh, the Hindu communalist party.[25]

That there were many difficulties impeding such an arrangement was clear: The Hindu fear of the 'historical ghost'; Pakistani fears of being 'submerged' by the Hindu majority in the subcontinent; Pakistan's declared sectarianism as opposed to India's professed secularism; and Pakistan's military alignment with the West in the Central Treaty and Southeast Asia Treaty defence pacts, as against India's avowed devotion to nonalignment almost as an end in itself.

[22] Cited, *The Statesman*, 2 September 1959.
[23] Cited, *Hindu*, 3 November 1959.
[24] *Hindu*, 14 November 1959.
[25] See *Times of India*, 26 November 1959.

President Ayub dealt with the latter problem at his Peshawar press conference on 6 November 1959, contending that joint defence did not necessarily mean association in foreign policy, as it was a 'simple and straight-forward matter' of 'simply defending the frontiers' and involved no politics.[26] Although such a contention lends itself to extensive debate, the important fact is that, not only did New Delhi show no interest, but it chose to regard the question, publicly at least, with that air of superiority and arrogance all too characteristic of the Nehru administration during the 1947–62 period.[27] Thus, for example, Nehru's response to General Cariappa's well-reasoned viewpoint of 1 November was to inform a press conference on 5 November that 'there is such extraordinary little sense in it that it amazes me. I think General Cariappa is completely off the track mentally and otherwise'.[28]

The incident evidenced Nehru's extreme sensitivity to implicit criticism of his own viewpoints, particularly on matters of foreign policy. It also reflected the view of the government that Pakistan still posed a threat and that a serious Chinese assault against the Himalayan frontiers was neither likely nor feasible in the near future, the latter view being shared by the Army on logistical grounds. The need for closer relations with Pakistan was not, therefore, viewed by the government as pressing. Nehru may have felt that any concerted effort to effect a reconciliation with Pakistan, though basically desirable, would at such a juncture entail a strategic realignment against China, who would interpret it as such and adopt an even more bellicose attitude in which a peaceful settlement of the border dispute would be impossible. He may also have feared that such a direct alignment with a member of the Western alliance against Peking would have alienated Moscow, towards whom he looked as a restraining influence on China's rulers and as a diplomatic counterweight.

NEHRU'S DOUBLE POLICY

The Prime Minister's response to the Himalayan challenge posed by China was cautious—the double policy of defending against

---

[26] Cited, *Thought*, 7 November 1959, p. 1.

[27] *Thought*, commenting on New Delhi's attitude in retrospect (3 November 1962), felt that it evidenced an incredible complacency and naïveté which had 'sprung from the confusion between basic interest and temporary predilection or pre-occupation'.

[28] Cited, *Hindu*, 6 November 1959.

further intrusions and demanding a withdrawal of Chinese forces from Indian territory while seeking a settlement of the issue by conference. This approach was, in effect, a restatement of the policy adopted in 1950–51 with the notable exception that there was no longer any attempt to conceal the military preparations being undertaken to counter Chinese designs. This new attitude was dictated by prudence, domestic politics, and the international attention focused on the dispute, as well as by considerations of national honour and self-respect to which the Nehru government was no less responsive than any other national administration.

Simultaneous with certain military precautions which did not basically alter defence policy towards Pakistan, steps were taken to strengthen the administration in the strategic border areas, accelerate their economic development, and improve communications.

Administrative Steps

Six border districts, modelled more or less on the pattern of the political divisions in NEFA, were established in 1960—Pithoragarh, Chamoli, and Uttarkashi in Uttar Pradesh, Lahaul–Spiti in Punjab, and Kinnaur in Himachal Pradesh. Senior Indian Frontier Administrative Service officers, deputed from NEFA to head the new districts, were given wide administrative and financial powers. A retired Chief of Army Staff, General S. M. Shrinagesh, was appointed governor of Assam on 14 November 1959 after the death of Saiyad Fazl Ali, thus becoming the first Indian military leader to hold the post under the Union government. In early 1960, NEFA, the Naga Hills, and the Tuensang area were united under a single administration.

Police Measures

The police patrolling the Indo-Tibetan border in the middle sector were placed under overall military control in late 1959, and steps were taken to strengthen this constabulary and to raise their efficiency to something approaching that of the Assam Rifles. Security measures were further tightened in January 1960 when the Union government extended the Punjab Security of the State Act 1954 to include Himachal Pradesh.[29] After the outbreak of disorders in the

* The act empowered the lieutenant-governor of Himachal Pradesh to take 'special measures to prevent activities prejudicial to the security of the State or the maintenance of public order'. A similar measure was already in force in Uttar Pradesh.

Anini area of the Lohit Frontier Division, which were suppressed by regular troops, it was decided in December 1960 to establish a NEFA police force of about twelve platoons to deal with the increasing lawlessness in the Agency.[30] In an order published in the Gazette of India of 31 March 1962, the Indian government declared that most of the districts of Pithoragarh, Chamoli, and Uttarkashi, the whole of the Darjeeling district in West Bengal, and what is known as the area beyond the 'inner line' in the Kinnaur district were to be 'notified areas' under the Criminal Law Amendment Act 1961—an action clearly aimed at facilitating control over the movements of persons suspected of being engaged in activities prejudicial to Indian security.

Further efforts were undertaken to quiet the Naga areas, where nearly 30,000 troops and police were occupied with controlling the Naga dissidents. Bowing to the demands of a Naga convention held in 1959, Nehru sanctioned the creation of a state of Nagaland, which was inaugurated on 15 February 1961. Development of the Naga area was accelerated; whereas Rs 4 crores had been spent on the area during the Second Five-Year Plan, the Planning Commission allocated Rs 7.15 crores for development programmes in Nagaland during the Third Plan (1961–66). A major reshuffle of the Nagaland administration was made in late 1961 after the assassination of Dr. Imkengliba Ao, the head of the Nagaland Interim Body, the legislative assembly.

Development Schemes

In early 1960 a committee was set up in the Cabinet Secretariat to ensure the Union government's effective co-ordination of development programmes in the strategic border areas. Development schemes prepared by the states concerned were examined at the Centre and authority was given to the states to proceed with urgent schemes in anticipation of approval from the Centre. For the period of the Third Plan, an outlay of Rs 5 crores was envisaged for roads, buildings, and irrigation works in Ladakh.[31] The Punjab state government increased its allocation for development schemes in the Lahaul–Spiti district for fiscal 1960 to Rs 2 crores (as against less

---

[30] *Times of India*, 16 December 1960.

[31] For details on the schemes outlined, see *Times of India*, 16 August 1960; *Hindu*, 30 December 1959, 24 July 1960; *Asian Recorder*, 23–29 January and 22–28 October 1960.

than Rs 1 crore for 1959), and it planned to develop 100 miles of roads at an estimated Rs 68.38 crores in this area during the Third Plan. The government of Uttar Pradesh undertook twelve road projects in the hill regions bordering Tibet which would ultimately involve an outlay of Rs 65.84 crores, The Center bearing half the cost. The expenditure on NEFA for the Third Plan was estimated at Rs 7.21 crores (double the amount expended during the Second Plan); plans were drawn up for the construction of further airport and landing-field facilities and for greatly increased expenditures on roads.

Communications

A central Border Roads Development Board (BRDB) was created in March 1960 to co-ordinate the various state construction projects with the Army's own hastily conceived road-building programme in the strategic border areas. The over-all plan was to construct 2,500 miles of new roads and improve 1,500 miles of existing roads at an estimated cost of Rs 120 crores over a three-year period. The implementation of the programme was assigned to various project units: *Vartak* (Tusker) in Assam and NEFA; *Dhantok* in Bhutan; *Dragon* in Sikkim; *Deepak* in Himachal Pradesh; and *Beacon* in Ladakh. The heavy burden on the Army engineering corps was partially alleviated by the recruitment, in mid-1960, of a semi-military construction force called the General Reserve Engineering Force (GREF) paid at bonus rates 50 per cent above the usual level. This force was assigned responsibility for primary work, leaving Army engineers to concentrate on the vital bridges. Extra bulldozers and excavators were diverted from the armed services and national development projects, and scarce foreign exchange was expended for United States-made helicopters and transport aircraft to supply these projects. Soviet-made helicopters and transports were bought with rupees.

From its inception up to June 1963, the BRDB carried out the cutting of nearly 1,600 miles of road, developed land communications over 600 miles, and surveyed and made a complete reconnaissance of about 2,700 miles for possible later roads.[32]

The 95-mile Dirrang–Along road was completed in 1960, and new roads were constructed in the foothills north of Sadiya, the military

---

[32] See statement by Defence Minister Y. B. Chavan in the Lok Sabha, 9 September 1963. *LSD*, 3d Series, vol. 20, nos. 16–20, col. 5097.

rail junction in northern Assam. The 79-mile Mokokchung road was completed in the spring of 1962. The track to Gangtok was improved to accommodate truck convoys, and work began in 1961 on an alternative Rangpo–Gangtok link via Pakyang, suitable for uninterrupted heavy vehicular traffic during the monsoon season. In October 1960 the BRDB relieved the Central Public Works Department of the responsibility for the 150-mile North Sikkim highway and completed the project, begun in October 1958, in 1962. On 13 January 1960, construction commenced on the 107-mile road from Phuntsholing in West Bengal to Paro, which is Bhutan's combination fort, Buddhist monastery, and winter capital. Formally completed on 13 February 1962, the road reduced travelling time between the two points from six days by mule and on foot to ten hours by jeep. The Dirrang–Tashigang project, initially undertaken by the Bhutanese, was completed by the BRDB in mid-1962, and, at the request of Bhutan, the government of West Bengal undertook in 1961 to improve the old road from Jalpaiguri to the Indo-Bhutan border so that it would be suitable for vehicular traffic. Communications were also improved along the Indo-Nepal border.

Work on the 153-mile Kargil–Leh pilot road was resumed in early 1959 by state authorities with the assistance of Army engineers, and the road was opened to traffic on 1 August 1960. Improvements were made to the 61-mile long motor road linking Leh and Baltal, the 67-mile Baltal–Kargil section was rendered suitable for three-ton vehicles, and work proceeded on a road to connect Leh with Nubra via Khardung La. A 75-mile jeep track was completed from Leh to Chushul on the eve of the border conflict, by which time work had also begun on a jeep track from Chushul to the border post at Dungti.

Relations with the Himalayan Kingdoms

The developments in Tibet and China's aggressive border policy caused the Indian government to develop even closer relations with Nepal, Bhutan, and Sikkim. On 24 August and 26 November 1959, Nehru restated the intention of his government to defend Bhutan and Sikkim against any act of aggression and, on 27 November, he declared again that any attack on Nepal would be regarded as an attack on India.[88]

---

[88] See *New York Times*, 26 August and 28 November 1959.

Sikkim

In August 1959, India gave Sikkim a grant equivalent to $6 million (U.S.), over half of which was allocated for transportation and communication. A former Indian consul-general in Lhasa, Major S. L. Chibber, was appointed first secretary at the Indian Political Office in Gangtok, and a military officer was appointed to the important post of administrative officer in the Kalimpong district. In response to a request from the Maharajkumar (Crown Prince) Palden Thondup Namgyal, an expert team from the Planning Commission visited Sikkim in April 1961 and drew up a five-year plan of economic development which involved the expenditure of an estimated Rs 8.2 crores. The entire plan was to be underwritten by India, Nehru apparently insisting that India provide the aid as a grant, although it had been envisaged as a loan when the plans were being drawn up.[34]

During his visit to Delhi in January 1961, the Maharajkumar proposed that a militia be raised in the northern frontier area of Sikkim as a means of associating his people with the defence of their country. However, for both military and political reasons, the proposal met with a cool reception from the Indian government. For the Indians it would mean some derogation of their role as sole defenders of Sikkim. Since such a militia would consist of Lepchas and Bhutias but exclude the important Nepalese community in southern Sikkim, it was feared that Indian support for the proposal would involve her in an internal political issue and exacerbate relations with Nepal.[35] New Delhi was, however, able to effect a compromise scheme in an agreement formally concluded on 9 June 1961 whereby the Maharajkumar's palace guard of 60 men under a junior commissioned officer would be expanded to two companies and commanded by an officer of the Indian Army. One of the companies was to function for normal palace duties and the other was to be attached to the Indian army for border security duties. The Indian government agreed to finance the expanded guard and to assist in its recruitment, training, and equipment.

[34] See statement by Thondup Namgyal at his monthly press conference in Gangtok, 3 November 1964. Cited, *Times of India*, 4 November 1964.

[35] *Hindu*, 20 April and 11 June 1961. The Nepalese majority in Sikkim only received Sikkimese citizenship with the passage of the Sikkim Subjects' Regulation legislation in 1961 and, even then, they were still prohibited from settling in the northern valleys.

An interesting sidelight to Indo-Sikkimese relations was provided by the engagement of Crown Prince Palden Thondup Namgyal to an American, Miss Hope Cook of New York City, in late 1961. The announcement was preceded by six months of negotiations between the governments of India and Sikkim,[36] indicating Indian concern at the presence of a foreigner (particularly a citizen of one of the major aligned powers) so close to the source of authority in strategic Sikkim. Perhaps more significant, however, is that the Indian government was unable to prevent the marriage—if it did, indeed, attempt to do so.

Bhutan

Bhutan's reaction to the Tibetan revolt and its aftermath was initially very cautious. Tibetan refugees were not welcomed in the country, and China's seizure of Bhutan's eight Tibetan enclaves in July appeared to instill in some Bhutanese officials a belief that there was a need to enter into closer relations with Peking.

Prime Minister Dorji did not apparently regard the situation as requiring such a drastic step, which would have required renegotiation of the treaty with India. He visited India in August and September in search of further economic aid and, according to one observer, a written guarantee of Indian support in the event of a Chinese attack.[37] At a Delhi press conference on 15 September, he undoubtedly relieved Indian anxieties concerning a possible divergence from the intimate relationship with India by placing great stress on the untroubled amity between India and Bhutan and making it clear that his government had not contemplated asking for aid from any other country.[38] An announcement released in New Delhi on 17 September stated that India had agreed to increase its annual subsidy to Bhutan from Rs 500,000 to Rs 1,200,000—the increase to replace *ad hoc* grants for development schemes—and would bear the estimated Rs 15 crore cost of five all-weather roads to link

---

[36] Pradyumna P. Karan and William M. Jenkins, Jr., *The Himalayan Kingdoms* (New York: D. Van Nostrand, 1963), p. 74.

[37] See despatch from George Patterson in the *Daily Telegraph*, 13 August 1959, in which he cites a personal interview with Bhutan's Prime Minister. It is not known whether Dorji was able to obtain a written guarantee from Nehru, but his request is significant as revealing that even Dorji, who was by no means cool towards India, held doubts as to whether New Delhi could be counted upon in a crisis.

[38] See *The Times*, 16 September 1959.

the two countries.³⁹ Dorji also revealed the intentions of his government to raise a standing army of 2,500 men with modern equipment to augment the country's 5,000 strong militia as soon as finances permitted.⁴⁰

Indo-Bhutanese relations subsequently underwent some strain because of Bhutanese sensitivities towards India's often overbearing attitudes, and Peking's indirect overtures to Dorji via some 'private persons' in 1960 for Sino-Bhutanese talks on their border dispute ⁴¹ clearly sought to capitalize on such feeling. The approach was ignored, however, and, in response to Chinese maps claiming 300 square miles of territory in northeast Bhutan and north of Punakha, the Bhutanese government in early 1961 completely sealed the border in the disputed area and increased the checkposts there.

In January 1961 the Maharaja of Bhutan made his first trip to India since 1954. Speaking to the press at Calcutta on 30 January, he declared that the Chinese proposal for direct talks on the border dispute had some merit in view of the present stalemate in Sino-Indian border discussions and that he might raise the issue with Nehru.⁴² He added, however, that Bhutan had not received offers of aid from any country save India and it did not at that time propose to seek aid from other sources. Either possibility was something which the Indian government clearly meant to prevent so as to preserve its position of dominant influence in the country.

A high-level meeting held in February, presided over by Nehru and attended by the Maharaja, Defence Minister V. K. Krishna Menon, and the three Indian Chiefs of Staff, reportedly worked out a new programme for the discharge of India's responsibility for the defence of Bhutan. Provision was made for a substantial increase in the Indian forces available for speedy despatch to Bhutan in a crisis; more modern helicopters were made available to Indian forces for possible operations in Bhutan; and an intensive study of the facilities for Indian Air Force operations over the state was undertaken.

---

³⁹ The projected roads would link Jaigon (West Bengal) to Paro (western Bhutan) via Hashimera; Dirrang (Assam) and Tashigang (eastern Bhutan); Farkigram and Sarbhang; Garubasha and Hatisar; and Rangi with Dorangmala.

⁴⁰ See his statement in Calcutta on 17 November 1959. Cited in *Times of India*, 18 November 1959.

⁴¹ See statement by the Maharajah at a Calcutta press conference on 30 January 1960. Cited in *ibid.*, 31 January 1961.

⁴² Cited, *ibid.*

Nehru persuaded the Maharaja not to seek direct talks with China. A press statement issued by the Bhutanese ruler before his departure from Delhi revealed that his government had requested the government of India to 'negotiate or take up any question with China' relating to the kingdom's northern border.[43]

In response to the Maharaja's request for experts to formulate development plans, a team from the Planning Commission visited Bhutan in June 1961. The result of the visit was a five-year development plan estimated to cost Rs 17.5 crores—which India agreed to underwrite—of which Rs 12 crores was allocated for roads.[44] A Survey of India team joined local authorities in preparing a detailed map of the state, including the hitherto undelimited and undemarcated (that is, from China's viewpoint) 190-mile Bhutan–Tibet border. At the invitation of the Bhutanese government, senior Indian military officers visited Bhutan in 1961 and made an elaborate survey of defence requirements; following their advice the Bhutanese government proceeded with the strengthening of its militia.[45] In September 1961 Bhutan and India signed a pact to harness the Jaldhaka River for hydroelectric power, Bhutan to receive 250 kilowatts free per year and also a royalty from India of Rs 8 per kilowatt per year from a project to generate 18,000 kilowatts of power annually.

Nepal

Nehru visited Nepal in June 1959 where, even while expressing the view that he did not see a threat to Nepal from the north because of developments in Tibet, he stated that Indian troops had been sent to man eighteen posts on the Nepal–Tibet border at the request of the Nepalese government.[46] In August Nepal announced a 14 per cent increase in its outlay on defence and accepted an Indian offer equivalent to $20 million worth of technical and economic aid, including equipment and training for the 10,000-man Royal Nepal Army. In November the two governments reached

---

[43] Cited, *ibid.*, 15 February 1961.

[44] The Bhutanese government reportedly requested the Indian government to channel to it some of the funds available from the United States under Public Law 40. Clearly desirous of monopolising aid to Bhutan, however, New Delhi informed Bhutan that there was no need for such a diversion, as India could meet all of the state's needs. Karan and Jenkins, *Himalayan Kingdoms*, p. 53.

[45] *Ibid.*, p. 55.

[46] *Daily Telegraph*, 15 June 1959. The Indian personnel were to be replaced as qualified Nepalis became available.

agreement on the Gandak irrigation project after three years' negotiation, with Kathmandu reportedly driving a hard bargain.[47]

Nehru's declaration of 27 November that any attack on Nepal would be regarded as an attack on India, though little more than recognition of geopolitics, touched off anti-Indian resentment in Nepal and forced Prime Minister Koirala to stress publicly Nepal's sovereignty. At the same time, he declared that Nepal would provide such assistance as New Delhi might seek in the event of an attack on India—an assurance viewed by a leading Indian daily as 'welcome evidence that the Government of Nepal is fully aware that the vital interests of the two countries coincide'.[48] Koirala visited New Delhi in January 1960 and secured an Indian pledge of Rs 18 crores in economic aid.[49] A communiqué issued on 28 January, at the conclusion of the visit, attested to the vital interests of each country in the other's 'freedom, integrity, security and progress', their similarity in approach to international problems and desire to co-operate with regard to them, and their agreement on the need for close consultation in matters of common interest.[50]

King Mahendra and members of his government visited New Delhi in April 1960 for further talks, and a joint communiqué issued at the conclusion declared the vital interest each country had in the other's sovereignty, independence, and territorial integrity and reaffirmed their intention to consult together on mutual assistance at the request of either party.[51] King Mahendra returned to New Delhi for a four-day private visit in early July, and Prime Minister Koirala held talks with Nehru in New Delhi on 9 August while en route to Israel. In an agreement signed in Kathmandu on 31 August, India extended a further Rs 91.5 lakhs in economic aid, and the two governments concluded a trade and transit treaty in Kathmandu on 11 September.

Indian aid could not however prevent, nor Indo-Nepali professions of mutual interest conceal, a perceptible and deliberate shift by Kathmandu into a neutral position on the Sino-Indian border dispute and into closer diplomatic and economic relations with both of India's suspect neighbours, China and Pakistan. Prudence dic-

[47] *Hindu*, 27 November 1959.
[48] *Times of India*, 1 December 1959.
[49] This figure included about Rs 4 crores unspent from the amount India had pledged to the previous plan and Rs 3–4 crores allocated for the Chatra Canal project, completed in 1965.
[50] Cited, *Hindu*, 30 January 1960.
[51] Cited, *Times of India*, 27 April 1960.

tated neutrality on the respective merits of China's and India's opposing border claims, and Nepal's conscious efforts to promote closer economic and political relations with China and Pakistan reflected a desire to lessen Nepal's economic (and, consequently, political) dependence upon India.

Prime Minister Koirala visited China in April 1960, winning a general agreement on a delimitation of the Nepal–Tibet border favourable to Nepal and a Chinese pledge of aid worth Rs 10 crores. Chou En-lai returned the visit between 21–29 April, during which the two governments agreed to establish a commission to demarcate the boundary and concluded a treaty of peace and friendship. Nepal declined, however, to include in the treaty a promise not to join a military alliance, on the grounds that this was rendered superfluous by the 1956 Sino-Nepalese treaty and by the fact that panch sheel was the basis of Nepal's foreign policy.[52] The appearance of Chinese claims to Mt. Everest and Chinese military operations against Khampa rebels near Nepal's northern border in the spring of 1960 resulted in border clashes in which some Nepalese frontier guards were killed. The action momentarily caused concern in Kathmandu and led to a strengthening of the posts on the northern border. The Chinese government was quick to apologize for the incidents, however, and paid compensation, with the result that relations were cordial at the time of King Mahendra's coup in December 1960.[53]

The coup provoked a tactless response from New Delhi and led directly to a concerted effort by King Mahendra to loosen the somewhat oppressive tie with India. The action may well have seemed, as one Indian daily described it, 'one step forward, two steps backward',[54] but the attitude adopted by Nehru understandably caused intense resentment in Nepal. On 16 December, while admitting that it was not for him to criticize the King's action. Nehru stated that 'obviously, it is a matter of regret for all of us that the democratic experiment or practice going on there has suffered a setback'.[55] Initiating the debate on foreign affairs in the Rajya Sabha on 20 December, the Indian Prime Minister came out in sharp criticism

[52] See *The Times*, 28 April 1960.
[53] On 15 December, Mahendra dissolved the elected Parliament in which the Nepali Congress party held a two-thirds majority, ordered the arrest of Koirala, other ministers, and a large proportion of the leaders of the political parties, and assumed emergency powers under the provisions of the 1959 Constitution and supplementary legislation.
[54] *Times of India*, 19 December 1960.
[55] Cited, *ibid.*, 17 December 1960.

of the coup and persisted with such comments in subsequent weeks.

In response, Radio Nepal blacked out Nehru's references to Nepal in his Rajya Sabha speech and an anti-Indian press campaign began in Nepal. As each side criticized the attitude of the other, relations were further strained by the beginning of a campaign in the fall of 1961 by armed followers of the Nepali Congress, who raided district arsenals and treasuries in Nepal and clashed with Nepali police and army units. Many of the raids were launched from Indian territory, as in 1950, and the absence of effective action by New Delhi to prevent such activity suggested at least tacit official support of, or acquiescence in, the rebel activity. The refusal of the Indian government to detain and hand over rebel leaders as per the latter's request was legally defensible. The refusal, however, to restrain rebel spokesmen from making statements against the Mahendra government from Indian soil [56] was inconsistent with the attitude adopted towards refugee Tibetan leaders, including the Dalai Lama, and certain Western correspondents (particularly George Patterson), concerning their expression of views on issues relating to Tibetan developments.

It is not at all surprising, therefore, that the King should have considered it to be in his country's short- and long-term interests to bring about closer ties with neighbouring China and Pakistan. He visited Pakistan in September 1961 and, during a visit to China in October 1961, signed an agreement for Chinese aid in the construction of a 45-mile road from Kathmandu to Koderi Pass.[57] In October 1962 Nepal signed a trade agreement with China. The strategic implications of the road were self-evident; it would link up with the Tribhuvan Rajpath and provide China with an all-weather highway through Nepal to the Indian plains. The Indian government informally communicated its views to Kathmandu on the subject [58] but to no apparent avail. Notwithstanding this setback, India continued her policy of economic aid to Nepal with the pledge of the equivalent of $40 million towards Nepal's second (but three-year) plan, which commenced in 1962.

[56] For example, Subarna Shumshere, Koirala's deputy Prime Minister, was permitted to set up the headquarters of the Nepali Congress in Calcutta, address press conferences, and make statements aganist Mahendra's coup.

[57] China undertook to provide the equivalent of $9.8 million in materials, machinery, technicians, and training during the 1962–66 period. The importance with which Peking viewed the project is evidenced by the speed with which the Chinese technicians pushed through surveys for the road in early 1962.

[58] See statement by Nehru in the Lok Sabha, 24 November 1961. *LSD*, 2d Series, vol. 54, col. 95.

Chapter Five

THE INDIAN ARMY, 1947-1962

The decision to partition British India into two sovereign states resulted in the division of the existing army[1] on a roughly 2:1 basis, with the larger share going to the Indian Union. India's share totalled about 280,000 personnel of all categories and included the 1st, 3d, 4th, 5th, 8th, and 9th Gurkha Rifles, retained under the provisions of a tripartite agreement concluded between the governments of Nepal, Britain, and India in November 1947.[2]

In the immediate aftermath of partition, the violent communal disturbances made it impossible for the Defence Ministry to undertake long-term planning for the armed forces. Pending the return of 'normal conditions', the Army was expected to be maintained at the existing level.[3] However, the onerous needs of internal security and the military operations against the princely state of Hyderabad and against Pakistani tribals and ultimately regular units of the Pakistan Army in Kashmir necessitated a considerable strengthening of the security and defence forces. The Army was augmented by fresh recruits for both temporary and permanent service, additional men were recruited from the State Forces, and troops were loaned by Nepal for internal security duties. A National Cadet Corps (NCC) was established in 1948, and a Territorial Army, modelled

---

[1] As of July 1947 the undivided Indian Army comprised about 500,000 men, and the divisional organisations consisted of the 4th, 5th, 7th, and 10th Infantry Divisions, 1st Armoured Division, and 2nd Airborne Division. An unofficial estimate of the communal composition of the Service at this time was, in percentage of officers and men: Hindus (47.8 and 55.7), Muslims (23.7 and 33.8), Sikhs (17.3 and 7.5), and others (12.2 and 3.0). Robert Trumbull, *New York Times*, 29 July 1947.

[2] See Appendix IX for the resultant military establishment of India. Britain retained the 1st and 2nd Battalions of each of the 2nd, 6th, 7th, and 10th Gurka Rifles. Pakistan's share comprised 34 engineer units, 8½ artillery regiments, 8 infantry regiments, and 6 armoured units totalling about 150,000 men.

[3] See statement by Finance Minister R. K. Shanmukham Chetty. *CAD*, vol. 2 (28 February 1948), p. 1337.

on the British organization, was constituted by an Act of Parliament in 1948 and was officially inaugurated on 9 October 1949.[4]

PROVISIONAL PLANS

In early 1949 the ceasefire in Kashmir and the return of general normalcy to the country permitted the government to give its first serious consideration to the question of the size and composition of the peacetime Army. Faced with the need for maximum economy in defence expenditure simultaneous with the development of an Air Force and Navy, the Defence Ministry proposed to effect economy at the expense of the Army. The authorities are understood to have envisaged a highly mechanized and mobile force of about 150,000 men backed by a large reserve, a Territorial Army, and various para-military formations.[5]

No decision was taken regarding the peacetime size of the Army, however, because of the Communist insurrections within India and throughout Southeast Asia, and the emergence of a united China under militant Communist leadership dedicated at least to the restoration of ancient glories and domains. In his first address to Parliament, delivered on 31 January 1950, President Rajendra Prasad admitted the concern with which the government viewed developments. He declared that, while it was the government's desire to reduce defence expenditure 'as a measure of economy as well as a gesture of peace', it could not risk 'putting the country in jeopardy at a time when evil forces were endangering its security both within and from outside'. 'The first essential of freedom', he concluded, 'is the strength to preserve it and no country can take any risk in such a vital matter'.[6]

This prudent attitude was reinforced by continuing poor relations with Pakistan. A sharp deterioration in this relationship in

[4] A persisting poor response to the Territorial Army led to the passage through the Lok Sabha on 23 November 1956 of the Territorial Army (Amendment) Bill, which provided for compulsory enrolment of government servants and employees of specified public utility concerns in selected age groups so as to relieve the shortage of technicians in the Territorial Army's urban units.

[5] During a visit to Ottawa in May 1949 at the head of an Indian military mission, Defence Secretary H. M. Patel was reported as stating that he was 'profoundly impressed' by the Canadian military system of a light defence force designed for rapid expansion in a crisis and that India would 'probably' adopt this system. Cited, *Hindu*, 12 May 1949.

[6] *CAD*, pt. 2, vol. 1, p. 24.

February and March 1950 followed serious communal rioting in West Bengal, a mass exodus of Muslims from that state to East Pakistan, and the outbreak of anti-Hindu riots there. As a precautionary measure against the possibility of war, Indian forces were moved towards the borders of West and East Pakistan, and a crisis was averted only by talks held in New Delhi in April between Nehru and the Prime Minister of Pakistan, Liaquat Ali Khan. Further caution was warranted by developments outside the subcontinent: the invasion of South Korea by North Korean Communist armies in June 1950,[7] the Chinese entry into Tibet in early October, and major Chinese intervention in Korea in November.

Shortly after Chinese troops entered Tibet, however, it was reported by a leading Indian daily that the government was considering a proposal to progressively reduce defence expenditure on the assumption that the Korean War would soon end and would not, in any case, develop into a world war.[8] The intention was officially confirmed on 17 November, when Nehru intervened during the question period in Parliament to declare that he had directed the Defence Ministry to reduce defence expenditure and the size of the Army, his government desiring a highly efficient and mobile Army which, he claimed, did not depend on numbers. Referring to the subject again in the same forum on 21 December, the Prime Minister stated that the government preferred a highly mechanized and relatively small Army to a large and ill-equipped 'foot' force and intended to reduce the size of the Army for economy reasons.

In accordance with this policy, about 50,000 personnel were demobilized in early 1951. Announcing the move in the Constituent Assembly on 26 March 1951, Defence Minister Baldev Singh declared that further demobilization would depend on many factors, including the internal situation, the international situation, and, above all, the question of Kashmir. Ostensibly because of Pakistan's 'war propaganda' and the absence of any corresponding reduction in her armed forces, a further Indian reduction proposed for 1951–52 (which, it is understood, would have involved some 100,000

---

[7] India's contribution to the United Nations' force consisted of the 60th Field Ambulance (Paratroop), which landed in Korea on 20 November 1950.

[8] *The Statesman*, 13 October 1950. According to the report, the government was considering a proposal to progressively reduce defence expenditure on the revenue side to Rs 165 crores (1951–52), Rs 160 crores (1952–53), and to a 'stable' figure of Rs 140 crores (1953–54 and thereafter). It was also proposed to fix capital outlay at about Rs 35 crores per year.

men) was not made.[9] Too much significance should not, however, be attached to the release of the 50,000 men in early 1951 or of other personnel between 1949 and 1953. The actual reductions were effected by demobilizing the Defence Battalions (an internal security force) and the Pioneer Corps (a labour group), returning to Nepal those forces borrowed from it, releasing 'unsuitable' officers and men from the State Forces, and resuming demobilization of personnel from the Second World War who either desired to return to civil life or were considered unsuitable for the peacetime Army, but whose release had been deferred after partition.

These releases were more than offset, however, by fresh enlistments, the integration of the State Forces into the regular service (effective 1 April 1950), and the reinduction (between 15 August 1947 and March 1953) of 441 officers and 121,322 other ranks who had been demobilized at the end of the Second World War.[10] One indication of the aggregate increase in the size of the Army between 1949 and 1953 is the steady increase in the outlay on pay and allowances during this period.[11]

Composition and Deployment, 1953–1956

As of 1953, the Indian Army comprised between 325,000 and 350,000 personnel of all categories, organized into the 4th, 5th, 10th, 19th, 26th, and 27th Infantry Divisions, the 1st Armoured Division, the 1st Independent Armoured Brigade, the 50th Paratroop Brigade, and several unattached battalions and brigades. These formations were, however, still in the process of consolidation and varied considerably in effectiveness. Three infantry divisions, reinforced in 1951, were sited in the Vale of Kashmir, Jammu, and the Poonch–Mendhar–Rajaori area, with an infantry battalion and supporting arms at Leh. The main counterstrike force against Pakistan, designated Punjab Force, comprised a corps which consisted of two infantry divisions, based at Ferozepore, Ambala, Jullundur, Amritsar, Khasali, and Gurdaspur, and the armoured division, sited in its

[9] See Nehru's statement in Parliament as reported in *The Times*, 25 July 1951. See also the statement by Defence Minister Menon, *LSD*, pt. 2, vol. 15, cols. 10, 257–258.

[10] Deputy Defence Minister S. S. Majithia, *LSD*, pt. 1, vol. 1 (10 March 1953), col. 897. During the period 15 August 1947 to 31 January 1953, 1,507 Indian officers were released. Deputy Defence Minister Satish Chandra, *LSD*, pt. 1, vol 2 (4 April 1953), col. 1745.

[11] See Appendix II.

training area at Jhansi, south of Delhi and 72 hours removed by train from its operational 'take-off' point in the East Punjab. The independent armoured brigade was based at Patiala in the East Punjab, and an infantry brigade group was located at Jaipur (Rajasthan) with one of its battalions at Jodhpur. There was an infantry brigade and a light (Stuart) armoured regiment in the vicinity of Calcutta; an independent infantry brigade group in Kutch; one infantry brigade at Secunderabad; one infantry battalion in each of Madras, Bangalore, and Trivandrum; and the paratroop brigade at Agra.

The deployment of these forces indicated a compromise between likely operational contingencies, the continuing demands of internal security, and financial stringency. From the purely military viewpoint, the concentration of the field army in a 100-square-mile area in Madhya Pradesh enclosing Agra and Gwalior would have resulted in the most effective defence, permitting rapid air to the civil power wherever required and a speedy concentration of forces against any threat to India's long land frontiers from west to east. For financial reasons, however, the government was not prepared to sanction such a measure, and considerations of civilian morale in the areas contiguous to Pakistani territory and the military sanction required for the administration of Indian-occupied Kashmir resulted in a 'tight' defence of the Indo-Pakistan frontiers, particularly in the west. Since the main operational theatre remained in the northwest, no major redeployment of the Indian Army was required, except for Kashmir. Thus, pre-1947 cantonments were utilized to a large extent.

The size and deployment of the Army remained fairly static from 1953 to 1956. In early 1956, however, its commitments were expanded to encompass the pacification campaign against rebellious Naga tribesmen in the strategically important region of eastern Assam. Initially, units were drawn from Eastern Command but, as the Army's involvement deepened, it was necessary to draft battalions from the Punjab and Kashmir and replace them through the raising of fresh units.

Adjustments to Meet Chinese Challenge, 1959–62

Between August and November 1959 the Army's responsibilities were greatly increased when it was directed to secure the Himalayan frontiers against hostile actions by China. In their assessment of the

Chinese military threat, India's military leaders viewed NEFA, the Sikkim–Bhutan sector, and Ladakh as likely 'danger areas', although it was felt that serious attacks were, for the moment, precluded by logistical factors. Large-scale redeployment of troops to these areas was, in any case, prevented by poor communications.

Planning for Ladakh aimed at the eventual development of an brigade group once a suitable operational infrastructure existed. As immediate measures, the Army strengthened the battalion at Leh, took over the existing checkposts from the Central Reserve Police, and established forward patrol bases in areas where logistics permitted: along the Shyok Valley up to Daulet Beg Oldi, near the southern entrance to the Karakoram Pass. Chushul was conceived of as the anchor for this system of posts, which were designed to check further surreptitious Chinese advances; it was flanked by about ten posts extending both east and west for a distance of some 40 miles in each direction. The Leh and Chushul airstrips were speedily recommissioned.

In the Sikkim–Bhutan sector the plan was ultimately to deploy an infantry division with one brigade and divisional headquarters at Siliguri, one brigade at Kalimpong, and one brigade at Gangtok with its forward elements extending as far as Natu Pass on the Sikkim–Tibet border. A force deployed in this manner was considered to afford defence in depth against an attack from the north while simultaneously covering the narrow corridor lying between the northern tip of East Pakistan and Bhutan from interference from East Pakistan. As the initial stage of this plan, an infantry brigade was shifted from Lucknow during the period December 1959–January 1960 and sited with brigade headquarters and one battalion at Siliguri, one battalion at Kalimpong, and one battalion at Gangtok with its forward elements extending up to Natu Pass.

With regards to NEFA, the 4th Infantry Division was shifted from Ambala during the period December 1959–January 1960 and sited with divisional headquarters at Tezpur, two brigades in the foothills, and one brigade forward at Tawang. This force was assigned to make a thorough reconnaissance of the area. The Army Command at Jorhat, which exercised over-all command of the border force with an advance command post at Foothills, was expanded and a new base was started at Misamari. The Army planned to gradually take over border security duties from the Assam Rifles, but this semi-military force, though strongly reinforced, was not immediately replaced by regular troops—ostensibly so as to avoid unrest among the tribals.[12] In the event of a serious Chinese assault against the forces along the border, it was decided to concede the untenable forward areas and retire to more defensible positions where artillery and tank support could be utilised to effect.

Further military contingency planning was undertaken by Army leaders in January 1961, at which time a sand-model exercise concerned with the defence of the McMahon Line was held in Lucknow (or Tezpur). The 'Chinese syndicate' employed as the most likely Chinese strategy a three-pronged attack similar to the one actually employed by Peking in October–November 1962. The force required to defend against such an attack was estimated at three infantry divisions, two on the line and one in reserve. For contingency purposes, the units allotted to the plan were the 4th (already in NEFA), the 'Naga' Division of approximately 14 battalions deployed against the Nagas, and the 5th Division from the Punjab. If and when an attack seemed imminent, it was proposed to implement the plan immediately. In such an event, the forward brigade at Tawang was to abandon all forward checkposts and fall back and join the other two brigades of the 4th in the vicinity of Bomdila; two of the brigades from Nagaland would fall back to positions near the 4th, picking up a brigade from Ranchi or Calcutta to replace the formation left in Nagaland, and the 5th Division would be rushed to act as the reserve at Bomdila, the main defence anchor. The main defence line would be strengthened with light tanks drawn from the armoured regiment at Calcutta and artillery drawn from the most readily available source, such as the paratroop brigade at Agra.

Contingency planning for the Sikkim area remained unchanged, although some provisions, details of which are not in the writer's possession, were made to counter any Chinese attack on Bhutan. As regards Ladakh, the military authorities remained of the view that the existing logistics deficiencies severely limited the preparation of a successful defence against a serious and sustained Chinese attack. In the event of such an attack, it was recognized that the troops in the area could only fight as best they could and would, in all probability, be forced to concede a major part of Ladakh.

All contingency planning was based upon the assumption that Pakistan would not seek to take advantage of any major Indian military involvement against China in the Himalayan region, thereby permitting the redeployment of the requisite forces against China.

[12] *New York Times*, 9 January 1960.

To enable the Army to meet its new Himalayan commitments, a programme was undertaken to increase the existing combatant and support arms and to raise a new infantry division—the 17th—to replace the 4th in Punjab Force. Although a shortage of officers and equipment limited the expansion to one division at a time, the fact that only one was raised during the three years preceding the border war in October 1962 suggests that the government was not seriously concerned with the prospect of open war with China.

This relative complacency about a Chinese military threat was characteristic of the government's attitude towards the country's security as a whole. Although Nehru had early declared his preference for well-equipped forces, he was strongly disinclined to concede requests from the Army for a phased re-equipment programme,[13] for reasons of finance. As he declared in the Rajya Sabha in September 1963:

When you are faced with extreme difficulty, like the Chinese invasion, you have to do it [undertake costly re-equipment] whatever happens. You can get it too from friendly countries. You can tax your people much more than normally you could. But, imagine in peacetime, how far can you create that atmosphere? How far will people bear such heavy burdens of taxation and how far will other countries be prepared to help you to that extent. It is only when danger comes and shakes you up that you can get more money by taxation, loans, credits and gifts from outside.

Thus, Nehru concluded, requests from Army authorities when referred by the Defence Ministry to the Defence Committee of the Cabinet were 'possibly' agreed to by the Committee to the extent of one-tenth what was asked.[14]

Tanks

The government was sympathetic to the idea of providing tanks, in the belief that these would be decisive in any Indo-Pakistan war.

---

[13] The last comprehensive assessment of the Army's equipment needs made up to October 1962 is understood to have been drawn up by Army headquarters in 1957–58 and to have been submitted to the Defence Ministry at that time. The proposals were for an outlay of Rs 500 crores and comprised, in order of priority: (a) replacement of the .303 rifle with a semi-automatic; (b) replacement of the 4.2-inch mortar, possibly by the Brandt; (c) re-equipment of the tank units with a universal light or medium model; (d) replacement of the 25-pound field piece; (e) acquisition of more mountain guns; and (f) replacement of the vehicle fleet.

[14] Cited, *Hindu Weekly Review*, 9 September 1963.

The need for newer tanks had been illustrated during the Kashmir conflict, when the obsolete Stuarts and Churchills and obsolescent Shermans had been kept operational (in spite of the Anglo-American embargo on arms shipments to both the disputants) only by the despatch of teams to acquire available spares from World War II theatres of action. With the lifting of the embargo India purchased at least 30 Shermans from the United States in 1953 as a stop-gap measure, and made enquiries about the availability of modern tanks and the possible indigenous manufacture of a foreign design under licence. The latter proposal was shortly discarded as premature, given India's technological backwardness, and negotiations commenced with Britain and France which culminated in the purchase of 200 British Centurion heavy tanks in 1956–57 and of 150 French AMX light tanks in 1957–58. After a subsequent decision to manufacture a modern tank during the Third Five-Year Plan (1961–66), assessments were made of the AMX and a light Panzer tank of West German design, but it was ultimately decided to accept an offer by the British company of Vickers-Armstrong for a factory producing a medium tank based on the Chieftain design and modified to Indian specifications.

Vehicles

The vehicular fleet was augmented by a few jeeps purchased from private British firms in the 1948–51 period and by an unknown number of general service trucks acquired from American sources in subsequent years. However, general reliance continued to be placed upon the large stocks of vehicles left from the Second World War, in the belief that the consequent heavy burden of repairs and maintenance put upon the Electrical and Mechanical Engineers (EME's) was preferable to spending scarce foreign exchange. A phased programme of replacement of vehicles was drawn up in 1956 but could not be implemented immediately because of India's acute shortage of foreign exchange in 1957–58 and her inadequate capacity for manufacturing four-wheel-drive vehicles. Sanction was thereupon given for the long-overdue streamlining of the existing vehicle fleet, and some 20,000 vehicles were reconditioned by Army engineers from spares provided by Levy Auto Parts of Canada. In the 1959–61 period, in order to meet the Army's requirements for light and medium vehicles, the government began the production, under licence, of Japanese Nissan patrol jeeps and one-ton trucks and West German three-ton trucks.

Weapons

The government did not seriously consider replacing the .303 rifle, the Army's standard infantry weapon in two world wars, until the Himalayan situation deteriorated sharply in late 1959. Army interest was considerable in the Colt AR-15, a lightweight American design which had first appeared in 1958; the Belgian FN was also highly regarded; and lesser interest was shown in a West German design and the indigenous Ishapore model then undergoing development. A number of models of each of the four types were acquired and were subjected to extensive tests by front-line units under all conditions. According to an informed source, the tests resulted in a consensus in favour of the AR-15, and Army headquarters accordingly submitted its recommendation for the adoption of the American rifle in late 1960.

The government, however, was not inclined to act upon the proposal; it remained very reluctant to expend foreign exchange. Certain of its hierarchy were emotionally opposed to dealing with a private arms supplier in the 'arms racket', and many had a long-standing aversion to the acquisition of 'offensive' armaments from either of the two major participants in the cold war. As an alternative, which appeared to be far more attractive, consideration was given to the possible licensed manufacture of the Belgian FN. While it is not known to what extent the proposal was pursued, the alleged involvement of the particular Belgian firm in a 'scandal' apparently confirmed the strong predelictions of certain influential members of the political executive concerning the immorality of private arms manufacturers. With the encouragement of the Defence Minister, V. K. Krishna Menon, the decision was taken to proceed with the development and production of the Ishapore design, despite the fact that Army circles regarded it as but a 'poor copy of the FN', too heavy and too bulky, and were not happy with the further delay inherent in the decision. Their fears were well-founded, as a satisfactory prototype of the Ishapore design was not forthcoming until mid-1962 and production had not commenced when the Chinese border conflict erupted.

Requests by the Army for new mortars met with no positive response from the government. The proposed purchase of the French Brandt heavy mortar in the early 'fifties was rejected on the grounds that it was too expensive and that it was preferable to develop an indigenous type. The Army became interested in a Finnish mortar which appeared in 1959 or 1960, but enquiries were apparently inhibited for political reasons; Israel was the only country licensed to produce it, and direct or indirect purchase from this source was considered by the government as a possible source of offence to the Arab bloc with whom there was a strong and continuing desire to maintain close relations.

Persistent requests from Army headquarters for consideration to the early replacement of the 25-pound field artillery and the acquisition of modern mountain howitzers provoked a qualified response from the government. It viewed the items as having a relatively low priority, rejected external purchase on financial grounds, and was content to await the production of designs being developed in the research sector of the Defence Ministry's ordnance establishment.

PERSONNEL

Chronic Shortage of Officers

The problem of suitably staffing the officer corps, which posed an acute issue even before partition, was considerably aggravated by the loss to Pakistan of all Muslim officers save 215 commissioned officers and 339 Viceroy's Commissioned Officers (VCO's) who opted for India.[15] (Their rank was later designated as JCO [Junior Commissioned Officer]). For political and psychological reasons, rapid Indianization proceeded, and by 1955 only a few British EME technicians remained in the Army. There continued to be an acute shortage of officers, however, because of the Army's inability to attract the required number of suitable applicants. The response for vacancies at the Inter-Services Wing of the Armed Forces Academy (Khadakavasala) was described in April 1949 as 'disappointing', as was the disparity in the response of the various provinces, whereby over 75 per cent of the officer recruits were coming from northern India.[16] This state of affairs persisted in later years.[17]

The initial shortage of officers was partially eased by granting

---

[15] Defence Minister Singh, *CAD*, vol. 1 (3 February 1948), p. 164.

[16] See statement by the Director, Selection of Personnel at Army Headquarters, Brig. N.D. Bilimoria at a Bombay press conference on 1 April 1949. Cited, *Hindu*, 4 April 1949.

[17] See statements by Defence Minister Gopalaswami Ayyangar, *LSD*, pt. 1, 11 June 1952, col. 799; Defence Minister Singh, *CAD*, pt. 1, vol. 2 (23 March 1950), p. 1014.

Short Service Permanent Regular Commissions to former officers and employing civilian engineers on a contract basis in certain technical services. Special List commissions were introduced in 1953, aimed at specialist JCO's and non-Commissioned Officers (NCO's); 2,000 officers holding temporary commissions were granted permanent ones in mid-1957; and retired officers were recommissioned for a maximum of three years, this period being extended in 1959 so long as no officer was retained beyond 55 years of age.

By 1960 the officer cadre was still about 3,000 short of a full complement, with some infantry battalions having only eleven or twelve officers out of a desired thirty or forty. The situation was made more acute by the expansion programme begun in late 1959 and by the release of World War II entrants who were nearing the maximum age limits, which for majors and below had already been extended by several years. The 1956-60 period had witnessed the virtual disappearance of the war-experienced NCO cadre, and the rural background and low educational standards of most of the recruits in the combatant arms precluded undue haste in the training of new NCO's.[18]

The situation prompted further action to augment the officer corps. The intake to the Indian Military Academy was increased by 50 per cent, and standards were lowered for entry to the National Defence Academy. Five Sainik schools—which offer the equivalent of an English public school education for boys wishing to enter the National Defence Academy—were established in 1961 and six in 1962. The Special List cadre was substantially increased, promotion for certain categories of NCO's was liberalized, and some JCO's were employed as Administrative Officers in National Cadet Corps units. The World War II Army Cadet College at Nowgong (Madhya Pradesh) was re-established in May 1960 to train suitable JCO's and NCO's so as to enable them to compete successfully with others for entry into the Indian Military Academy and for regular commissions.

The character, organization, and 'outlook' of the Army remained largely unchanged during the fifteen years from the reconstitution of the service in 1947 to the border war with China in 1962.

Recruitment Policy

Shortly after independence, recruitment to the Army was opened to all persons of Indian domicile irrespective of class, creed, or reli-

[18] See article by an Indian military correspondent entitled 'The Indian Army', *Round Table*, no. 211 (June 1963), pp. 217-218.

gion. The practice introduced during the Second World War of 'mixed' artillery, signals, administrative, and other ancillary and support arms and services was retained, and a Brigade of Guards [10] and a parachute regiment were formed as 'mixed units'. The class-caste basis of the infantry regiments was, however, not tampered with, in recognition both of the effects of such a policy on *esprit de corps* and the peculiar social patterns of India. This tradition was applied to the Jammu and Kashmir Regiment raised after partition, this unit recruiting only Sikhs, Dogras, and Muslims from that state. The Gurkha Rifles, once despised by Congress politicians as mercenaries, were retained and are coveted.[20] The Viceroy's Bodyguard was retained as the President's Bodyguard, with the Asoka lion replacing the imperial crown and insignia on the breastplate of the uniform. The only structural change occurred with the conversion of the Mahar Regiment from an infantry to a machine-gun formation. Thus, while the so-called 'non-martial' classes were well represented in the noncombatant arms, the frontline infantry remained dominated by the 'martial' classes of the north and northwest: Sikhs, Jats, Dogras, Rajputs, Garhwalis, and Gurkhas. India's large Muslim community contributed only a few thousands to the successor of the Army in which their members (albeit largely from the northwestern areas incorporated in West Pakistan) were once so prominent.[21]

Organization and Character of the Army

Various suggestions put forward from time to time regarding changes in the organization and character of the Army included a reduction in the logistical branches, the replacement of the divisional organization by brigade groups, and reliance upon large mili-

[10] Modelled on the British unit, the brigade has the same function, protection of the head of state.

[20] The abilities of these Nepali are well known; their retention would appear to be due to various factors: recognition of the importance of remittances from the Gurkha Rifles to the economy of the poverty-stricken areas of Nepal from which their recruits have been traditionally drawn; the effects on Indo-Nepalese relations of any termination of their services; the substantial link thereby created between India and the strategic Himalayan state; and the neutrality of such a force in Indian national politics and communal disorders. Many of the Gurkhas are domiciled in India, however, and are thus classed as Indian nationals.

[21] For brief comments on the classes and castes recruited to the Army, see Brig. Rajendra Singh, *History of the Indian Army* (New Delhi: SAS, Army Educational Stores, 1963), pp. 257-283.

tia-style forces as either a temporary arrangement pending the indigenous manufacture of modern costly armaments or as a permanent policy. The brigade group proposal provoked some discussion in Army circles, but the divisional organization was retained. The establishment of the Lok Sahayak Sena (National Volunteer Force) in May 1955 with the declared aim of reducing dependence upon the standing Army (the Army being given no control over the force) suggested a political desire to prevent a concentration of authority in Army headquarters. It is doubtful, however, if the position of the professional Army was ever threatened for either political or economic reasons, India's responsible political leaders undoubtedly recognizing that a large and half-trained peasant militia was in no way a credible substitute for a modern regular army.

MILITARY PROPOSALS FOR HIMALAYAN DEFENCE

The need for some units trained and equipped for operations in the mountainous and jungle terrain of the Himalayan region was advanced by a British officer in an article published in early 1947.[22] In the aftermath of China's occupation of Tibet in 1950–51, at least a section of the Army leadership realized that it would be prudent to form a small specialized force to maintain a constant surveillance of the Himalayan frontier. Political disinterest was primarily responsible for the pigeonholing of the proposal. Army headquarters also felt the need to make at least some preparations against the contingency of future operations in this area, and decided in 1951–52 on the preparation of a manual on Chinese infantry tactics, organization, and equipment; material was to be obtained from British and American sources and based upon their experience in Korea. Upon learning of the project, however, Nehru ordered it to be dropped.[23] Political attitudes towards military precautions during this early period were in accordance with Nehru's strong belief (which virtually amounted to a conviction) that the Chinese military threat to India's Himalayan frontiers and interests in the hill states was distant and should not be stimulated by any Indian

[22] Lt. Col. A. Green, 'The Case for a Himalayan Division', *USI Journal*, 78:327 (April 1947), pp. 324–326.
[23] In appreciation of the political aspect, Army headquarters proposed to keep the existence of the pamphlet a tightly guarded secret and to issue it only when, as in 1959, there was no danger of compromising the government's political and diplomatic objectives.

actions or attitudes that might be regarded by Peking as provocative.

As the Himalayan situation steadily deteriorated after 1954, there was increasing concern in military circles at the seeming refusal by the political authorities to appreciate the need for phased adjustments.[24] The Army moved to acquaint its personnel with the problems of mountain and jungle warfare by establishing a Jungle Warfare School at Dehra Dun in 1958 and introducing a course on guerilla tactics at the Infantry School at Mhow in the same year. In the latter part of 1960 the Chief of Army Staff, General K. S. Thimayya, was permitted to make a long-desired study of alpine troops, organization, and tactics in the Mount Blanc area at the invitation of the Italian government. Upon his return to India, General Thimayya is understood to have recommended to the Defence Ministry the raising of some mountain divisions and to have made proposals regarding their organization, training, and equipment. The resulting scheme of Himalayan defence would consist of lightly equipped and mobile infantry deployed in forward areas and backed by a strong and highly mobile mechanized force based in the plains.

The proposal was rejected by the government for reasons which had become quite irrelevant. Defence Minister Menon and Prime Minister Nehru seem to have felt that the formation of such divisions would constitute a basic shift in strategy with far-reaching and unwelcome repercussions on foreign policy. The cost of such a measure would also increase the country's already heavy defence burden. Desirous of an eventual peaceful settlement of the border dispute and having ruled out the possibility of large-scale Chinese attacks in the immediate future and even beyond, the political leadership of the ruling Congress party viewed the Army's expensive proposal as not warranted.[25] The only adjustment to the Army training programme after 1959 that related to Himalayan operations was the establishment of a High Altitude Warfare School in March 1962, although the need for mountain formations deployed in the Himalayas continued to be advanced by officers in responsible journals.[26]

---

[24] See chapter ix for the background to the Thimayya–Menon rift in 1959.

[25] The belief that Himalayan operations would remain at the level of patrol clashes was widespread even in the officer cadre of the Army and was reflected in the disinterest with which many officers are understood to have viewed the courses on jungle warfare and guerilla tactics.

[26] See, for example, Maj. M. L. Tuli, 'Reorganization of an Infantry Battalion', *USI Journal*, 92:386 (January–March 1962), pp. 33–39; Lt.-Col. M. R. P. Varma, 'The Himalayan Frontier Force', *ibid.*, pp. 12–17; Gen. K. S. Thimayya, 'Adequate Insurance', *Seminar* (July 1962), pp. 13–15; Gen. K. M. Cariappa, as cited in *Times of India*, 20 November 1961.

THE ARMY ON THE EVE OF CONFLICT WITH CHINA

On the eve of the border conflict in October 1962, the Indian Army comprised some 550,000 personnel, including about 35,000 unenrolled (civilian) personnel and a substantial body of enrolled noncombatants. The service was organized in three commands, and field formations consisted of eight infantry divisions, one armoured division, an independent armoured brigade, a paratroop brigade, and various unattached formations. There were approximately 1,000 tanks (150 AMX, 200 Centurions, 600 Shermans and Stuarts, and a number of Churchills) spread in operational, training, and reserve categories. This regular force was backed by a Reserve of 250,000 officers and men serving seven-year engagements (of which only about 30,000 could be regarded as front-line reservists), two battalions of the Jammu and Kashmir State Militia, the semi-military Assam Rifles with perhaps 15,000 personnel, 15 battalions of the Central Reserve Police, and a number of battalions of Armed Police from the various states.[27]

Para-military organizations embraced several million civilians. The Territorial Army consisted of 177 units with an actual strength of 419,580; the Lok Sahayak Sena scheme had given elementary military training to 619,114 by March 1962; the National Cadet Corps consisted of 27,811 officer-teachers and 1,791,237 cadets as of 31 March 1962.[28]

The regular service continued to reflect its development as an adjunct to the imperial British military system. British weapons, drill manuals, unit tables of organization, and British-style uniforms remained in use. There was great stress on the regimental tradition, and the infantry continued to be recruited largely from the so-called 'martial' classes. Although Hindi was eventually to replace English as the language of command, English remained the vehicle of administration, operation, and training, and Hindustani continued to be the *lingua franca* of the service. The distinction between the senior (King's Commissioned Officer and Indian Commissioned officer) and junior (JCO) forms of commission remained in vogue. By virtue of their long service and their conservative and rural origins, the JCO's continued to knit together the regimental structure and to perpetuate the traditional flavour of the service.

[27] For further details on the composition and nature of the service at this time, see Appendix X.
[28] Details cited from Ministry of Defence, *Reports*, 1959–64.

The formal regimental mess was retained, complete with traditional taboos and ceremonies like the 'Loyal Toast' to the head of state. Formal ceremonies like 'beating the retreat' and the presentation and trooping of the colours continued to be performed with meticulous care for tradition.

The weapons and ancillary equipment of the Army dated from World War II and, in some cases, before. Communications equipment was old and suited for static conditions. The vehicles were generally old and well-worn, 15 per cent of the jeeps having been acquired before 1948, as were 38 per cent of the three-ton general service trucks and 68 per cent of the one-ton general service type.[29]

Combat formations were deployed to meet the demands of frontier defence against Pakistan in the west and east and China in the northwest and northeast, of internal security (against the Naga dissidents), and of certain international obligations voluntarily assumed by the government. Contingency planning had been prepared to meet the requirements of operations against Pakistan in Kashmir, Punjab, and Rajasthan with precautionary measures along the borders of East Pakistan, and to counter possible Chinese attacks in Ladakh, the Sikkim–Bhutan sector, and the Tawang area of NEFA.

The Army was fairly well-prepared for conventional operations against a markedly smaller Pakistani adversary possessing similar organization, training, and equipment and deployed defensively.[30] In the event of attacks by tribals, Azad Kashmir forces, or Pakistani regulars across the ceasefire line in Kashmir, the garrison in that area (with possible support from the armoured brigade at Patiala) would seek to contain the attacks and to regain the initiative by means of offensive operations directed towards Sialkot and perhaps also Peshawar and Rawalpindi. In the meantime, Punjab Force would strike towards Lahore and seek decisive action with the opposing Pakistani forces. The resultant pincer movement, coupled with India's superior military power, was regarded as adequate to deal a crippling blow to Pakistan's field army and force an early peace. Only watch and ward duties appear to have been envisaged toward East Pakistan.

[29] *Ibid.*, 1963–64, p. 37.
[30] Pakistan's army was largely deployed in the Lahore–Sialkot–Rawalpindi–Peshawar area with small bodies of troops in the Quetta and Karachi areas and in East Pakistan. It comprised about 225,000 men organized in six infantry divisions (one of which was in East Pakistan), two independent infantry brigades, one paratroop brigade, one armoured division, and one independent armoured brigade. There was also a militia of 250,000 and 25,000 to 30,000 Azad Kashmir troops.

For the contingency of Himalayan operations against China, however, the service was ill-prepared. The forces in Ladakh consisted of an infantry brigade based at Leh with perhaps two other battalions dispersed among some forty small posts spread over nearly 400 miles of difficult terrain extending from the Karakoram Pass to Demchok, with Chushul as base and anchor point. The primary purpose of these posts was to demarcate the forward line and discourage further Chinese advances; they were not designed to withstand any serious attack. Srinagar and Leh were linked by road via Kargil and Dras, and Leh was connected by road with Chushul and thence to Demchok and also to Manali. Air supply originated at Chandigarh (Punjab) with airfields of variable capacity at Srinagar, Kargil, Leh, and Chushul. The forward outposts were almost exclusively dependent upon this means of supply which, for reasons of weather, was operative for only about 180 days of the year.

The frontier in the middle sector was guarded by a number of small police checkposts under Army control, linked to rear areas only by horse and mule trails.

In the Sikkim area, the approach route from Natu La was covered by a brigade deployed in staggered fashion from north to south and assisted by two companies of Sikkimese militia totalling about 280 men. Supplies and transport for this meagre force were dependent upon the road extending north from Siliguri to Natu La via Gangtok.

In NEFA, there were two brigades in the Tezpur–Bomdila–Dirrang Dzong area with a third brigade deployed from Tawang to Dhola, near the junction of NEFA, Bhutan, and Tibet. The frontier was guarded by a series of small posts manned chiefly by the Assam Rifles, backed by several strongpoints garrisoned by regulars. Positions on the Namka Chu River were only 15 miles from the Tibetan border but five days' march from Tawang. The defensive positions in this most threatened of areas were weak; heavy trenching tools had only begun to arrive shortly before the major Chinese attack, there were no wire obstacles, ammunition was in short supply, the troops were not acclimatized to the 14,700-foot altitudes, and warm clothing was generally conspicuous by its absence. The logistical support in the Kameng Division was restricted to the newly completed 220-mile road linking Tezpur with Tawang via Se La, Dirrang Dzong, and Bomdila, which was barely capable of taking one-ton traffic. A series of defensive posts were in the process of being established along this route.

The remaining forward posts extending eastwards along the Mc-

Mahon Line were isolated and, although some were interconnected by goat and mule tracks, they were dependent for their main requirements upon air supply. The border post at Kibithoo in the Lohit Division was 15 miles (at least two days' march) from Walong, with forward positions on a 15,000-foot-high ridge near the banks of the unfordable Lohit River. Walong was 100 miles, or about two weeks' march, from the nearest roadhead and was dependent for supply upon a small airstrip.

Contingency plans prepared in 1960–61 remained unchanged, but the capacity of the Army to carry out successful defensive and offensive actions against sizeable Chinese forces on a major scale was virtually nonexistent. The shortage of officers had inevitably led to a deterioration in the quality of the corps which was aggravated by its apathy and complacency arising from the government's efforts to project a pacific image in international affairs, from low pay as compared to the civil service and private industry, from obsolete equipment, and from the conduct of the Defence Minister towards the service in general and promotions in particular. Few officers evinced serious interest in techniques useful for operations against a Chinese opponent who, according to the politicians, really posed no serious threat. The shortage of qualified officers had inhibited Army headquarters from establishing a planning group, and the government's refusal to allocate suitable training areas had limited the ability of the Army leadership to ascertain service effectiveness on a continuing basis and under various physical conditions. There was an inadequate appreciation of the logistics requirements of modern warfare; supplies were located in scattered depots often sited with only marginal relevance to likely operational needs and to possible despatching delays to the front lines caused by weather and mechanical and human errors.

Many of these deficiencies were illustrated by Operation Vijay, launched against the Portuguese enclave of Goa on 17 December 1961. The action was used by the Defence Ministry as a tactical exercise on a tri-service basis on a scale that was lavish relative to operational needs. According to reports,[81] the 17th Division took nearly a month to prepare for the operation and the troop movements so disorganized the railway system in central India that the steel mills at Ahmedabad ran out of coal and had to shut down temporarily. Four days after the attack, the roads leading into Goa from Savant-

[81] See Stephen Barber, *Daily Telegraph*, 20 November 1962; Frank Moraes, *Indian Express*, 7 May 1962.

vadi, Maneri, Colemn, and Polem were choked with columns of medium artillery, trucks, and tank transport. A considerable number of troops arrived for action equipped only with canvas shoes because of a shift in the contract for army boots from a major recognized firm to a smaller company that failed to fulfill its obligations. Some troops were without field rations for 48 hours because of a breakdown in the supply system, and inadequate co-ordination between the air and ground forces resulted on one occasion in aircraft being nine miles off target and discharging their bombs onto Army transport.

It is understood that the exercise was subject to considerable scrutiny and comment in service (particularly Army) circles, and that various proposals were made to the Defence Ministry regarding their correction. As the events of October–November 1962 were to reveal, however, little action was sanctioned in the interim period to increase the Army's effectiveness.

Chapter Six

THE INDIAN AIR FORCE, 1947-1962

India retained at partition roughly two-thirds of the Royal Indian Air Force, comprising seven fighter squadrons, one transport–communication squadron, and miscellaneous aircraft but few of the prewar training establishments and permanent air force stations.[1] The development of the service had necessarily to be a phased and expensive undertaking, and its size and composition were dependent upon the strategic role assigned it by the government.

Partition and the altered strategic requirements consequent on the poor relations with Pakistan do not appear to have altered New Delhi's conception of the type and size of the air force required by the Union. The Indian Defence Minister, Baldev Singh, informed Parliament in early 1949 that it was the government's intention to create a balanced air force of twenty squadrons by 1960.[2]

DEVELOPMENT, 1947-1953

One hundred British-built Spitfire and Tempest fighter aircraft —33 constituting India's share of the old RIAF and 67 representing purchases from surplus British stock—were shifted from Royal Air Force bases at Karachi to Bombay in the spring of 1948. There de Havilland Vampire F.3 fighters were obtained in late 1948, 52 Vampire F.B.9's and N.F.54's in 1949-50, and 71 French-built Dassault MD-450 Ouragan fighter-bombers in 1953-54. Several heavy bomber and reconnaissance units were formed from American-built B-24J Liberator heavy bomber aircraft reconstituted by Hindustan Aircraft Limited (HAL) from World War II salvage yards at Kanpur. The C-47 (DC-3) transport–communication unit was expanded to

[1] See Appendix IX for specific details. Pakistan received as her share of the old RIAF the 5th and 9th Fighter Squadrons, the 6th Transport Squadron, one air observation post flight, one communication flight, all the prewar training establishments and permanent stations, and the only repair and maintenance workshop, located at Drigh Road, Karachi.
[2] Cited, *Flight*, 27 January 1949.

perhaps 40 aircraft shortly after partition; a number of de Havilland Devon light transports were purchased in 1948–49; and in 1953–54 the transport arm was augmented through the purchase of 26 American Fairchild C-119G short- and medium-range transports and six American Sikorsky S-55 helicopters.

Simultaneously with the acquisition of new aircraft, training establishments were set up to replace the facilities of the old RIAF, which had been located within the boundaries of the new state of Pakistan. The British Percival Prentice was selected in 1948 as the interim trainer pending the availability of the Hindustan HT-2 primary trainer then undergoing development at HAL; 62 units were received from HAL during the period from 1948 to 1953. Indianization of the service proceeded, the resulting shortage of officers being alleviated by recruiting civilians, commissioning qualified senior NCO's, and retaining British personnel in key posts. By March 1953, only nine officers and 54 civilians of British nationality remained in the Indian Air Force,[3] and the top post of Chief of Air Staff was assumed by Air Marshal Subroto Mukerjee in April 1954. The service continued to have difficulty, however, in attracting suitable recruits, and the problem was aggravated by the introduction by various states of local languages as the medium of instruction in preference to English, the knowledge of which was important in such a highly technical service.

RE-EQUIPMENT AND EXPANSION, 1953–1962

The appointment of Air Marshal Mukerjee coincided with the general completion of the first phase of the Air Force programme and was followed by the re-equipment and expansion of front-line operational strength.

Fighters

The IAF appears to have been initially interested in procuring 80 Dassault Mystere IVA interceptors or, as a possible alternate manufacturing the British Folland Gnat lightweight fighter-bomber.[4]

[3] See statement by the Minister of Defence Organisation, Mahavir Tyagi, *LSD*, pt. 2, vol. 1 (25 March 1953), col. 2815.

[4] *Aviation Week*, 4 July 1955, p. 7. Special correspondent Philip Deane reported in *The Scotsman* on 16 February 1954 that the Ouragans had not given complete satisfaction and that the IAF had 'let it be known' that orders for new types would likely go to Britain if India could get satisfaction on delivery limits and prices.

In any event, the government purchased another 33 Dassault Ouragans, ordered 110 Mysteres as replacements for its older Ouragans, and commenced negotiations with Folland Aircraft for a licence to produce the Gnat in India. India's hesitation to sign a firm order with Folland over the summer of 1956 provoked speculation that Russia had made an attractive offer of MIG's, but in September the Indian government contracted for 20 'whole' Gnats, 20 sets of components for assembly in India, and the licensed manufacture of 100 units by HAL at Bangalore.[5] Even as the first Mysteres and further Ouragans were arriving and the Gnat project was getting underway, India placed an order in Britain for 160 Hawker Hunter Mk 56 FGA's (fighter-ground attackers) and 22 Mk 66 two-seat trainers.[6]

Bombers

Negotiations with Britain for the English Electric Canberra as a replacement for the obsolete American Liberator began in 1954 and continued through 1956. Although Russia reportedly offered the Ilyushin Il-28 bomber at one-quarter to one-half the market price of the Canberra,[7] the Indian government decided in principle on 1 April 1956 to obtain the Canberra.[8] In January 1957 the government placed an order for 54 B(1).58 light bombers, eight P.R.57 photoreconnaissance aircraft, and six T.4 dual-control trainers, and deliveries began in the early summer. A supplementary order for twelve more B(1).58's was placed in September 1957, and it is understood from a reliable source that a further 20 to 30 Canberras of all types were ordered in 1961, with deliveries of this latter order continuing through 1962.

Transport and Communications

The transport capacity of the Air Force was substantially increased during the 1955–62 period. Twenty-six Canadian de Havilland DHC-3 Otter utility transports were purchased in 1956 to augment and replace the Devons, and four American Bell 47G-2 helicopters were acquired in 1957. Two British Vickers Viscount 730 commercial transports were obtained in 1955–56 for the use of important officials, and the Soviet Union presented India with two Ilyushin Il-14

[5] The delivery of the 'whole' units from Britain commenced in April 1957 and was spread over a two-year period.
[6] Deliveries of the Mk 56 began in October 1957, and of the Mk 66 in 1959.
[7] *Aeroplane and Astronautics*, 15 February 1957, p. 222.
[8] *The Times*, 2 April 1956.

commercial transport aircraft at about the same time. Both the Viscounts and the Ilyushins are believed to have been tested by the IAF for possible military use, but the British Avro-748 had been selected as the DC-3 replacement by early 1959; an agreement signed by representatives of Hawker Siddeley and the Indian government in Delhi on 7 July 1959 provided for the licensed production of the Avro-748 in India.

The Army's commitment to Himalayan security operations in late 1959 caused the Defence Ministry to initiate a search for helicopters and transport aircraft capable of high-altitude operations. In May 1960 India was reportedly examining a Sikorsky proposal to build the S-62 model in India,[9] and an Indian technical delegation visited the Sikorsky plant in June during the course of a United States tour in which 29 more Fairchild C-119G transport aircraft were purchased. The placing of an order for two Sikorsky S-62's in August appeared to presage a larger order with provision for licensed production in India, but the Indian government subsequently obtained from American sources only six S-62's. It bought six Bell 47G-3 units in mid-1961 and six more in August 1962. For most of its increased transport requirements, New Delhi turned to the Soviet Union. An eight-man Indian mission visited Moscow in October 1960 and negotiated the purchase of 10 Mi-4 Hound helicopters, 24 Il-14 transports, and 8 Antonov An-12 heavy air freighters. A further order for 8 An-12's and 16 Mi-4's was placed in early 1962 despite reported Indian dissatisfaction with the performance of the Soviet aircraft at the high Himalayan altitudes.[10] To conserve foreign exchange, the Defence Ministry also purchased a number of used aircraft (probably DC-3's) from Indian civil and private sources.

Air-to-Air Missiles

At about the same time the government was engaged in augmenting its transport capacity, it was reportedly making enquiries about the availability of air-to-air missiles from American sources.[11] Requests for Sidewinder air-to-air missiles for use by the IAF's subsonic

---

[9] *Aviation Week*, 23 May 1960, p. 37.

[10] See, for example, *ibid.*, 20 February 1961, p. 50; 17 July 1961, p. 23.

[11] The enquiries were evidently prompted by the IAF's lack of a world-class fighter with supersonic capabilities and by expected delays in the indigenous HF-24 project undertaken in 1955; the addition of missiles to the IAF's subsonic fighters would be an economical substitute for their lack of supersonic capabilitity.

fighter arm were made in 1960 and 1961, but were evidently refused by American authorities.[12] Three separate requests to the State Department for permission to obtain detailed data on the Hughes HM-55 air-to-air missile system were also apparently rejected.[13] Mr. Nehru's claim in the Rajya Sabha on 23 August 1961 that India could have 'easily' bought some guided missiles from America, Britain, or Russia but preferred to develop her own would, therefore, appear (with regard to the United States and Britain) to be as misleading as another claim made by him on the same occasion—that India was reaching the stage where she could produce such missiles in abundance.

Indian Interest in Soviet Aircraft

In any case, by early 1962 the Indian HF-24 jet fighter project, begun in 1956, was progressing only slowly as the search continued for a suitable engine to power the Mk 2 supersonic version. At some point in the early spring of 1962, the Indian government accepted the view—which the IAF must have been putting forward for some time—that several squadrons must be re-equipped as quickly as practicable with a world-class supersonic fighter comparable to the American Lockheed F-104 Starfighter, which was in service in a number of Western air forces and in Pakistan, the latter having obtained twelve of these aircraft in 1961-62. In May 1962 several Indian newspapers reported that the government was interested in the Soviet MIG-21 fighter.[14] After the appearance of these reports, which provoked immediate reaction in the United States, the Indian government maintained a discreet silence for reasons that were clearly not unrelated to Congressional discussion of American economic aid to India. Nehru left for a Kashmir vacation on 16 May without comment on the MIG issue, while Menon's only remark to newsmen after seeing the Prime Minister off was to declare that India had the right to purchase arms wherever she wished.[15]

With the passage of the aid bill through the United States Con-

[12] *New York Times*, 11 June 1960; George Wilson, *Aviation Week*, 5 November 1962, p. 26.

[13] George Brownlow, *ibid.*, 26 November 1962, p. 30. He stated also that the IAF mission sent to London in July 1962 ostensibly to evaluate the Lightning reportedly discussed with British officials the possible purchases of Bloodhound surface-to-air missiles as an interim weapon pending re-equipment of the IAF with supersonic aircraft.

[14] See the *Indian Express*, 8 May 1962; *Times of India*, 6 May 1962; K. Rangaswami in *Hindu*, 9 May 1962.

[15] Cited, *New York Times*, 17 May 1962.

gress, Indian political leaders became more ready to offer opinions on the relative merits of the MIG. Menon admitted publicly, for the first time, in the Lok Sabha on 23 May, that the government was indeed weighing the purchase of Soviet jet aircraft. He listed price, ease of maintenance, and other advantages that the MIG possessed over comparable Western types. At a press conference on 13 June, Nehru expressed the view that he was leaning towards acceptance of the Soviet 'offer' for reason that the MIG's were most suited to India's needs,[16] but he admitted in the Rajya Sabha on 20 June that Russia had actually made no 'formal offer' to supply MIG's and that his government had only stated its 'intention' to obtain them.

While the attitude of the government remained ambiguous and seemingly aimed at convincing the public that their political leadership would assert its independence of judgement, British and American official circles were concerned at the possibility that India might acquire Soviet military aircraft. Prime Minister Macmillan and President Kennedy reportedly undertook urgent bilateral consultations involving an attractive counteroffer to India of British or French jets.[17] The British Secretary of State for Commonwealth Relations, Duncan Sandys, flew to New Delhi on 15 June and held talks with Nehru and Menon over a period of three days, during which time 'diplomatic sources' revealed that Nehru had assured Sandys that India would consult Britain and the United States before making any decision on the purchase of MIG's.[18] Sandys announced on 19 June that Britain would make 'precise proposals' to counter the MIG offer.[19] According to one press source, Britain was willing to provide the Lightning at a unit cost of $750,000 (about one-half the market price) and to discuss production of the model under licence in India.[20] Another report stated that the British had offered one squadron of Lightnings (twelve aircraft) to India but on the condition that the Royal Air Force immediately receive an equivalent number of F-104's from the United States.[21]

'Informed sources' reported that the Defence Ministry was 'inclined' to shelve the MIG purchase indefinitely or at least until Britain's counterproposals could be evaluated,[22] and a three-man

[16] Cited, *Hindu*, 15 June 1962.
[17] A. M. Rosenthal, *New York Times*, 13 June 1962.
[18] *Ibid.* (city edition), 16 June 1962.
[19] *Ibid.*, 20 June 1962.
[20] *Aviation Week*, 23 July 1962, p. 24.
[21] K. Rangaswami, *Hindu*, 7 July 1962.
[22] *New York Times* (city edition), 1 July 1962.

mission led by Air Vice-Marshal Harjinder Singh left for Britain on 7 July, ostensibly to evaluate the Lightning. Simultaneously, the Indian government reportedly made an exploratory approach to the U.S. State Department for McDonnell F-101 Voodoos [23] and enquired of the Dassault Company of France concerning the possible purchase of about 50 Mirage III's.[24] No satisfactory arrangement eventuated from Western sources, however, and an Indian evaluation team left for Moscow on 31 July to discuss the possible purchase of two squadrons of operational MIG-21's, their production under licence in India, and the purchase of air-to-air missiles to arm them. An agreement was concluded in August which provided for Indian purchase of twelve MIG-21's and for Soviet technical assistance in establishing production facilities for this model in India.[25]

THE AIR FORCE ON THE EVE OF CONFLICT WITH CHINA

On the eve of the border conflict with Communist China in October 1962, the Indian Air Force constituted the largest and most effective national air force in the Indian Ocean region. As nearly as the writer has been able to ascertain, the IAF comprised about 30,000 regular personnel and about 400 front-line and 600 reserve, training, and miscellaneous aircraft [26] organized in 25 regular and 7 reserve squadrons.[27] The two operational commands were Western Air Command, based at Palam (New Delhi), and Eastern Air Command, formed at Calcutta in 1960 to meet the growing commitments of the IAF for air defence and support operations in the areas bordering China, Burma, and East Pakistan. In addition to the Auxiliary Air Force, the reserve included the Air Defence Reserve, consisting of technical and flying personnel associated with aviation, and the Regular Reserve of IAF personnel who had either retired or been released from the regular service.

The service had been less affected by financial stringency than

[23] *Aviation Week*, 23 July 1962, p. 24.
[24] *Dawn*, 6 July 1962.
[25] The nature of the agreement was not revealed at the time, but it was apparently largely one of principle, requiring extensive further negotiations.
[26] Aircraft in service with the IAF or available to it comprised roughly 110 Mysteres, 60 to 75 Gnats, 182 Hunters, 100 Vampires, 104 Ouragans, 100 Canberras, 53 C-119G's, 30 C-47's, 26 Otters, 12 Devons, 16 An-12's, 62 Prentices, 30 Texans, 26 Il-14's, 15 to 20 Austers, about 60 helicopters, a few B-24's, and several Viscounts.
[27] See Appendix X for a detailed breakdown of the Service.

were the Army and Navy. The first phase of the programme conceived at independence was implemented within the limitations imposed by the scarcity of trained personnel and suitable aircraft rather than money.[28] The re-equipment and expansion phase, comprising stage two, began uneventfully in 1954 with the placing of the orders for Canberras, Gnats, and Mysteres, but the Hunter purchase and the supplementary orders for further Ouragans and Canberras represented an expansion in the bomber and fighter-bomber formations which does not appear to have been envisaged in the original scheme.[29] As the Hunter purchase followed upon reports of Pakistan's impending receipt of North American Aviation's F-86F Sabre day fighters from the United States, leading Indian newspapers were inclined to view the order as directly attributable to American aid to Pakistan [30] or as 'largely' reflecting official anxieties regarding Pakistan's intentions.[31]

There were probably several actual motivations leading to the expansion of the bomber and fighter formations. It is understood that the initiative for the Hunter order came from Defence Minister Menon and was not even referred to the Chiefs of Staff Committee. The Army and Navy were of the view that Pakistan's receipt of the Sabres did not warrant a further and unplanned allocation of scarce foreign exchange for the IAF, and the Finance Minister argued against the purchase on financial grounds. In the circumstances, Menon's motives were apparently related to the political advantages to be gained by countering Pakistan's increased capabilities in a sphere where information about developments was readily available to the general public. Nehru's reasons for sanctioning a further drain on foreign exchange reserves depleted by other aircraft and tank purchases are less clear. He was certainly not insensitive to the mood of the public, which was easily alarmed by any strengthening of the power of the 'historical ghost'—Muslim Pakistan—and he may have viewed the Hunters as necessary reassurance to the Indian people

[28] The British Commander-in-Chief of the RIAF, Air Marshall Sir Thomas Elmhirst, was reported to have stated at a New Delhi press conference on 19 February 1949 that Britain had given higher priority to India's aircraft needs than it had to any other Commonwealth country. Cited, *Hindu*, 20 February 1949.

[29] The Hunter order apparently surprised even the usually well-informed British aircraft industry. See *Aeroplane and Astronautics*, 13 September 1957, p. 398.

[30] *Hindu Weekly Review* leader, 15 December 1958.

[31] *The Eastern Economist*, 13 March 1959.

of the government's determination to protect the country. He may also, however, have had an eye to the deteriorating regional situation (trouble in Laos, instability in Burma, strife in Viet Nam, and Chinese policies in Tibet) and felt it prudent to strengthen the ultimate sanction behind Indian diplomacy—her armed forces. Public emphasis upon the threatening regional situation as the reason for the purchase of the Hunters may have raised doubts internally and externally as to the government's sincerity about panch sheel and its persistent criticism of power diplomacy and the arms race. It was expedient, therefore, for Nehru to let the Indian public arrive at its own conclusions on Pakistan.

The subsequent orders for more Ouragans and Canberras would also seem to be explainable on these more general grounds with the added factors that the Ouragans were probably obtained at extremely favourable prices because they were regarded as virtually obsolescent in Europe. It was reported at the time that the IAF felt that an even larger bomber force was required if India was to possess 'secure superiority' over Pakistan [32] and the possibility of Pakistan acquiring American-built B-57 (Canberra) bombers undoubtedly strengthened the service's argument with the Cabinet. The factor of national prestige, however, must not be overlooked; New Delhi placed far greater reliance upon at least the image of strong military forces than it was prepared to concede publicly.

The interplay of prestige and prudence, particularly in view of Chinese policies in the Himalayan region and Southeast Asia, is also apparent with regard to the order for Canberras placed in 1961 and the almost frantic search for supersonic fighter aircraft in the spring of 1962. The 'sudden' interest in several squadrons of supersonic fighters in the spring of 1962 followed upon Pakistan's receipt of twelve F-104 supersonic fighters and was generally regarded at the time as a direct reaction to that issue; in fact, it was publicly explained as such by official spokesmen.

For political considerations, upon which the Air Force must have played, the government may have been disinclined to concede superiority to Pakistan in such a prestigious weapons system. However, at the same time it must also have recognized that Pakistan's weapons system could not threaten India's general industrial and military superiority in war. More important motivation for the MIG agreement would seem to lie with the continued delays in the proposed re-equipment of the fighter arm with the HF-24 and the rapidly

[32] Rawle Knox, *The Scotsman*, 9 February 1957.

worsening situation along the long frontier with China. Continued reliance upon the HF-24 to re-equip the Air Force would have entailed the maintenance of an increasingly obsolescent fighter arm for at least two years, with serious doubts as to whether the HF-24 project would come to fruition at all and whether the model would be world-class even if it did. New Delhi was well aware of the numerous intrusions into Indian air space in the Himalayas by Chinese aircraft [33] and, viewed against this background, the aim of purchasing some operational world-class fighters and ultimately producing them in India suggests a desire to maintain an efficient and effective fighter arm against any contingency that might arise. While China did not at that time possess operational aircraft faster than the MIG-19 (maximum speed 900 mph), Indian officials probably thought that only markedly superior aircraft would suffice to offset the quantitative superiority of the Chinese People's Armed Forces Air Forces (CPAFAF).

The purchases of transport aircraft and helicopters from 1960 onwards were directly related to the commitment of the IAF to fly in supplies to the Army troops deployed in Ladakh and NEFA—a contingency for which the IAF was not prepared. As the C-47's were not suitable for operations at Himalayan altitudes, the Indian government was forced to procure additional planes. Even then, however, no provision had been made for possible large-scale operations in NEFA; the C-119's, An-12's, and various helicopters—particularly the Mi-4's—were acquired for, and primarily committed to, supply operations in Ladakh.

The IAF as of October 1962 possessed an extraordinary complexity of aircraft—some thirty types of British, French, Russian, American, Canadian, and indigenous manufacture. It is hard to see the reasons for such a policy in a country seriously short of technically qualified personnel. British aircraft were generally preferred and were acquired despite the availability of comparable types from other sources. The Ouragan purchase in 1954 only followed a failure to obtain Gloster Meteor F.4 fighters from Britain and, apparently, Sabre Mk 30's Australia.[34] Canberras and Mysteres were pur-

[33] India charged China with 127 intrusions of her air space between 19 September 1959 and 3 June 1961. See *White Papers*, nos. III–V.

[34] According to *The Times* (15 December 1953), Britain was unable to supply these aircraft at the time because of the priority given its own needs and those of its NATO allies. *Aviation Week* (26 July 1954, p. 7) reported that the Commonwealth Aircraft Corporation had been unable to accept an Indian order for 50 Sabres because it had committed its complete production to the Royal Australian Air Force for 'some years' hence.

chased despite the availability of Soviet MIG-17's and Il-28's at far cheaper prices.[35] The Hunters were acquired despite IAF preference for the Mirage and possibly reflected Menon's known preference for British equipment and corresponding bias against French sources of supply. The Mystere order would seem to have constituted a deliberate decision to reduce excessive dependence upon a single source (that is, Britain) which might not always be able or willing to meet Indian requests for aircraft of a particular type. India's disinterest in Soviet aircraft until 1959 probably reflected a desire to adhere to Western weapons systems and, perhaps more importantly, to avoid misinterpretations in the West (on whose support India's economic plans were heavily dependent) and particularly the United States (by far the greatest contributor of aid) concerning the political implications of resort to such a source of supply.

India's purchase of Soviet equipment during the 1959–62 period is partly explicable on practical grounds: the Mi-4 possessed advantages over the Sikorsky S-62 in capacity, ease of maintenance, and price, while the An-12 was, in the view of certain Western military personnel interviewed by the writer, comparable in performance for Himalayan conditions to any similar Western aircraft, with the probable additional advantage of price and rupee payment. The decision in favour of the MIG-21 reflected certain attractions in price and rupee payment and the willingness of the Soviet Union to meet India's request for licence rights and technical aid in establishing the factories [36]—arrangements which Western manufacturers and governments were apparently not prepared to meet for a variety of financial, political, and technical reasons. However, the MIG possessed no obvious operational advantages over the Lightning, Mirage, or F-104; it was essentially a day fighter with a more limited operational radius and less versatility than the three Western types and is understood to have provoked little enthusiasm in IAF circles

[35] The decision in favour of the Canberras may have been partly influenced by Britain's willingness to release the 'blue study' radar bombsight. See statement by Mahavir Tyagi, cited in *The Times*, 9 May 1956. This factor alone, however, would not seem to account for the rejection of the Il-28 at a third to half the price in the context of a particularly acute shortage of foreign exchange.

[36] In view of India's subsequent difficulties with the Soviet Union over implementation of the project, however, it may well be that Moscow sought to obtain short-term political advantages with no intention of pursuing the matter in more concrete fashion; it may have shared Western doubts as to India's ability to implement such a sophisticated project and relied upon eventual Indian recognition of this fact to halt the project before it really began.

beyond the negative view that, if Western types could not be acquired, the MIG-21 was at least a decided improvement upon the existing aircraft in front-line service with the IAF.

Such factors had been ignored previously, however, with respect to the Il-28's and MIG-17's and MIG-19's, and it was no mere coincidence that the political interest in Soviet aircraft followed the appearance of a recognizable Chinese threat to India's territorial integrity. In such a context, it must have appeared highly advisable to Indian political leaders to obtain at least symbolic assurance of Russian friendship with the possibility that such a demonstration would impose a brake upon any hasty action which Peking might otherwise contemplate. Moscow's sale of aircraft and helicopters for obvious use in the Himalayan region against China was thus an excellent diplomatic move.

The Indian political implications of the MIG deal are less easy to assess, as official spokesmen made few references to the need to counter Chinese air power in Tibet,[37] and this aspect appears to have gone largely unnoticed by the public and press. Convinced of the need for supersonic aircraft and for its indigenous production under licence, New Delhi appears to have taken up the Soviet offer as the only one that met the desired conditions of price and manufacture.[38] The government and the Indian public may have felt satisfaction that the arrangement reinforced nonalignment, exerting an 'independent' line in the face of undisguised Western concern and perhaps indicating resentment at Western support for another United Nations resolution involving the question of a plebiscite in Kashmir.

The general effectiveness of the Indian Air Force in the performance of its assigned responsibilities was compromised in various ways. The multiplicity of aircraft, each with different maintenance schedules and spare parts and service requirements, necessitated continual retraining of ground and air crews. Technical and equipment procedures had been largely adopted from other air forces, and little

[37] At Calcutta on 29 July 1962, however, Nehru described the desire for supersonic aircraft as motivated by the Pakistani threat and China's 'grasping' part of India's mountain territory. Cited, *The Nation*, 31 July 1962.

[38] The usually well-informed Prem Bhatia charged in an article published in late 1962, however, that while the IAF mission was in London in July the manufacturers of the Mirage III offered to set up a production line in India to match the Soviet offer but were turned down by Menon on the grounds that he was 'committed' to the Russians. 'The Harvest of Menonism', *The Reporter*, 22 November 1962.

effort had been made to develop procedures more in accordance with Indian conditions. There was little appreciation of logistics procedures and of the need for detailed and accurate forecasting and records of spares requirements. This lethargy was aggravated by government reluctance to provide funds for the stocking of reasonable supplies of spares and was particularly dangerous for an air force equipped with many obsolete aircraft for which spares were difficult to obtain. The result was, according to one confidential source, that, at the time of the Chinese attacks, the Harvard trainers (acquired shortly after partition) and most of the Vampires were grounded for lack of spares and the Hunters escaped a similar fate only by the narrowest of margins. As one Indian newspaper has observed, during the border war with China the aircraft base repair depot at Kanpur could not perform its basic function of repair for lack of spare parts; the depot had sufficient foreign exchange for new projects but not for its primary needs of repair.[39]

The operational squadrons were deployed and trained for actions against Pakistan in primarily a tactical role in support of the Indian Army in the Punjab and Kashmir. The air defence system appears to have been rudimentary in view of the absence of any radar warning system—only the Delhi and Calcutta airports possessed radar of any kind—and reliance seems to have been placed upon early strikes against the Pakistan air bases with the aim of delivering a crippling blow to the PAF.[40] Most of the activity of both air forces, however, would probably be closely related to the land battle upon which the outcome of any Indo-Pakistani conflict would depend. The almost 2:1 superiority enjoyed by the IAF over the PAF would have left little doubt as to the outcome of any prolonged clash between the two air forces.

The contingency of war with China on even a limited scale, however, had been almost completely ignored in practice, if not in theory. Defence of the heavily populated northern Indian plain and its heavy industries, particularly in the Calcutta area, was nonexistent, although China, unlike Pakistan, could not be expected to be deterred from such action for fear of much more destructive reciprocal counteraction. The air squadrons were not deployed to put up any

---

[39] *Overseas Hindustan Times*, 30 April 1964.
[40] The PAF comprised about 15,000 personnel manning eight squadrons of F-86F Sabre subsonic fighter-bombers, one squadron of F-104 supersonic strike fighter-interceptors, one or two squadrons of B-57 (Canberra) tactical bombers, and reconnaissance, transport, and coastal search units.

effective defence against an air attack launched from Tibetan bases. The possible use of bomber and fighter-bomber units in tactical support of the Army in NEFA was precluded by the inability of the IAF to deploy and maintain at short notice more than four or five squadrons and by the fact that the service lacked training in support tactics in the rugged jungle and mountain terrain of NEFA and Assam. Even transport capacity was fully committed to supply operations in the secondary Ladakh theatre and thus was unable to provide appreciable assistance to the forces in NEFA. Against China, the IAF provided no deterrent, had little if any strategic role (in view of the need to avoid any escalation of a military conflict from which India could hardly benefit), and was so deployed and trained as to be of marginal value in either a tactical or supply role.

Chapter Seven

THE INDIAN NAVY, 1947–1962

At partition, the Royal Indian Navy was divided between India and Pakistan in the rough proportion of 2 to 1, with India's share comprising 32 vessels of various types,[1] the naval dockyard at Bombay, and approximately 1,000 officers and 10,000 ratings, or seamen. The naval establishment was completely unbalanced in almost every respect, and the development of a modern navy had necessarily to be a long-term process that would require the full co-operation of an advanced naval power like the United Kingdom.

OFFICIAL CONCEPTIONS OF INDIAN NAVAL REQUIREMENTS

Differences of opinion concerning India's naval requirements appear to have arisen at the very outset between the Indian government and British naval planners assigned by the Indian government to the task of developing the Indian Navy. According to one writer, who preferred to use a pseudonym, the Admiralty wanted the Navy to conform to some Commonwealth pattern. The Admiralty visualized a force of escort vessels and local flotillas of minesweepers, the extension of base repair facilities at Bombay and possibly Calcutta for the use of large ships of the Commonwealth navies, and the development of considerable assembly and supply arrangements for escort forces at Cochin.[2]

The leadership of the Indian government, however, purportedly made it clear that they wanted a navy which in the event of a war would provide not merely the 'missing bits' of a larger naval scheme;

[1] See Appendix IX for a breakdown of vessels by type. Pakistan received two sloops, two frigates, four fleet minesweepers, two motor minesweepers, four motor launches, one training ship, the gunnery, radar, and tactical navigation schools, the Boys' Training Establishment, and about 180 officers and 3,400 ratings.

[2] 'Tughlak', 'The Birth of the Indian Navy', *Naval Review*, 44:2 (April 1956), pp. 173–174

they felt that India, by virtue of its location, potential wealth, and vast population must inevitably be of immense strategic significance in world problems and could be centrally influential in local ones. India accordingly desired 'a preponderance of naval power vis-a-vis her Asiatic neighbours to ensure that (though she herself firmly and truly disclaimed any aggressive policy) where they were concerned she would have a reasonable assurance of freedom of the seas through the Arabian Sea, Indian Ocean and Bay of Bengal for her own shipping'.[3] The Nehru administration therefore appeared to subscribe to the policy of securing and maintaining naval superiority over neighbouring nations. Such a strategic role necessitated a navy possessing the nucleus of a striking force, as well as escort vessels and local flotillas to safeguard base areas. With direct reference to the threat that would be posed to communications and shipping in the Indian Ocean by Soviet-bloc submarines, the Indian Navy was to be developed with primary emphasis on anti-submarine warfare.

In accordance with an official directive, Indian Naval Headquarters under the direction of Vice-Admiral W. E. Parry drew up a ten-year plan of naval expansion in late 1947. The proposed programme involved the Indianization of the Navy as soon as practicable and its gradual development into a carrier task force comprising two light fleet aircraft carriers, three light cruisers, eight to nine destroyers, and the necessary support vessels.[4] The force was to be capable of expansion when the necessity arose and, though designed primarily for a defensive role, it was to be capable of offense against an enemy in the Indian Ocean.[5] Its specific wartime roles were defined in March 1949 as the protection of merchant convoys, assistance to the Army in amphibious operations, and offensive operations against enemy ports and installations.[6]

The naval programme was accepted and begun by the Indian gov-

[3] *Ibid.*, p. 175. Lord Mountbatten seems to have supported the Indian view. In an address to officers and ratings of the Navy at Castle Barracks, Bombay, on 17 December 1947, he expressed the view that India's new international position required a 'great and powerful navy'. Cited, *The Times*, 18 December 1947.

[4] Vice-Ad. W. E. Parry at a New Delhi press conference, 8 October 1948. Cited, *New York Times*, 9 October 1948. This appears to have been the first public revelation of the plan.

[5] Parry, 'India and Sea Power', *USI Journal*, 79:334–335 (January–April 1949), p. 27.

[6] See report of an interview with Capt. H. C. Ranald by a correspondent in *Hindu*, 26 March 1949. Ranald was a Royal Navy fleet air arm expert deputed to organize such an arm for the Indian Navy.

ernment in 1948. A few samples of landing ships and craft—one LST and six LCT's—were retained, 'ready for the day when we can prepare for any landing operations needed in the future'.[7] A light cruiser and three 'R' class destroyers were purchased from Britain in 1948, the cruiser arriving at Bombay in September of the same year and the destroyers in January 1950, after refitting.[8] Two oilers were acquired in 1948, and the four trawlers and six of the twelve fleet minesweepers retained at partition were discarded by 1950. A directorate of Naval Aviation was established in 1948; as the Royal Navy was unable at that time to meet an Indian request for suitable fleet aircraft, it was decided to form a fleet air arm nucleus for the future. Provision was accordingly made in the defence budget for 1949-50. As of late March 1949, it was expected that the first aircraft carrier would 'probably' be purchased from the Royal Navy in 1955 and the second in 1957—by which time it was hoped that the fleet air arm would comprise 300 modern naval fighters, fighter-bombers, and anti-submarine aircraft with a front-line strength of 54 units in two carrier groups. The first 40 naval aircraft were expected to arrive in India before the end of 1950.[9]

The deterioration in the international situation during the 1948-51 period, as manifested in the Berlin blockade, the formation of NATO, and the Korean War, introduced uncertainties about the availability of the required naval vessels. During a visit to Britain in the summer of 1949, Vice-Admiral Parry was unable to make definite arrangements for further ships because the Admiralty was unable to specify the types of ships that would be available for sale.[10] The situation became even tighter in 1950-51,[11] presumably as a result of the Korean War, but a pause was in any case required for the recruitment and training of further Indian personnel needed to man future acquisitions.

In the meantime, the government had reconsidered the naval programme from a financial standpoint and had reached the conclusion that it was beyond the country's immediate resources and needs. De-

[7] Parry, 'India and Sea Power'

[8] For presumably accurate reports concerning the composition of the Indian Navy, see Raymond V. B. Blackman (ed.), *Jane's Fighting Ships* (London: Sampson Low, Marston).

[9] See report of the Ranald interview in *Hindu*, loc cit.

[10] See remarks by Parry cited in *Hindu*, 8 April and 15 August 1949.

[11] See report by Press Trust of India of a statement by Parry cited in *ibid.*, 4 June 1951.

tails of the revised programme were revealed by Vice-Admiral Parry at a Bombay press conference on 21 January 1950. He stated that the Navy now planned to develop a small carrier task force of the 'hunter-killer' (anti-submarine) type that would comprise one light fleet carrier, three light cruisers, eight to nine destroyers, and the necessary support vessels.[12]

With the slightly revised scheme India proceeded in 1953 to purchase from Italy a fleet replenishment vessel and to borrow from Britain three ex-escort destroyers of the 'Hunt' type 2 class.[13] A second light cruiser was purchased from Britain in April 1954 and underwent extensive refit before joining the Indian fleet in 1957. Two inshore minesweepers were transferred from the Royal Navy in 1955.

SIX-YEAR BUILDING PROGRAMME, 1955-1961

The details of a six-year building programme for the Navy in British shipyards were revealed by the Chief of the Indian Naval Staff, Admiral Sir Mark Pizey, in Delhi on 11 July 1955. He stated that, during the 1955-61 period, the Navy expected to receive twelve anti-submarine and anti-aircraft frigates as replacements for the 'R' class destroyers and older frigates, eight coastal minesweepers to replace the obsolete types then in service, and an unspecified number of inshore minesweepers.[14] The delivery of ships under this programme proceeded as the individual units were completed. Four 'Ton' class coastal minesweepers were transferred from the Royal Navy in 1956. Two 'Whitby' class anti-submarine frigates were received, one in May and one in August 1960, and single 'Blackwood' class anti-submarine frigates arrived in Bombay in each of 1958, 1959, and 1960. A 'Leopard' class anti-aircraft frigate was received in each of 1959, 1960, and 1961.

No further ships were acquired for the ambitious modernization and expansion scheme, which thus fell considerably short of the initial proposals. The third cruiser envisaged from 1947 also failed to materialize. The reasons for not purchasing these vessels would seem to be financial stringency and the acute foreign exchange problem, which involved a deficit of $650 million in 1957-58 and threat-

---

[12] Cited, *ibid.*, 22 January 1950. See also *Jane's Fighting Ships*, 1949-50, p. 95; 1950-51, p. 104.

[13] The vessels were loaned for an initial period of three years subject to extension by agreement.

[14] Cited, *The Times*, 11 July 1955.

ened to ruin any prospects that the Second Five-Year Plan would be fulfilled. The Indian naval programme underway in British shipyards was an early casualty of Indian efforts to reduce external procurement of what were regarded at the time as nonessential items.

The Indian government subsequently purchased the three 'R' class destroyers hitherto on loan from the Royal Navy and planned ultimately to construct minesweepers, frigates, and destroyers in Indian shipyards,[15] which were already building minor craft for the Navy. A mooring vessel and a survey vessel were commissioned from Hindustan Shipyard Limited (Calcutta) in November–December 1959, a repair ship was commissioned in May 1960, and three seaward patrol craft were commissioned between September 1960 and January 1962. Two diesel tugs were handed over to the Navy in February 1962, and miscellaneous water boats, ferry craft, ammunition barges, and pontoons were also acquired from Indian sources.

Development of a Fleet Air Arm

The development of the fleet air arm progressed slowly, for a lack of both money and suitably trained personnel. The first naval air station, INS *Garuda*, was commissioned on 13 May 1953 at Venderuthy, Cochin. A Fleet Requirements Unit was formed in the same year, when ten Short Sealand light amphibians, which had been ordered the previous year, were received. Five Fairey Firefly T.T.1 and five Fairey Firefly T.T.4 target-tug aircraft were acquired for the Unit in 1955,[16] and the formation was augmented several years later by a flight of Vampire jet trainers taken over from the Indian Air Force and by a number of locally produced Hindustan HT-2 jet trainers.

For some time the government was apparently undecided whether to proceed with the acquisition of an aircraft carrier. Defence Minister Gopalaswami Ayyanger stated in 1952 that no specific date for the purchase could be given.[17] Defence Minister N. N. Katju informed the Lok Sabha on 5 April 1955 that a proposal had still not been made regarding the purchase and claimed that he could not

---

[15] See p. 135.

[16] The purchase followed a demonstration of naval anti-aircraft fire in which the last ship in line had to resort to firing a rocket down the line of ships to compensate for the lack of proper target drones. The inadequacy of such a procedure provoked an on-the-spot resolution by a visiting parliamentary delegation to provide the Navy with proper target drones. See Adm. Sir Mark Pizey, 'The Indian Navy Today', *Asian Review*, 52:189 (January 1946), p. 48.

[17] *LSD*, pt. 1, vols. 1–2 (29 May 1952), p. 326.

foresee future developments. Further evidence of government indecision in the matter was revealed by Admiral Pizey on the INS *Hamla* in June 1955, when he declared that perhaps his last big job with the Indian Navy would be to convince the government of the need for aircraft carriers and fast modern aircraft.[18]

The matter was subsequently taken under consideration, and the hulk of the Royal Navy's light fleet carrier *Hercules* was purchased in January 1957. The unit was modernized and completed at Belfast and was commissioned on 4 March 1961. The purchase of jet aircraft for the carrier was under consideration by August 1958;[19] 24 Sea Hawk FGA Mk 6 jet fighter-bombers were ordered in late 1959, and further units in 1961. British-built Gannet anti-submarine/reconnaissance aircraft and Westland Wessex anti-submarine helicopters were initially favoured, but the decision was ultimately taken to obtain French types: 15 Breguet 1050 Alize turbo-prop aircraft were ordered early in 1960 and four Alouette 3 helicopters in 1962. Naval air squadrons 300 (equipped with Sea Hawks) and 310 (equipped with Alizes) were commissioned on 6 July 1960 and 9 January 1961, respectively, and joined the *Vikrant* (ex-*Hercules*) in August 1961.

SUBMARINES

The establishment of a submarine arm was envisaged in the original naval plan, but with a lower priority than aircraft carriers.[20] Official spokesmen persistently refused to clarify policy concerning submarines on the grounds that it was not in the national interest to do so.[21] It seems clear, however, that financial priorities precluded the acquisition of any submarines and forced the Indian Navy to rely upon periodic visits by British submarines for its training in anti-submarine operations. In a statement at Bombay on 9 May 1962, the retiring Chief of Naval Staff, Vice-Admiral R. D. Katari, indicated the Navy's dissatisfaction with its dependent role by publicly advocating the establishment of an Indian submarine fleet.[22]

[18] Cited, *Hindu Weekly Review*, 6 June 1955.
[19] See statement by Defence Minister Menon, *LSD*, vol. 19 (30 August 1958) col. 3648.
[20] See Comm. N. Krishnan, 'Strategic Concepts of Indian Naval Expansion' *USI Journal*, 88:327 (July–September 1958), p. 217.
[21] See, for example, Deputy Defence Minister S. S. Majithia, *LSD*, pt. 1, vol. 5 (28 July 1956), cols. 506–507; Menon, *ibid.*, vol. 3 (23 May 1962), col. 6068.
[22] Cited, *Hindu*, 10 May 1962.

Development of Training Establishments

Simultaneously with the acquisition of new ships and aircraft, the Navy developed training establishments to replace those of the old Royal Indian Navy retained by Pakistan at partition. Until 1952, all naval officers were sent to Britain for training but, by 1955, India possessed ten training centres which were adequate to meet most of the Navy's general needs. The numbers of personnel sent to Britain for training steadily declined from 108 (1954-55) to 42 (1959-60),[23] as only specialists continued to be sent abroad.

The replacement of British with Indian personnel in the service proceeded within the limitations imposed by the availability of qualified Indian officers and technicians. By January 1948 all naval ships were commanded by Indians, but an acute shortage of officers necessitated the retention of former British officers of the Royal Indian Navy and the loan of officers from the Royal Navy. The 120 British naval officers and Admiralty civilians still employed in July 1949 were gradually replaced by Indian personnel as the latter attained the necessary standards, and by March 1953 only 46 naval officers and ten civilians of British nationality remained. Captain R. D Katari was appointed to the position of Deputy Chief of Naval Staff on 18 March 1954 and became the first Indian Naval Chief of Staff in April 1958, with the rank of Vice-Admiral. With the appointment of an Indian as Chief of Naval Aviation in April 1962, the Indian Navy became an entirely Indian-staffed service.

The Navy on the Eve of Conflict with China

The commissioning of the *Vikrant* in August 1961 completed the existing re-equipment and expansion programme of the Navy, as the Chief of Naval Staff, Vice-Admiral B. S. Soman, informed a press conference at Coimbatore on 17 August 1962.[24] At the moment he spoke, the Indian Navy constituted the most effective naval force of any country located within the Indian Ocean region—some 50 warships of all types manned by about 1,450 officers and 14,550 ratings.[25] There was also a Naval Reserve and a Naval Volunteer

---

[23] See statements by Majithia, *LSD*, pt. 1, vol. 2 (9 April 1956), col. 1985; Menon, *ibid.*, vol. 45 (20 August 1960), col. 3678.

[24] Cited, *Hindu*, 18 August 1962.

[25] See Appendix X for further details regarding the nature of the Navy.

Reserve. The service functioned under four operational commands, of which one was afloat; the fleet was based at Bombay and Cochin on India's west coast.

The vessels were entirely of British construction with the exception of a fleet replenishment ship of Italian origin, the 'Savriti' class seaward defence boats of mixed Italian, Yugoslav, and Dutch origin, a Portuguese frigate seized during the Goa operation and undergoing repair, and miscellaneous craft built in Indian shipyards. The reliance upon Britain for vessels, equipment, and training facilities was attributable to the origin of the service and the co-operation of the Royal Navy in its development. The Sea Hawk fighter had been chosen not least for the reason that at the time of purchase it was the cheapest proven carrier-borne jet fighter in existence. The choice of French-built Gannet and Alouette units, instead of British types, seems to have been based primarily upon technical considerations.

The service was responsible for the defence of India's coasts and coastal trade, in co-operation with the Air Force and the Army, and for the protection of India's maritime trade and communications.

The Indian government saw its Navy as an implicit part of a Commonwealth–United States naval defence of the lines of communications passing across the Indian Ocean. Although the Indian government had every desire to avoid involvement in any East–West conflict, it clearly appreciated that in such an eventuality neutrality would be almost impossible because of India's heavy dependence on maritime-borne commerce, which was largely carried in ships of the Western bloc maritime countries to and from Western ports. Thus the Indian Navy had been conceived and developed as an anti-submarine force aimed at countering Soviet submarines and in at least implicit co-operation with Western and regional Commonwealth nonaligned states. While India entered into no contingency planning with prospective allies and probably declined even 'understandings' for political and diplomatic reasons, the annual naval exercises with other Commonwealth navies in the Indian Ocean facilitated co-operation in defence of communications in the region lying between Aden and Singapore in the event of an East–West conflict.

The Indian Navy's operational planning during the period 1947–62, however, seems to have contemplated operations, if at all, only against Pakistan; the contingency of conflict with Communist China or Indonesia involving naval actions appears to have been ignored in practice although it is not unlikely that either or both countries figured in staff exercises. The naval threat posed by Pakistan was marginal [26] and could have amounted to little more than one foray by the fleet from Karachi against Indian coastal shipping and perhaps a short bombardment of some west coast city. Following this the Pakistani vessels would have had to concede India's superior naval strength and retire to Karachi, to be 'bottled up' pending the outcome of the decisive land campaigns, or continue eastwards around India, to face the same fate in Chittagong under constant attack from Indian carrier- and land-based planes or perhaps internment in a neutral port. Any serious challenge to India's maritime shipping interests would be effectively precluded by these events and by the difficulty in making attacks on short notice and under pressure against shipping lanes in which Indian-registered vessels would be intermingled with a variety of foreign-owned ships. Uninterrupted Indian access to Middle Eastern oil would be further assured by the fact that India's oil imports are carried almost exclusively in foreign bottoms, only two Indian oil tankers being in existence in 1962.

The very complacency with which the contingency of naval operations against Pakistan were viewed, however, had permitted financial considerations to become of paramount importance in determining budgetary allocations for the Navy. The government failed to provide the necessary ships and facilities, so that the responsibilities of the Navy were considerably in excess of its actual operational capabilities. There was no continuous refit of units of the fleet, and an outbreak of hostilities would have found few ships of the Indian Navy able to quickly take up stations or to maintain them for any useful period of time. The absence of adequate docking or repair facilities aside from Bombay and Cochin on the west coast virtually precluded any sustained action against hostile forces in the Bay of Bengal. Because of government refusal to provide funds to maintain adequate stocks of spare parts,[27] the fleet would be faced with progressive immobilization in a crisis in which external sources of sup-

---

[26] The Pakistan Navy was actually an anti-submarine force and, like the Indian Navy, had been conceived and developed primarily to combat Soviet-bloc submarines in a general war. It comprised one light training cruiser, seven escorts, six minesweepers, and miscellaneous smaller craft.

[27] An example of the subordination of efficiency to financial considerations was the 'Leopard' class anti-aircraft frigate *Brahmaputra*. Acquired in 1958 even as the Royal Navy was obtaining ships of this type, the *Brahmaputra* like its sister ships developed clutch problems. The government was reluctant to release the foreign exchange to effect the necessary repairs, and this vessel remained, to all intents and purposes, unoperational.

ply were interfered with or cut off. India had absolutely no answer to the powerful *Irian,* Indonesia's Sverdlov-class Russian-built cruiser.

In operations conducted against submarines or surface ships, many of the Indian naval units would have been liabilities rather than assets to the more modern units of the fleet and allied navies. The cruiser *Delhi,* although refitted in 1955, possessed little operational value and rarely left harbour even in its training capacity. The three 'R' class destroyers and the three 'Hunt' class frigates were obsolete and quite incapable of detecting or destroying modern conventional submarines, much less nuclear-powered ones. The cruiser *Mysore* would have been exceedingly vulnerable to submarine attack and incapable of undertaking action against a Sverdlov cruiser. As true in 1962 as in 1953—when it was made—was the observation of one Indian commentator that 'the most comforting thing about our navy . . . stout-hearted though . . . officers and . . . ratings are, is that the British and American fleets guard the Western and Eastern entrances to the Indian Ocean'.[28]

[28] 'Odysseus', *Eastern Economist,* 6 February 1953, p. 210.

Chapter Eight

DEFENCE PRODUCTION, 1947–1962

The ordnance establishment was not affected by partition, as all the functioning plants (sixteen ordnance and one clothing) were located within the political boundaries of the Indian Union.[1] The government was well aware that the country's industrial base was narrow and its manpower deficient in many of the specialized skills required in modern armaments production. While striving to rectify these inadequacies as an integral part of economic development,[2] official policy was: first, to ensure the indigenous production of basic items of military equipment that were likely to be required in sufficient quantity to make their production economically feasible; and second, to produce items which though in small demand, were essential. It was considered wiser to continue to purchase those military items that were extremely costly and in which new developments were taking place rapidly and unceasingly, such as fighter and bomber aircraft, gunsights, and guided missiles. The spare peacetime capacity of the ordnance factories was to be used for the manufacture of civil items, but it was intended to maintain close contact with civilian industry to permit future planning for defence production to proceed on a realistic basis.[3]

PROMOTION OF DEFENCE SCIENCE RESEARCH

The government proceeded to prepare a scientific organization upon which to base its proposed modern ordnance establishment. A

---

[1] The Union government agreed to compensate Pakistan for a proportion of the value of these plants, but subsequently declined to honour its obligations completely in the context of strained Indo-Pakistan relations.

[2] The Industrial Resolution Policy of the Indian government, issued in 1948 and revised at the start of the Second Plan in April 1956, designates munitions, aircraft, and shipbuilding as 'industries whose future development would be exclusive responsibility of the state'.

[3] H. M. Patel, *The Defence of India* (Bombay: Asia Publishing House, 1963), pp. 15-16.

Science Research and Development Organization was established in 1948, and in 1952 a Defence Science Service was created to attract young scientists into undertaking defence-oriented research. The Institute of Armament Studies was established at Kirki in 1952 to familiarize selected military officers with science and technology as applied to armaments and to promote the dissemination of basic defence information. A factory was set up at Ambarnath in 1954 to serve as the foundation of an armaments plant aimed at enabling ordnance establishments to design and adapt existing types of equipment in small quantities. A reorganization was effected in January 1958 in which the technical development establishments of the three Defence Services and the Defence Science Organization were replaced by the Defence Research and Development Organization (DRDO). In 1959–60, the government constituted the Defence Minister's (Research and Development) Committee to consider all policy matters affecting the DRDO and created a Research and Development Advisory Committee to replace the Defence Research Policy Board and the Defence Science Advisory Committee. In 1959, the government approved a defence research fellowship scheme, to give grants to universities and to persons undertaking defence-oriented research.

PROGRESS FROM 1947 TO 1954

Between 1947 and 1954, the existing ordnance factories were apparently balanced and brought up to a satisfactory state of efficiency, 'one or two' were expanded, and several new factories were planned and approved by the Defence Committee of the Cabinet but were not proceeded with at the time 'for one reason or another'.[4] Pursuant to a decision taken in 1952, Bharat Electronics was set up in April 1954 as a limited company in the public sector under the control of the Defence Ministry; technical assistance for the project was provided by the Compagnie de Telegraphie sans Fils of France. Production increased in value from Rs 5 crores in 1947 to Rs 27.5 crores in 1953. By 1953 the requirements of the armed forces obtained from local sources had been met and the government was considering the retrenchment of semiskilled and unskilled workers. The aim continued to be 'to expand civil production in directions which will be helpful also to meet the defence requirements of the country in an emergency', but the government had started a drive to use the

[4] *Ibid.*, p. 15.

surplus ordnance capacity to produce goods for other government departments and for civil industry—provoked partially by delays in civilian production in providing sufficiently advanced basic materials, components, and semi-manufactured parts.[5]

In mid-1954 the government reportedly considered an offer from Daimler–Benz of Stuttgart for a joint enterprise with the Tata Iron and Steel Company to produce light armoured vehicles and light tanks.[6] Serious consideration of this proposal was kept in abeyance because of the reorganization of the ordnance factories following the report by the Ordnance Factories Re-organization Committee headed by Baldev Singh.

REORGANIZATION OF ORDNANCE FACTORIES, 1955–1961

The report of the committee was submitted to the government in 1955 and, while not a secret document,[7] has for some unexplained reason never been made public. According to informed sources, however, the report included recommendations for establishing a Defence Production Board, modernizing equipment, producing for the civilian market, and decreasing the number of semiskilled and unskilled workers. With the exception of equipment modernization, which was deferred largely for financial reasons, the committee's proposals seem to have been subsequently implemented. About 5,000 workers were laid off by September 1956,[8] and the production of civilian items was extended to include such things as coffee percolators, pressure cookers, and Meccano sets. It was announced in August 1955 that the Defence Production Board had been created to assume management of all ordnance factories, co-ordinate research and development in the three armed services, and secure effective liaison with civil industry to meet defence requirements.

Bids were invited from manufacturers of tractors, with the proviso that such units were to be produced in ordnance plants. Komatsu of Japan was selected over Marshall, a British firm, and the scheme was sanctioned in March 1959.

A scheme for the production of three-ton Shaktiman trucks, signed

[5] See the statement by the Minister of Defence Organisation, Mahavir Tyagi, *LSD*, pt. 2, vol. 2 (25 March 1953), col. 2822.
[6] See report by the Bonn correspondent in *The Times*, 21 June 1954.
[7] See the statement by Defence Minister Menon, *LSD*, 2nd sess., vol. 3 (25 July 1957), col. 5212.
[8] *Ibid.*

with Maschinenfabrik Augsburg–Nurenberg AG (M.A.N.) of West Germany in September 1959, resulted from government dissatisfaction with the performance of private Indian suppliers. After 1949 the Defence Ministry had placed substantial orders with Premier Automobiles and Hindustan Motors with hopes of ultimately obtaining military vehicles of 100 per cent Indian manufacture. After eight years Premier was unable to achieve more than a 30 per cent local manufacture of parts for their military vehicles. The firm manufacturing Studebaker trucks (largely through assembly) had supplied 4,000 units to the Army up to 1957, when they abandoned their manufacture, leaving the Army with a large number of trucks for which they were not assured of spares. Protracted negotiations with TELCO for 1,000 three-ton trucks foundered when the company refused to reduce its price; after extensive tests conducted by the Army, the agreement was signed with M.A.N.[9] The first Shaktiman truck rolled off the assembly line at the gun carriage factory at Jubbulpore on 21 June 1959.

Expenditure on the manufacturing and research establishment remained fairly constant for the period ending in 1959,[10] but the output of the ordnance factories fell in value to Rs 14.57 crores (1956–57) before recovering to Rs 19.57 crores (1958–59).[11] The gradual decrease in production was accompanied by a decrease in idle capacity from Rs 63 lakhs (1956–57) to Rs 9 lakhs (1958–59).[12] The nature of production eased India's dependence on foreign (primarily British) sources, which accounted for no less than 90 per cent of her military equipment and stores in 1950.[13] By March 1953 India had reportedly attained general self-sufficiency in nonlethal stores and equipment,[14] and the Commander-in-Chief of the Army, General M. Rajendrasinjhi, declared in Calcutta on 22 June 1953 that 80 per cent of the Army's light equipment was then being produced in India.[15]

The deteriorating border situation with Communist China, however, prompted the government in late 1959 to undertake an am-

[9] See Menon's statement in Parliament on 5 December 1958, *LSD*, 2d sess., vol. 23, cols. 3403–3414.
[10] See Appendix II, Main Head 5.
[11] Ministry of Defence, *Report*, 1960–61, p. 24.
[12] *Times of India*, 19 January 1960.
[13] *Hindustan Times*, 25 April 1950.
[14] See statement by Deputy Defence Minister Satish Chandra, *LSD*, pt. 1, vol. 1 (5 March 1953), cols. 754–755.
[15] Cited, *Overseas Hindustan Times*, 2 July 1953.

bitious modernization and expansion programme in its ordnance establishment. Speaking at a New Delhi meeting of the Congress Parliamentary party on 8 February 1960, Nehru explained that the government had sought to economize in the past few years by postponing the manufacture of certain items but that, because of the border situation with China, top priority was to be given to defence and the defence industries in the 1960–61 budget and in the Third Plan.[16]

About Rs 20 crores were sanctioned for the modernization and expansion of defence factories in the 1960–61 fiscal year in a plan to produce new items, renovate old plant and equipment, establish a new explosives factory at Bhandara, and develop a plant for steel and special alloys.[17] These plans led one Indian daily to comment that 'the year 1960 has all the portents of coming off as a significant landmark in the history of the Defence industries'.[18]

In February 1960, the production of one-ton trucks was undertaken in collaboration with the Nissan Motor Company of Japan. Projects sanctioned during fiscal 1961 included a clothing factory at Avadi and the alloy and special steels plant.[19] In an agreement made public on 16 December 1961, Nissan agreed to collaborate with the Defence Ministry in the assembly in India of small (800-pound) patrol jeeps, and the first of these 'Jongas' was pressed into service on 24 January 1962. On 1 February 1962 the foundation stones of a cable factory and base repair depot were laid at Chandigarh; the repair depot was to manufacture helicopters in addition to repairing and maintaining aircraft.

Renewed interest was shown in the indigenous production of tanks. A team of defence experts headed by the Chief of the Army General Staff, Lieutenant-General L. P. Sen, visited Britain and West Germany in January 1961 to assess possible types. The West German firm involved, a subsidiary of Daimler–Benz, was prepared to design a panzer tank suited to Indian conditions, but the offer by Vickers–Armstrong of Britain to modify the Chieftain medium tank to meet Indian specifications proved more attractive.[20] The resulting

[16] Cited, *Times of India*, 9 February 1960.
[17] *Ibid.*, 19 January 1960.
[18] *Hindu*, 26 January 1960.
[19] Ministry of Defence, *Report*, 1961–62, p. 36.
[20] An important consideration in decisions on equipment purchases from abroad, however, was noted by Nehru at a Delhi press conference in April 1956, when he admitted that 'Indian forces had in the past been developed largely on the basis of British equipment and for practical reasons it was convenient,

agreement, as revealed in a London announcement on 21 August 1961, involved the manufacture of 1,000 37-ton medium tanks at a heavy vehicles plant to be established for this purpose at Avadi, near Madras. The first 40 units would be built in Britain, the components of subsequent units would be shipped to India for assembly, and, ultimately, the manufacture at Avadi with the minimum of imported components.[21] The plant would have the capacity to manufacture 100 units per year.[22]

AIRCRAFT MANUFACTURE

Even before independence, the nationalist political leadership indicated its hopes for national self-sufficiency in the manufacture of aircraft for the Indian Air Force and civil aviation within twenty years, that is, by about 1967.[23] In 1946 the interim government invited a British technical mission to India to advise it concerning the establishment of an aircraft industry. The committee recommended the repair and overhaul plant of Hindustan Aircraft Limited (HAL) at Bangalore as the nucleus for the industry, and its advice was accepted by the government.

While a modern design and development department was being established, HAL undertook the assembly of various aircraft required by the IAF. Fifty Percival Prentice basic trainers were assembled during the 1947–50 period and twelve were produced for the Indian Navy between 1951 and 1953. Some 150 de Havilland DH-82 Tiger Moth primary trainers were turned out up to 1951. A licensing agreement was concluded with de Havilland Aircraft of Canada in 1950, and assembly of Vampire F.B.9 fighter-bombers and T.55 conversion trainers began in 1953 and 1956, respectively. By the time production ceased, during the 1959–60 year, a total of 230 fighter-bombers and 50 trainers had been produced.

Negotiations were undertaken in 1955 with Folland Aircraft and Bristol Siddeley Aero-Engines of Britain for a licence to produce the Folland Gnat lightweight fighter and its powerplant, the Orpheus

other things being equal, to continue on this basis'. Cited, *The Times*, 3 April 1956.

[21] See *The Times*, 23 August and 13 September 1961.

[22] See statement by the Minister of Defence Production, A. M. Thomas, at Wellington (Nilgiris) on 7 November 1964. Cited, *The Hindu*, 9 November 1964.

[23] See Leonard Bridgman (ed.), *Jane's All The World's Aircraft* (London: Sampson, Low, Marston, 1947), p. 103c.

701 turbojet. The licences were acquired in September 1956, new factory buildings for the project were completed in 1959, and production of the airframe commenced in 1961 from imported components. The first Orpheus 701 came off the production line on 21 November 1960, and type approval was granted by the Defence Ministry nine months later. After concluding a licence agreement with Hawker Siddeley in Delhi on 7 July 1959, the Indian government initiated a project to manufacture a military version of the Avro-748 short- and medium-range transport at the Aircraft Maintenance Depot established for this purpose at Kanpur. A licence for Indian production of the Rolls Royce Dart RDa7 turboprop, the proposed powerplant for the Avro series, was secured in an agreement signed in London on 30 December 1959. In the spring of 1962, the Indian government obtained the right to produce Sud-Aviation's SE-3160 Alouette III general-purpose helicopter.

Simultaneously with the assembly and production of foreign aircraft under licence, HAL developed its own design section under its government-appointed chief designer, Dr. V. M. Ghatage. In September 1948 the government decided that HAL should proceed with the development of three aircraft types, designated the HT-2 primary trainer, the HT-10 three-seat advanced trainer, and the HT-11 advanced trainer.[24] The first prototype of the HT-2 all-metal two-seat trainer flew on 13 August 1951, and a total of 160 units were subsequently produced for the IAF, Indian Navy, and civil aviation training centres until lack of orders caused the production line to be virtually closed down in early 1962. For some reason the HT-10 and HT-11 trainers were never developed, nor was the proposed Navy amphibian, which was to have been similar in design and power to the Short Sealand;[25] a number of Short Sealands were purchased instead. HAL developed the two-seat Pushpak monoplane for flying clubs and private owners, and the more powerful four-seat Krishak for artillery observation and spotting. The first demonstration of a light communication aircraft, the Kanpur, took place on 4 February 1961.

During the Second Five-Year Plan (1956–61) HAL undertook to design and manufacture a jet trainer, an advanced jet fighter, and aero-engines. The trainer was intended as a single replacement for the HT-2, Harvard, and Vampire, while the fighter was to be pro-

[24] *Ibid.*, 1949–50, p. 102e.
[25] *Ibid.*, 1950–51, pp. 107–108c.

duced in two series to meet the Air Force's requirements for a transonic ground attack fighter-bomber and a Mach 2 interceptor.[26]

Official approval for the development of the HJT-16 two-seat basic-intermediate jet trainer was given in December 1959—the first jet design to be undertaken in India without the help of non-Indian consultants. Detailed design work began in April 1961, when Dr. V. M. Ghatage, HAL's chief designer, assembled a group of fifteen designers, who were increased to thirty-five personnel the following year. Development also commenced on the HJE-2500 turbojet engine for the trainer, on a six-cylinder piston engine for the Krishak, and on the PE90H four-cylinder pistol engine for the Pushpak—the first production model of the latter engine being started up by Defence Minister Menon on 11 March 1959.

Development of the HF-24 fighter began in 1956 under the direction of Dr. Kurt Tank, former technical director of the famous Focke–Wulf organization and designer of the Kondor maritime bomber and F.W.190 fighter. The team was initially comprised of eighteen German engineers, three Indian senior design engineers, and about twenty-two other Indian engineers with design experience. Initial plans were to use two Orpheus 703 turbojets for the transonic Mk 1 version and a single Orpheus 12 turbojet for the supersonic Mk 2. The Orpheus 12 engine was being developed by Bristol for the NATO competition, and its completion by Bristol was conditional on its acceptance by NATO countries.

Within 22 months of the start of the project, glider trials were begun to test the full-scale wings and fuselage of the HF-24 design, which had previously been model-tested in wind tunnels and had been tested for low-speed behaviour in the tunnel of the Indian Institute of Science at Bangalore. Assembly of the first prototype began in April 1960 and was completed in eleven months, after which ground trials were held. The aircraft took its maiden flight on 24 June 1961, powered by two Orpheus 703 turbojets.

Indian technicians had reportedly built some twenty-five Orpheus 12's virtually by hand [27] when it became clear that NATO no longer had any interest in the engine. Bristol Siddeley was thereby faced with a further expenditure of about $10 million to complete develop-

---

[26] In early 1961, a study was also in progress regarding development of a naval version of the HF-24 as a replacement for the Sea Hawk. Ministry of Defence, *Report*, 1960–61, p. 13.

[27] *Aviation Week*, 18 December 1961, p. 23.

ment of an engine [28] for which India alone offered a market, and a limited one at that. Although under no obligation, contractual or otherwise, to India to complete development of the model, Bristol Siddeley was prepared to expend up to $1 million further on development [29] but advanced the perfectly reasonable suggestion that the Indian government either accept further financial liability or request a subsidy from the British government.[30] For reasons that can only be ascribed to pique, New Delhi refused to assume the costs of further development. And, according to a well-informed aviation magazine, 'An effort by Britain to compromise by offering India a loan for the general purpose of aviation development and not specifying the Orpheus project as beneficiary was rejected by India's Defence Minister, Krishna Menon'.[31] India reportedly showed no interest in an offer by the French firm, Snecma, of the Atar 9 turbojet (which powers the Mirage III and IV) [32] but turned to the Soviet Union for a suitable power plant.

Several Klimov VK-7 turbojets, which develop a thrust comparable to the Orpheus 12, were obtained and subjected to evaluation tests at Bangalore. The centrifugal-flow VK-7 could not, however, be fitted to the existing HF-24 airframe without major design changes, so that India shifted its attention to the Russian RD9-F axial-flow engine; six of this type were imported in late 1961 and bench-tested. The use of this power plant was also dependent on a modification of either the engine or airframe, but, for reasons of prestige and the problems of time and finance involved in a redesign of the airframe, the Indian government was strongly disinclined to undertake such a measure except as a last resort. In an apparent about-face, however, Moscow finally agreed to modify the engine to fit the existing HF-24 airframe [33] and an agreement was concluded in the Russian capital in July 1962 for the licenced manufacture of the Mach 1.4 engine in India. The Soviet authorities agreed to supply a few models by the

[28] *Ibid.*, 23 July 1962, p. 24.
[29] *Ibid.* According to the report, development of the engine had been started with U.S. Mutual Aid funds, which were terminated by America when India purchased Soviet transports and helicopters.
[30] Discussions between Bristol Siddeley and the Indian government were reportedly held in 1960 and 1961 with a view to completing development of the Orpheus 12 or of continuing development of the much later BS. 75 turbofan. *Flight*, 2 July 1964, p. 17.
[31] *Aviation Week*, 23 July 1962, p. 24.
[32] *Ibid.*, 18 December 1961, p. 23.
[33] *The Statesman*, 14 July 1962.

end of 1963, and production was initially envisaged in 1963 but was subsequently deferred. Indian enquiries about the feasibility of acquiring a Soviet power plant for the HF-24 indirectly led to interest in the MIG-21, Russia reportedly proposing that it provide the whole airframe and engine of a supersonic fighter.[34]

NAVAL CONSTRUCTION

The indigenous construction of naval craft and warships was evidently given a lower priority than aircraft and little serious consideration was publicly evidenced in such projects until 1955, when an order was placed locally for a survey vessel and consideration was given to Indian construction of a mooring vessel, seaward patrol craft, and some inshore minesweepers.[35] In April 1960 the government purchased the entire assets of Garden Reach Workshops Limited (Calcutta) and Mazagon Dock Limited (Bombay), planning to build small naval vessels like minesweepers and, later, destroyers.[36] Orders were subsequently placed with these yards for various yard craft and six seaward patrol craft. Firm orders for two inshore minesweepers were placed with Mazagon Dock in 1960–61, and it was reported as 'likely' that an order for a destroyer would soon be placed with the same yard.[37] Negotiations were also undertaken with Britain for technical and financial assistance in the proposed construction of three 'Leander' class frigates at Mazagon Dock, and discussions were still in progress at the time of the border war with China.

DEFENCE PRODUCTION TO 1962

On the eve of this conflict, India's defence industries were occupied with diverse and ambitious production schemes. The aircraft industry, comprised of HAL and the Aircraft Manufacturing Depot, had underway or in the planning stage the production of Pushpak and Krishak light monoplanes, the Kanpur Logistics Air Support type, Gnat transonic fighters, HF-24 transonic fighter-bombers and supersonic fighters, MIG-21 supersonic fighters, HJT-16 advanced

[34] *Aviation Week*, 23 July 1962, p. 24.
[35] See statement by Deputy Defence Minister Satish Chandra, LSD, pt. 1, vol. 1 (1 March 1955, col. 360.
[36] See statement by Menon in Parliament on 9 April 1960, LSD, 2nd sess., vol. 42, col. 10, 824.
[37] Ministry of Defence, *Report*, 1960–61, p. 37.

jet trainer, Avro-748 transport, Alouette III helicopters, and Orpheus 701 and 703, Dart RDa7, and PE9oH aero-engines. The state-owned Mazagon Docks and Garden Reach shipyards were engaged in the construction of yard craft and patrol vessels and contemplated the building of minesweepers and destroyers in the near future. The ordnance establishment comprised 22 factories—seven general engineering, five metallurgical, five clothing and leather, two chemical, two chemical-cum-engineering, and one cable [38]—which produced small arms and ammunition, artillery, sea mines, depth charges, bombs, one-ton and three-ton general service vehicles, 800-pound patrol jeeps, tractors and a variety of civil items including pressure cookers, Meccano sets, and hair clippers. The research organization consisted of 25 research laboratories and technical establishments, two training centres, and three field research stations, and its efforts were directed toward the development of a mountain gun, the Ishapore rifle, and universal gun and mortar sights.

India had made substantial progress in developing local sources of defence equipment, particularly after 1959, on a foundation that was built in less spectacular fashion between 1947 and 1958. HAL's Aero-Engine Division had achieved the distinction of being the first organization in non-Communist Asia to manufacture a gas turbine aero-engine. The HJT-16 was the first jet aircraft designed by an Afro-Asian country without help from either of the two power blocs. The HF-24 project gave India the 'distinction' of being one of only four or five countries to proceed with the development of a supersonic fighter aircraft.

India was still far from achieving self-sufficiency in defence production, however, and officially inspired claims to the contrary [39] were grossly misleading. India remained dependent upon external sources of supply for designs, vital armaments components, all sophisticated equipment, and many of the basic chemicals and intermediates required for the manufacture of ammunition and explosives. The production schemes for Komatsu tractors, Shaktiman and Nissan trucks, and Nissan patrol jeeps were considerably behind schedule and heavily dependent upon foreign components.[40]

[38] *Ibid.*, 1963–64, p. 13.
[39] Such misstatement was not restricted to the politician; Air Vice-Marshal Harjinder Singh, A.O.C.-in-C. of Maintenance Command was reported as informing airmen of the IAF at Avadi in early 1962 that India would be self-sufficient in the manufacture of aircraft within five years and would even be able to export. Cited, *Hindu*, 21 February 1962.
[40] For details, see Ministry of Defence, *Report*, 1960–61, 1961–62, 1962–3, 1963–64; *Economic Weekly*, vol. 40, no. 12 (29 March 1963), p. 628.

The aircraft industry was geared largely to the assembly of imported components. Neither special-quality steel nor aluminium—both vital to aircraft production—was manufactured in India, and all instrumentation, undercarriage, braking systems, communications, and electronic equipment had to be imported. HAL had not been able to undertake the repair and overhaul of jet engines until 1960 or to overhaul and inspect a Canberra bomber until 1961. The HF-24 fighter project was proceeding in a halting fashion; the first prototype of the Mk 1 had been flight-tested with great fanfare in June 1961 but had been unable to attain a supersonic speed in level flight; the second prototype had only been flight-tested in October 1962. The future of the Mk 2 remained uncertain, as no decision had yet been taken on a power plant and it was at least four years removed from the stage of full production. The Avro scheme was on the verge of chaos. The test flight of the first unit on 26 November 1961 had been hailed by government and project authorities with the claim that three or four units would be produced each month in 1962—but the second unit was not in fact to be flight-tested until March 1963. Furthermore, most of HAL's factory equipment was of pre-1945 origin and the Aircraft Maintenance Depot's tools and jigs had been fabricated from stores left behind by the United States Army Air Force in 1945, with some additions from the Punjab and Hindustan Machine Tools plants.

India's defence production organization was also afflicted with a series of other ills which inhibited efficiency and the establishment of soundly based defence industries consistent with the country's resources and immediate needs. India remained badly deficient in technicians and very short of first-rate design engineers and scientific workers despite the considerable efforts of the Defence Science Organization. The modernization of the ordnance establishment undertaken in 1960 was making only slow progress, and efficient operations were being seriously compromised by the absence of proper cost accounting and depreciation allowances which concealed the heavy costs being absorbed for moderate gains. Low pay scales and slow promotions were reflected in the flight of sorely needed personnel to the greater attractions afforded by civil and private industry. A country that remained dependent on gifts of American grain to meet persistent food shortages and on massive foreign aid to underpin its economic development was committed to two supersonic plane projects at a time when nations with greatly superior financial, technological, and industrial resources were limiting the types of fighter aircraft in service.

Planning for defence production must always be related to existing and potential capabilities, to a careful evaluation of likely military requirements, and their projection over a period of time. The available evidence suggests that New Delhi generally ignored these truisms in the latter half of the 1947-62 period. Maximum self-sufficiency in military needs was desirable to enable the country to pursue its foreign policy objectives free of the limitations imposed by the virtual arms embargoes applied by external powers, as during the Kashmir conflict. Desired armaments could not always be acquired when needed or at a price deemed reasonable. Acutely conscious of India's size, convinced of its importance and great potential, and sensitive to the country's economic dependence upon the goodwill of the more prosperous and committed countries of both the Soviet and Western blocs, India's political leadership developed what amounted to an obsession to achieve maximum self-sufficiency in defence equipment and thereby provide substance to her policy of nonalignment.

The considered approach to broadening indigenous defence production during the first decade of Indian independence gave way, about 1955, to ambitious schemes which were not warranted either by India's immediate military requirements or by the capacities of local technology and industry. The HF-24 project and the decision to initiate a MIG-21 scheme were quite premature and involved the actual or proposed diversion of scarce funds and technical skills to projects that have been described as 'nothing short of a huge fraud on the gullible public':[41] Professed official beliefs notwithstanding, there is really little difference between dependence upon external weapons systems and dependence upon external sources for blueprints and vital parts, as both require the co-operation of a foreign company and at least tacit approval of the particular foreign government. From the standpoint of time, external purchase from a substantial production programme permits faster acquisition of items undergoing progressive and revolutionary development. Such external purchase is far less expensive than the establishment of a limited local production line at great cost for a very limited domestic market. The popular argument that indigenous production permits appreciable savings of scarce foreign exchange is hardly relevant here, in view of the massive foreign aid India was receiving from the very countries from which she obtained military stores and equipment.

---

[41] Madhu Limaye, 'National Apathy', *Seminar* (July 1962), p. 34.

It is apparent that politics emerged as a primary determinant in defence production during the period that coincided with Krishna Menon's tenure (1957–62) at the Defence Ministry. The vigour with which he approached the issue of defence production, and the constant stress he placed upon the supposed progress being made, suggests that he perceived that only thus could political capital be made from a portfolio that was, from the viewpoint of domestic politics, hardly a stepping-stone to higher political office. The Avro project affords an example of his approach as, according to one political commentator, Menon wanted the first Indian-assembled Avro to fly even before it was thought fit for the first prototype to do so in Britain.[42] The result was that project officials set out to manufacture a full production model to certification standards instead of proceeding by the route of a pre-production development prototype. Work began in January 1960 but sanctions for the buildings were not given until 30 months later, with the result that equipment arrived but could not be installed and, as late as January 1964, production and construction were going on simultaneously in some hangars.[43]

There would also appear to be sufficient evidence to support the widely held view that Menon deliberately sought to create a private industrial empire within his ministerial control. Although the production of various items for civil trade was undertaken by the Defence Ministry before Menon's tenure, the items involved at this early stage—road rollers, rail carriages, and so on—appear to have complemented existing civil government and private facilities. After Menon's appointment, however, production was undertaken of such items as film projectors, briefcases, mailbags, microscopes, and coffee machines. The production of such items in ordnance could scarcely be considered warranted by the absence of such capacities in the private sector, and the expense involved in the limited production of such items could not possibly have been competitive with the larger capacities of the private sector if proper cost accounting and depreciation methods were followed. The argument that such production by ordnance was required to preserve spare capacity against the contingency of war would also appear to have been overworked; the private sector could employ the same argument even more effectively. Ordnance would have undoubtedly been more effective in its

[42] G. K. Reddy, *Times of India*, 11 August 1961.
[43] B. G Verghese, *Times of India*, 22 May 1964.

essential task—the development and production of military items—if it had not diverted its attention to petty items of civil trade in competition with established private facilities.

The production schemes for one- and three-ton trucks allegedly resulted from unsatisfactory deliveries and prices from private suppliers. Defending these projects during the debate on 9 April 1960, Menon claimed that two of the three manufacturers of trucks in India had delivered 'almost nothing' of the orders placed with them by the Defence Ministry while the third, although making more regular deliveries, had increased his price 'very considerably'. Menon claimed that the types of trucks under production in ordnance were better in performance and price than those supplied by the private sector.[44]

It would have been cheaper, however, to have resolved the issue through penalty-clause contracts with the private manufacturers than to have established such facilities independently in ordnance. As the annual requirements of the Army at the time amounted only to about 2,000 trucks, it seems highly doubtful that an ordnance scheme of, say, 2,000 vehicles per year could be operated as efficiently or as economically as private production lines serving a market of 40,000 civilian vehicles per year. This is particularly so when one takes into account the profit motive underlying the efforts of private manufacturers—an incentive not likely to be so compelling in a miniature 'ordnance empire' where the input–output efficiency scale method of computation was much more difficult to ascertain and where production schemes were undertaken on various items in the 'national interest' even if they were not economical. Menon's well-known bias against the private sector was not absent from defence production policy and, it can be argued, it did not facilitate the formulation and execution of policy calculated to achieve maximum results for the human, financial, and material resources expended. Insofar as policy was reflected by the HF-24 and MIG-21 projects, efforts were seemingly directed towards the projection of an image of industrial power and technical skill which in fact did not exist—and which contributed very little, if at all, towards alleviating India's pressing social and economic problems. The contradiction between a supersonic aircraft from an ordnance factory and emergency grain shipments from the West (over and above the massive grain shipments which the United States has been providing since 1951 under Public Law 480) needs no elucidation.

[44] See Menon's statement as reported in *Hindu*, 11 April 1960.

Chapter Nine

CIVILIAN–MILITARY RELATIONS, 1947–1962

The pattern of civil–military relations in India during the period 15 August 1947–20 October 1962 closely approximated the accepted norm in the English-speaking countries of the West. There was a stable subordination of the military establishment to the civil power, in which the channels of advice from the military to the civil authority were institutionalized in a manner compatible with a democratic policy-making process. In this achievement, India provided a rare exception among the newly emergent states [1] and a useful comparison with neighbouring Burma and with Pakistan, where the inheritance of a similar military tradition did not preclude an army *coup d'état* after just over a decade of civilian government.[2]

Under British rule, the armed forces had constituted a professional body which, though regarded by Indian nationalists as an instrument of sectionalism in internal politics, and as a mercenary force loyal to an alien rather than to a popular indigenous authority, evoked genuine national pride by its exploits in two world wars and countless minor ones. Their contribution to Indian independence from British rule, though generally ignored by publicists, was an important one

[1] For a useful survey of military–political developments in selected emergent states of the Middle East, Southeast Asia and sub-Saharan Africa, see John J. Johnson, (ed.), *The Role of the Military in Underdeveloped Countries* (Princeton: University Press, 1962). One observer has commented that 'with the exception, of course, of Pakistan and the Sudan, no newly independent state has so far rivalled India in military preparedness, in terms of officers, for complete autonomy. For this reason, perhaps, India ought to be taken consciously as the point of reference when considering the role and place of the military leadership in Afro-Asian societies'. William Gutteridge, 'The Indianisation of the Indian Army, 1918–45', *Race*, 4 (May 1963), p. 39.

[2] It must be noted, however, that Pakistan lacked the substantial educated middle class and able civil service which India acquired at partition and faced economic problems even more severe than India's.

and perhaps of greater significance than the frequently irresponsible actions and attitudes that characterized the nationalist movement.

The contribution of the armed forces to an independent and bifurcated India has also been extensive. Amid the chaos of partition the Army—though it failed to remain as impartial to communal strife as was hoped—nonetheless constituted the only sanction for official authority. It was the symbol of national purpose in the Hyderabad, Junagadh, Kashmir, and Goa operations. In Korea, Gaza, Indo-China, and the Congo, Indian military personnel have given expression to their country's support for peace-keeping activities and symbolized her international role. The image of military power projected by the British Indian Army before 1947 and inherited by the Indian Army at independence has been a major (if frequently overlooked) contributor to the status accorded to the country and its representatives in a power-conscious world. The Army, and to a lesser extent the Navy and Air Force, have continued to be the ultimate sanction of civil authority in a country that has remained at least as prone to civil disturbances as during the era of British rule. The armed forces have provided a model of discipline, efficiency, and resource for a civil India deficient in these very respects.

The government indicated its appreciation of the need for an efficient and nonpolitical military (and civil) establishment after independence when it rejected proposals from less responsible sections of opinion to prosecute members of the civil and military hierarchies for their loyalty to the British during the period of nationalist activity aimed at securing the removal of that alien authority. It readily accepted the need to retain the existing civil and military bureaucracies, rejected proposals to replace the professional Army with a more politically conscious force along the lines of the wartime Indian National Army (INA) and made no attempt to interfere with traditional recruitment patterns. Congress leaders paid tribute to the patriotic motives of the men and officers of the INA by permitting them to join the police, the state forces, and the civil service—but barred them from re-employment in the Army.

DECLINE IN STATUS OF THE ARMED FORCES

The status of the armed forces nevertheless declined after independence, both in society and the state.

The traditional aversion of Hindu society to regarding the military as superior to either royalty or the priestly order was strengthened by the post-independence period. The absence of any apparent real threat to Indian security during at least the first decade of independence reinforced the belief that Gandhi had shown the superiority of moral over physical force; there was thus a philosophic barrier to attaching undue glamour or importance to the military uniform. This attitude was reinforced by the government's moralistic postures, antimilitarist attitudes, nonaligned stance, and stress on economic development as the ultimate source of a nation's strength. In the sociological sense, India's inheritance of able political leadership, a well-trained bureaucracy, and a capable middle class with increasing competence in administration, business, and the professions served to lessen the value of the military as a vehicle of modernity and progress. The relatively modest stature of the military in Indian society was partly reflected in the marriage market (a useful barometer of career status in a society where marriages are still arranged), which rated young men in the armed forces in third place behind those in foreign firms and in the Indian foreign administrative services.

The relative status of the military officer in society was confirmed by various government measures directed at reducing the position of the armed forces in the state and the privileges and benefits given to military personnel. On 1 April 1955 the Commanders-in-Chief of the three services were redesignated as Chiefs of Staff (a much less prestigious title), and the comparative position of military officers in the Warrant of Precedence was sharply lowered. Lieutenant-Generals lost their former entitlement to gun salutes, and military officers' leave and travel concessions, family and other allowances, and accommodation scales were terminated or reduced. A new Pay Code, introduced in 1948, reduced the pay scales of ICO's (the vast bulk of the officer corps) to the levels prevailing in 1939, while the pay scales of the small but senior group of KCO's remained untouched.[3]

[3] Defence Minister Singh informed the Constituent Assembly in 1949 that the pay discrepancy between KCO's and ICO's dated to prewar days, that the parity given to ICO's during the war had been valid only for the duration of the conflict, and that the reductions were necessary as the Government was unable to maintain the wartime pay scales. *CAD*, pt. 2, vol. 2 (7 March 1949), p. 1220. Subsequent upward revisions in pay scales did not remove the discrepancy and, as of early 1964, the pay scale for Lieutenant-Generals was Rs 2,700 per month for ICO's and Rs 4,000 per month for the few remaining KCO's.

The position of the armed forces in the apparatus of state underwent a sharp reduction from 1946. With the formation of the interim government in September of that year, the Commander-in-Chief of an integrated service command ceased to function as Vice-President of the Executive Council, being replaced by a civilian Defence Minister. On 15 August 1947 the integrated service command was broken up, each service passing under a separate and independent head. In 1950, under Article 53 (2) of the new Constitution, the President of India became the Supreme Commander of the armed forces in a ceremonial supersession which symbolized civilian control.

From a position having direct access to the highest level of the British Indian government, the military were reduced to a position in the executive in which they constituted the base of a hierarchical structure of committees arranged in a pyramid with the Defence Committee of the Cabinet as the apex.[4]

In the opinion of H. M. Patel, a former Defence Secretary, the policy-making organization of the Defence Ministry was 'sufficiently flexible to ensure that every relevant point of view has a chance of being presented at appropriate level and to have it considered at the highest level if necessary'.[5] The theory is rarely if ever translated into practice, however, and this had been true of the formulation and implementation of Indian military policy to the detriment of the nation's defence preparedness.

The system of financial control met with the satisfaction of financial officials. Speaking in 1955, one of the Financial Adviser's staff declared that 'the coat is a little more stylishly cut and stitched if a friendly and well-informed critic helps the tailor at various stages before the finishing touch is given to it'. He admitted that occasional differences of opinion had existed but claimed that the system worked well in practice.[6] His claim would seem to require some qualification, however, in light of the conclusion arrived at in an officially sponsored investigation of Indian public administration published in 1953 [7] and the annual reports of the Public Accounts Committee, which noted persistent savings in the sanctioned grants. Noting that

[4] For a brief discussion of the policy-making machinery, see Appendix XI.
[5] H. M. Patel, *The Defence of India* (Bombay: Asia Publishing House), p. 3.
[6] Batuk Singh (Additional Financial Adviser) at the Defence Services Staff College on 5 April 1955. Lecture reprinted as 'Finance and the AFHQ' in *USI Journal*, 86:363 (April–June 1956), p. 134.
[7] Paul H. Appleby, *Report on Public Administration in India* (New Delhi: Government of India Press, 1953).

the Financial Adviser has a virtual right of veto over military expenditure, H. M. Patel has himself implicitly criticized the system of financial controls with the admission that 'many difficulties ensue from this [Financial Adviser's] position . . .'[8]

The 1958 report of the Estimates Committee pointed out that the military contribution to policy was further vitiated by 'the possibility of proposals emanating from a senior level at Services Headquarters being examined by officials in the Ministry who are either junior or lack the necessary expert knowledge'. The report also drew attention to 'an imbalance in the distribution of responsibilities between the Ministry and the Services Headquarters and also a lack of sufficient delegation of authority and powers to the Services Headquarters which are presided over by officers of the status of the Chiefs of Staff'.[9] The reception accorded to service views in the Ministry was also compromised by the tendency of senior bureaucrats to regard the outlook of the Indian military leadership as being excessively coloured by prevailing thought in British military circles.[10]

It is perhaps not surprising, then, that an Indian military writer has charged that civilian officials in the Defence Ministry have sometimes put a new complexion on a position stated by the Chiefs of Staff.[11] Confirmation of this is suggested by H. M. Patel, who claimed in 1953 that the Air Force and Navy obtained 'fair play' on several occasions only as a result of their being able to present their respective cases 'fully and frankly'[12] to the appropriate civilian officials like himself, who clearly made the decisions. The ability of the average civilian official to make such decisions, however, must be judged against Patel's own admission that the ignorance of civilian officials (to which may properly be added that of the politicians) about military matters is so complete as to be a self-evident and incontrovertible fact.[13] Efforts to correct this deficiency bore fruit very

[8] 'Balance of Hopes and Fears: A Review of the Past Five Years', *USI Journal*, 82:352, 353 (July–October 1953), p. 140.

[9] Cited, Brig. B. S. Bhagat, 'Reorganization of Defence Services', *ibid.*, 89:375 (April–June 1959), p. 168.

[10] See, for example, H. M. Patel, 'Balance of Hopes and Fears'; Nehru's statement in the Rajya Sabha on 9 November 1962.

[11] Brig. B. D. Kapur, 'National Preparedness', *USI Journal*, 87:367 (April–June 1957), p. 82.

[12] 'Balance of Hopes and Fears', pp. 140–41.

[13] An IDC for India, *USI Journal*, 84:355 (April 1954), p. 249. The first Indian civil servant was only appointed to the Defence Department in 1939. (See n. 25, below.)

belatedly, for reasons, it would appear, of general apathy. The scope and timing of such schemes as mutual liaison visits by civil and military officers in the three Army Commands and the establishment of the National Defence College in New Delhi in 1960 were such as to contribute little to the relationships between the civil and military bureaucracies during the 1947–62 period.

The advisory function of the military leadership was further compromised by the absence of a unified service command, which virtually precluded a consensus permitting forceful professional arguments on budgetary allocations. Instead of a single Commander-in-Chief as in the British period, there were three autonomous services, each formulating its own policy, competing with each other for budgetary allocations from an economy-minded and markedly apathetic political executive, and maintaining parallel bodies with the most scrupulous canons of parity. Interservices committees were no substitute for common instruments of joint action.

Such a system placed a heavy responsibility upon the Defence Ministry to effect compromises within the budgetary ceilings laid down by the Cabinet. As the Defence Secretary and the Financial Adviser are primarily concerned with matters of administration and financial procedures, it is the responsibility of the Minister to balance the services in a manner consistent with their respective operational roles through the apportionment of available resources. He thereby inevitably becomes the focus of service resentments over budgetary allocations, and this is bound to be true in a poor country desirous of possessing effective armed forces relative to its size but reluctant to expend the sums required to achieve the desired level of military power. In such a context, a satisfactory working relationship requires that the Minister be possessed of a congenial but businesslike manner, willing to recognize the experience of subordinates, capable of making reasonable assessments of conflicting service representations, and able to subordinate personal ambitions, predilections, and prejudices to the larger responsibilities of his office. The situation also requires that the Minister be able to present decisive arguments to the Defence Committee of the Cabinet and to the full Cabinet when he is convinced of the need for adjustments in military policy. The available evidence strongly suggests that not a single holder of the Defence post during the 1947–62 period managed to combine the desired assets.

THE DEFENCE PORTFOLIO

The Defence portfolio seemingly carried little weight in the Cabinet, perhaps for reasons advanced by a former officer in an article published in 1960. The officer, Major-General Y. S. Paranjpe, expressed the view that the appointment in Defence was not politically attractive because the appointee 'has to get into something that he knows nothing about; secondly, everything done in the Ministry is of a secretive nature and he cannot advertise himself, except occasionally by showing a rise in the production on the Defence Factories and, thirdly, he always faces criticism if anything goes wrong with nothing to compensate for it'. He thus felt that it was not surprising that such a Ministry should always get persons who possessed neither the necessary qualities nor aptitudes, and charged: 'It remains a neglected ministry, run mainly by the civilian secretariat staff. The minister in such cases remains a nonentity influenced by party politics and guided by his secretaries with whose intimate assistance he must function. His decisions are due more to political and financial considerations than to a mature understanding of military problems. He cannot therefore be convincing enough or force an issue amongst his colleagues'.[14]

In the complacent atmosphere towards defence which characterized India at least up to 1959, the post was certainly not one in which an individual could appreciably enhance his political stature. On the contrary, the post was subjected to persistent criticism for the heavy expenditure it incurred at a time when, according to the official interpretation, India was secure against attack. Nevertheless, the individuals who held the portfolio during the period were persons of considerable political stature. Sardar Baldev Singh (1946–52) occupied the office by virtue of his political standing in the Punjab and the heavy Sikh representation in the armed forces; he was not reappointed after the 1952 general election for reasons that probably reflected both a relative decline in his political stature and a desire by Nehru to shift the post away from a representative of an important military class and from the volatile Punjab. Gopalaswami Ayyangar was an important political figure; Nehru's assumption of the post after Ayyangar's death on 10 February 1953 placed Defence for two years under the nominal control of the most important po-

[14] 'Military Awakening in India is Very Fitful', *Organisor* (Delhi), 29 August 1960, pp. 3–4.

litical figure in the country. Dr. Nailus Nath Katju came to the post in 1955 with the experience acquired in the ministries of Home and Law (1950–51) and Home and States (1952–55); his appointment suggested Nehru's belated recognition that Defence was a major post.[15] The 'impression created was that the department would enjoy a fairly stable and continuing guidance'.[16]

For various reasons, however, none of these individuals appears to have been a forceful ministerial representative in the Cabinet. Singh was widely regarded as amiable but lacking both in initiative and administrative skill, with the result that the able Defence Secretary, H. M. Patel, virtually ran the Ministry to the point even of submitting briefs to the Cabinet. Ayyangar was viewed as a good administrator, but his tenure was very brief—from May 1952 to February 1953. Nehru's assumption of the portfolio from 1953 to 1955 should have augured well for a sympathetic hearing for military requirements but, while he retained overall Cabinet responsibility for the Ministry, the actual running of Defense was assigned on 15 March 1953 to Mahavir Tyagi, the (junior) Minister for Revenue and Expenditure from Uttar Pradesh. In view of Tyagi's minor status, it is probable that during this period the Ministry was largely run by the Secretary, M. K. Vellodi. The capabilities of Dr. N. N. Katju, the next incumbent, were judged differently by each person whose views were solicited by the writer, but in any case his tenure was also relatively brief and it is doubtful that it enabled him to acquire more than a superficial understanding of the Ministry's functions.

On Dr Katju's departure for the more attractive post of Chief Minister of Madhya Pradesh in February 1957, there was speculation that Morarji Desai might assume the Defence portfolio. Commenting on this possibility, one journal admitted that it would bring the office high political prestige, but that 'it appears the department is still not being looked upon as a very important one . . . what is

---

[15] Commenting on Dr. Mahmud's appointment to succeed G. S. Bajpai as Secretary-General of the External Affairs Ministry, *The Times* (6 December 1954) expressed the view that the appointment 'shows that Mr Nehru had failed to persuade his colleagues in the Cabinet to accept Mr Krishna Menon. Dr Katju will probably go to the Defence. If he does Mr Nehru will relinquish the Defence portfolio which he took over in the first place, it is said, to defend the armed forces from the Congress Party prejudice'.

[16] 'The Changing Defence Portfolio', *Thought*, 12 January 1957, p. 2

even more depressing is that Mr Nehru and his colleagues seem to apply no strict test of qualification to such an appointment'.[17] The journal regarded S. S. Majithia as an eminent Sikh second to none in popularity and felt that he had acquitted himself well as Katju's deputy and was the best choice: 'As a Defence Minister he can prove an effective rebuttal to the suspicion, unjustifiably entertained in some quarters, of minority representatives being deliberately kept from important portfolios.[18] It concluded that 'it is time the portfolio of Defence was recognized as of major importance, undeserving of whimsical improvisation'.

What then was the significance of Krishna Menon's appointment to the post in April 1957? One English observer described the post as 'India's key portfolio',[19] thereby implying that the appointment was significant, while the Delhi correspondent of the *Daily Telegraph* referred to the 'surprise announcement' of Menon's appointment.[20] The *Daily Express* saw it as a demotion from foreign affairs to 'what Indians pretend to regard as a junior post'.[21] An American press source interpreted the appointments of Menon and S. K. Patil—the latter to Irrigation and Power—as a balancing act between Left and Right in the Cabinet: 'Mr Krishna Menon, as Minister of Defence, will continue to deal with the scene of India's main military preparedness, the Kashmir land . . . It will doubtless make him available as an even closer adviser to the Prime Minister than he has been in the past . . .' The source concluded, however, that it was felt that Menon was likely to circulate less in international circles, where many Indians felt he had not advanced India's relations.[22] Expressing a similar view in retrospect, the *Montreal Gazette* stated that the appointment 'might have been labelled a gentle kick upstairs' for the reason that, in his relationships with the West as Foreign Affairs Adviser, Menon was often too extreme even for Nehru.[23]

The Defence post, however, did not cause any apparent decrease in Nehru's employment of his confidant in international diplomacy

[17] *Ibid.*
[18] *Ibid.*
[19] Elisabeth Partridge, *News Chronicle*, 18 April 1957
[20] 17 April 1957.
[21] 18 April 1957.
[22] *Christian Science Monitor*, 20 April 1957.
[23] 2 September 1959.

—nor was it, in all likelihood, ever intended to do so. At the same time, the appointment was clearly not in response to any crisis or impending crisis in defence, as official complacency about the nation's security had probably reached its zenith by this time. Quite to the contrary, the appointment appears to have been a device whereby Nehru could utilize Menon's experience in foreign affairs while providing him an office of greater prestige than was attached to the position of Minister without Portfolio to which he had been appointed on 3 February 1956. Politically ambitious, Menon must have long desired an office in which he could have national exposure and the fillip to his political stature which escaped him as a consultant and roving ambassador. In view of the hostility which Menon generated in Congress, Nehru had from the outset of independence proceeded to ease his confidant into appointive office, first as High Commissioner in London, and then as head of India's delegation to the United Nations General Assembly in 1953. The domestic acclaim that greeted Menon's presentation of the Indian case on Kashmir at the U.N. in early 1957 was clearly regarded by Nehru as offering the atmosphere in which to elevate Menon to a senior portfolio, despite the fact that he did not have the normal credentials for one, that is, a political base of sufficient importance in India.[24]

The range of senior posts open to Menon was, however, limited by the need for a position that would both permit him sufficient freedom to remain an adviser and special envoy of the Prime Minister in the field of foreign affairs and that would not require extensive administrative experience. This ruled out every post of importance except Defence which, at that time, appeared to be one that could easily be left to the civil secretariat. It was subsequently rumored that Menon would revert to his former portfolio so as to have more freedom to move on the international scene,[25] but this, and a later rumor that he had agreed to become High Commissioner in London on condition that the jeep scandal dating from his earlier

[24] The one exception to the rule is the Finance portfolio, the most important post in Indian government (External Affairs carrying the stature of the Prime Minister, without which it can claim second ranking at best) and one which is assigned on the basis of competance rather than political stature, although several holders of the portfolio have had both characteristics.

[25] *Thought*, 15 February 1958, p. 19. A likely replacement, according to this report, was C. L. Trivedi, the former Governor of Andhra Pradesh (and first Indian civil servant to be appointed to the Defence Department, serving as Secretary during World War II), who had the reputation of being a 'troubleshooter'.

posting in that capital be buried,[26] were evidently without foundation.

OUTLOOK OF THE OFFICER CORPS

In the context of national complacency about defence, financial stringency, and civilian 'pinpricks' regarding pay and benefits, there was understandable resentment on the part of military officers. One officer wrote in 1953 that the armed forces 'were to be tolerated only so long as conditions made it advisable to do so'.[27] Another officer charged that the 'combatant . . . is treated not as a symbol of the security of the country but as a drain on the country's resources'.[28] In such circumstances, there was a strong desire among officers to seek better-paying and more personally satisfying civilian employment whenever the opportunity presented itself. Even the Minister for Defence Organization, Mahavir Tyagi, admitted in the Lok Sabha on 25 March 1953 that 'a feeling is growing among our men that they are not paid the same attention which they had under their alien employers. It may be an unfortunate impression, but the impression is there'.[29]

Less apparent was the reaction of the officer corps, which comprised perhaps 13,000 in the Army and 6,000 to 8,000 in the other two services combined as of October 1962, to issues of policy. The officer cadre of the Army consisted of a small hierarchy of Sandhurst-trained KCO's commissioned before 1939, a middle echelon dating from a crash recruitment scheme from the universities during World War II, and a junior group which had entered the service after 1947 upon completing the training programmes at the military academies. The KCO's were generally of well-to-do family backgrounds, drawn from all parts of the country and strongly nonpolitical; the middle echelon was less grounded in tradition and perhaps inclined towards a mild radicalism in outlook; and the junior officers were largely

[26] 'Beachcomber's Diary', in *ibid*, 2 April 1960, p. 19. During the 1948–51 period, Menon in his capacity as High Commissioner contracted with some private British firms for several thousand jeeps for the Indian Army. The contracts were only partially fulfilled and were characterized by financial irregularities. For some details and comments, see Welles Hangen, *After Nehru, Who?* (London: Rupert Hart-Davis, 1963), pp. 75–76.

[27] Brig. B. S. Bhagat, 'Officer Recruitment in the Armed Forces of India', *USI Journal*, 83:350-351 (January–April 1953), p. 13.

[28] Maj. J. Nazareth, 'Fighting Spirit in the Armed Forces', *ibid.*, 85:358 (January 1955), p. 12.

[29] *LSD*, pt. 2, vol. 1, col. 2813.

from poorer, more urban, politically minded, and bourgeois origins, but steeped in military tradition by virtue of their training in the military academies. While there were undoubtedly some differences of outlook among the various class, caste, regional, and generational groups, the corps appears to have been fairly cohesive, disciplined, and professional. The officer cadres of the Navy and Air Force, who were probably better educated than their Army counterparts by virtue of the more technical orientation of their services, came from middle-class and largely urban backgrounds, with closer social and working relationships with the urban middle classes who comprised articulate public opinion.

Although reliable generalizations concerning the attitudes of the officer corps are difficult, certain observations seem permissible from the nature of the corps and from interviews with various members of it.

The services are the most Westernized element in a society with strong conservative tendencies. They embody modernity in organization, operational planning, general efficiency, and technical knowledge. They are not rooted in an indigenous military tradition and do not appear to have sympathy either for Gandhian precepts or for ideologies of the extreme Left or Right. They have a vested interest in stability and order, in national unity, development, and technological progress.

The comradeship of the old Indian Army survived partition and the clash in Kashmir; the officers have a less emotional view of Pakistan than do many civilians, although this is less likely to be true of the post-partition recruits and of the Sikhs, who cannot be expected to forget the events surrounding partition easily or quickly. The 'old Commonwealth' is well-regarded and the British tie remains strong with the aid of training courses in Britain, attendance of senior officers at the Imperial Defence College and British staff colleges, the annual conference convened by the Chief of the Imperial General Staff, service literature, weapons systems, and regimental and unit links developed over a period of association spanning two centuries for the Army and several decades for the Navy and Air Force. There is no real anti-Americanism, and the various bitter exchanges between the two governments from time to time do not appear to have left any lasting impression; there is even a moderate desire to turn to American military experience and methods. There is also an acute awareness that close relations with the United States are essential in view of India's ultimate reliance upon American military aid in any major conflict with China. Russia has never been viewed as a reliable friend, much less an ally, but there is a premise that good relations are prudent. Since independence the officer class has viewed China with a mixture of contempt and disinterest, having little sympathy for the view that intimate ties between India and China were a natural goal. Nonalignment was regarded as not detrimental to national security per se, on the assumption that Western military aid in a crisis was axiomatic. The manner of carrying out a policy of nonalignment was regarded with some concern, however, since it appeared to strain relations with India's sincere friends in the West for only short-term advantage among the nonaligned and Communist states, made the Kashmir issue even more intractable, sapped India's will to maintain defence preparedness, enhanced the attraction of the 'naive' Gandhian legacy, led to the policy of refusing military aid as incompatible with nonalignment (although such aid was viewed in military circles as basically indistinguishable from the economic assistance which the government eagerly solicited) and afforded no credible deterrent to a Communist attack nor to Communist policies designed to extend Soviet, and particularly Chinese, power and influence at the expense of India and her implicit Western allies.

During the decade following independence, however, civilian complacency about defence would seem to have been shared by the military to a considerable degree. This view, coupled with the recognition of the need for rapid economic development and the apparent belief that larger appropriations would eventually be made for defence, inhibited the military leadership from arguing too forcefully for sharply increased grants. In the absence of a clearly identifiable threat from China until the later 'fifties, Pakistan provided an expedient strategic rationale without which, given the pronounced nonaligned posture of the government, sound and efficient military policies would have been difficult to formulate and implement. The civilian fear and distrust of Pakistan thus appeared as a 'blessing in disguise' in preventing even greater economies in defence outlay and was used to good effect.[30]

[30] The three services used the politicians' sensitivity to Pakistan to defend requests for new appropriations that otherwise might have been deferred or reduced for financial reasons despite the government's general policy of developing a strong military establishment. Even in the context of strained Indo-Pakistan relations, however, the Army was generally unable to acquire new equipment and the Naval programme was sharply reduced—on financial grounds.

THE MENON–THIMAYYA EPISODE

While the military, for reasons of logistics, were not unduly concerned with an immediate threat from China after its reabsorption of Tibet in 1950–51, they were professional enough not to allow their opinions to be coloured by wishful thinking as to the intentions of other states—which are, in any case, political in nature, hard to assess, and unpredictable. Thus, while acutely aware of the severe difficulties in preparing a cautious response to the extension of Chinese power into Tibet, the Indian military professional had necessarily to conceive of the possibility of eventual military conflict with China in the Himalayan region and to support measures aimed at making adequate preparations against just such a contingency, however remote it was believed to be. Concern with Chinese intentions slowly increased from 1954, and China's Aksai Chin road project confirmed the suspicions of at least the informed senior officers that India's territorial integrity was being threatened and that a situation was developing in which an Indian military presence would be required as a deterrent to further Chinese intrusions in the near future and as a defense against at least minor overt attacks over a longer and indefinite period. Dissatisfaction with the continuing passive response of the government was a major contributing factor to the controversy, revealed by banner headlines in leading Indian dailies on the morning of 1 September 1959, which announced the resignation of General K. S. Thimayya, Chief of Army Staff, and the impending resignation of the other two service heads. According to the political correspondent of *The Statesman*, there was discord between the COAS and the Defence Minister, due partly to recent promotions in which considerations other than merit might have prevailed; the 'resignations' were attributed to the 'result of prolonged and evidently unsuccessful efforts to keep politics out of the army, navy and air force'.

Nehru's preoccupation with his proposed meeting with Ayub Khan at Palam airport and a discreet silence by the three Chiefs of Staff stimulated intense press speculation, and New Delhi was rife with rumours. The Defence Minister, Krishna Menon, declined to comment on the issue in Parliament, and a Press Trust of India (PTI) release in the afternoon announced Menon's resignation—an announcement withdrawn late that evening. At

4 P.M. a report from London revealed that the Chief of Air Staff, Air Marshal Subroto Mukerjee, had denied knowledge of, and involvement in, the affair.

In Parliament the next day, the Prime Minister offered an explanation which characteristically left the matter clouded. He admitted that the COAS had tendered his resignation but declared that he had withdrawn it at the request of Nehru himself. Nehru claimed that the issues involved were 'rather trivial and of no consequence', that they arose from temperamental differences and did not include promotions. He implied otherwise when he conceded that, while the civil authority is and must remain supreme, it should pay due heed to the expert advice it receives. This statement, coupled with his refusal to table a copy of Thimayya's letter of resignation—which specified the contentious issues—added to the speculation.

Press comment revealed a common reaction, well-expressed by *The Times* (London): 'He [Thimayya] is not the kind of soldier who can easily be imagined trying to relinquish his post for reasons that could be described as "trivial and of no consequence" '.[31] Available evidence suggests that, Nehru's claim notwithstanding, more basic issues were involved which centred around the conduct of the controversial Defence Minister and close confidant of Nehru, Krishna Menon.

Given Menon's intelligence and energy, his administrative drive, and his intimate relationship with Nehru, his appointment to the Defence portfolio in early 1957 should have augured well. Chinese actions on the northern frontiers and in Southeast Asia required a fresh perspective on defence, and Menon's influence with the Prime Minister should have achieved it. His tenure was indeed to coincide with increased budgetary allocations for the services, increases in service pay and benefits, some new equipment, and an accelerated programme for ordnance plants and production—achievements which, though not primarily due to his personal initiative (save the acquisition of Hunter fighter-bombers), apparently received his full support.[32] Unfortunately, Menon's strong

---

[31] Delhi correspondent, 3 September 1959.

[32] Even he was generally complacent about defence, however, and declined to support increased appropriations when it seemed more personally rewarding to appear as an economy-minded minister striving to reduce over-all expenditure in defence. See, for example, his claim to have initiated the reduction in defence demands proposed for fiscal 1959 as against the expenditure during

predilections in foreign policy, his vested interest in a nonaligned position for India, his political ambitions and his universally acknowledged arrogance were to exert a negative influence on defence during the very period when clear thinking and close co-operation between the political, military, and civil arms of government were required as never before. The military circles who viewed his appointment with misgivings because of his Leftist views and difficult temperament were quickly to have their suspicions confirmed.

The main figure in the 'promotional storm' which was to be a recurring feature of Menon's tenure in Defence was Brij Mohan Kaul, a Kashmiri Brahmin, scion of a wealthy family and a relation of Nehru by blood and marriage.[33]

Self-confident, well-educated, charming but ruthless, Kaul shared with the 'old guard' in the Army hierarchy a Sandhurst training, a good family background, an appreciation of the class and caste infantry organization as the basis of its esprit de corps, and an opinion that the Army was a disciplined force in an otherwise undisciplined country. In other respects, however, he was distinctive among the Sandhurst cadre. He allegedly regarded a popular mandate as unreal in an underdeveloped and largely illiterate nation, viewed the military takeovers in Burma and Pakistan with no misgivings, and was believed to have no inhibitions about an Army seizure of power in India in the event that civil authority proved ineffectual or a Communist bid for power appeared imminent or possible. Although he had been an early participant in student demonstrations against the British, he retained a strong affection for them after his years as a cadet at Sandhurst.

He served on the North-West Frontier and in the Burma theatre during World War II, but first attracted public attention in 1946 when Nehru appointed him as military adviser in Washington and he concurrently served as military adviser to the Indian delegation during the Kashmir debate in the Security Council. Returning to

fiscal 1958. *LSD*, 2d sess., vol. 29 (9 April 1959), col. 10,866. He added that the savings were being effected through greater efficiency and better of equipment. This was not borne out by the Finance Minister's claim, in presenting the budget, that the reduction in the demands for defence was largely due to adjustments in the manner of bookkeeping. See statement by Morarji Desai in *ibid.*, vol. 26, cols. 3600-3601.

[33] The information concerning Kaul's background and outlook has been obtained largely, but not exclusively, from Welles Hangen, *After Nehru, Who?* pp. 242-272.

India later in the year, Kaul organized and led irregulars in Kashmir until he had differences with the Prime Minister of Kashmir, Sheikh Abdullah—whom he was to arrest in a midnight episode five years later on Nehru's orders. His activities as Chief of Staff to Thimayya on the United Nations' Repatriation Commission in Korea (in which he allegedly was less than impartial to the Communist viewpoints) [34] appears to have led to differences with his superior culminating in his reposting to India as commander of the 4th Division in the Punjab, a post he was to hold for three years.

It is quite conceivable that Kaul may not have risen much further in rank and responsibility had not Menon assumed the Defence portfolio. When his efforts to cultivate the 'old guard' at Army headquarters proved unavailing, the Defence Minister tried to manœuvre one service against another by playing upon the inferiority complex of the Navy and Air Force vis-à-vis the Army and making arbitrary decisions regarding military priorities aimed, primarily it would seem, at promoting his popularity with the Air Force. At the same time, Menon cultivated more junior officers who were susceptible to his influence or were prepared to support him in the hopes of faster promotion; one of these was Major-General Kaul. The two men do not appear to have met before 1957, but their friendship clearly blossomed after their first meeting. Desirous of making the armed forces as 'productive' as possible to answer his political critics, Menon was attracted by Operation Amar I, an Army housing project undertaken at Ambala by Kaul's command with the enthusiatic support of the Defence Minister and the somewhat reluctant permission of the COAS, the reluctance of Army headquarters being due to a belief that employment of front-line troops in such tasks was scarcely cheaper than civilian labour and was detrimental to morale.

The first step in the promotional 'storm' occurred in early 1959 when the COAS, after the customary consultation with the Army commanders, presented to the Ministry for advancement to the rank of Lieutenant-General the names of Major-Generals P. S. Gyani, P. S. Kumaramangalam, and B. M. Kaul in that order, Kaul incidentally being the junior of the three. In June the Cabinet,

[34] Kaul was invited to pay a visit to China during his Korean engagement and claims he did so because Nehru felt that it would be impolitic to refuse and that his answers to reporters' questions on his return were misinterpreted. See *ibid.*, p. 254.

clearly acting upon the recommendation of the Defence Minister, elevated Kumaramangalam and Kaul only, the latter having in the meantime been appointed Quartermaster-General. Kaul's appointment to QMG was consistent with his seniority, but the supersession of Gyani provoked comment both in and out of Parliament and in the service. At issue was not the fact that Gyani's seniority had been ignored, as such must inevitably be the fate of many officers in the course of a military career. In this case, however, an outstanding artillery officer with extensive experience and senior commands in that branch and in the UNEF in Gaza had been superseded by an officer of very limited experience. Gyani had not commanded a division, which was normally a desired prerequisite for promotion to Lieutenant-General, but Army headquarters clearly did not regard this factor as an obstacle to his promotion. The politicians had obviously interfered in a promotional issue for reasons having strong political overtones, and it is perhaps significant that, shortly thereafter, Gyani was promoted to Lieutenant-General commanding an infantry division.

The June promotions affair provoked considerable comment in the Army at all levels, with open discussion of Menon's 'interference' and speculation as to why Thimayya permitted it to continue without protest. An immediate and natural result of the issue was to damage Army morale and the discipline and respect for superior rank which are the foundations of an efficient service. It was evident to senior officers that further political interference of this type would have a serious effect on the Army.

The promotions issue was aggravated by Menon's persistent misrepresentation of service views on military policy to Nehru. The Aksai Chin discovery required, in the eyes of the military authorities, immediate counteractions so as to avoid further infiltration and the inevitable dangers of a 'last-minute' panic action to compensate for years of neglect. The Tibetan revolt and its outcome were foreseen by Army headquarters in a report prepared in early 1959, in which they proposed specific counterpreparations similar to those actually implemented late in 1959 and including recruitment of special units from the Khampa refugees expected to seek asylum in India. Nehru and Menon remained convinced, however, that Peking must under no circumstances be provoked; thus India's response was limited to stepped-up policing by the border police and Assam Rifles and fresh consultations with the hill states. Such a response added to the frustrations of the armed forces (particularly the

Army), who felt that the politicians were refusing to accept the fact that even minimal military precautions in the Himalayan region could not be effected at a moment's notice. There was concern that, while India talked, the Chinese were developing such a powerful position along the Himalayan front that they would be able to act with virtual impunity.[35]

The three service chiefs, in accordance with their professional responsibilities, had often discussed general policy and also the matter of Menon's conduct. In July 1959 they decided to bring the whole question to the attention of the Prime Minister, who, they believed, was not being properly briefed by Menon. To avoid the appearance of a tri-service ultimatum, it was agreed that Thimayya—as the officer whose service was most concerned—should make the approach and call upon support only if it was necessary to convince Nehru of the seriousness of the matter. Vice-Admiral Katari and Air Marshal Mukerjee were prepared to support their Army colleague even to the point of submitting their resignations, if such a drastic step were required. Various Cabinet ministers, who were aware of the situation and had few reasons to like Menon, advised the COAS to discuss the issue directly with Nehru. They promised such support as they personally might be able to give.

The opportunity for a meeting of the Prime Minister and the COAS apparently occurred by chance at a garden party in late August. It was the first meeting of the two men in some time, and Nehru invited Thimayya to his house the following day. During the course of this conversation, Thimayya informed the Prime Minister of his concern with Menon's interference in Army matters and its effect on service morale, and his opinion that it was an 'impossible situation' which could not continue. Thimayya told Nehru that the other two service chiefs were available by telephone to confirm his contentions, but Nehru professed no need to contact the two men and promised to speak to Menon about the issue the next day.

What transpired in the Nehru–Menon talk must remain speculation, but three days later Menon sent for the COAS. In the highly

[35] The head of the Army at this time, General Thimayya, was by no means an advocate of conflict with China, as he recognized that, because of China's superior strength, 'It must be left to the politicians and diplomats to ensure our security'. 'Adequate Insurance', *Seminar*, no. 35 (July 1962), p. 14. He felt, however, that it was necessary to show the Chinese that India meant to preserve its territorial integrity and thereby provide the Indian diplomat a position of at least minimal strength.

excited state of mind frequently exhibited on the world stage, Menon criticized Thimayya for taking the matter to Nehru and referred to the possible political repercussions if the issue became public; he argued the need to resolve such differences privately and on a bilateral basis. Thimayya replied by making his views 'abundantly clear' to the Minister. In a series of regular meetings with Menon at 2:30 P.M. on subsequent days, Thimayya recognized that the Defense Minister had no intention of amending his conduct. Faced with this situation and the apparent indifference of Nehru, Thimayya decided to tender his resignation on the assumption that it would be accepted but hoping that it might focus attention on the seriousness with which Menon's conduct was viewed.

The letter of resignation, which specified the complaints about Menon's interference in internal Army affairs, was drawn up on the morning of 31 August 1959 and typed in Thimayya's residence by his personal assistant. The letter was shown to Katari and Mukerjee, who unsuccessfully sought to dissuade the COAS from pursuing the matter, and was then delivered by one of Thimayya's military assistants to Nehru's residence, where it was left with a member of the Prime Minister's staff. During the course of the 2:30 P.M. meeting with Menon that afternoon, Thimayya informed him of the letter and refused Menon's 'urgent request' to withdraw it before it came to Nehru's attention. The Prime Minister appears to have read the letter at about this same hour and summoned the COAS at 7 P.M. He stated that such an action must add to his already heavy burdens of office—with Ayub's visit scheduled for the next day—and that he wanted no issue of this magnitude to become public. He requested Thimayya to withdraw his resignation on the grounds that Menon was scheduled to leave for the United Nations shortly (and would thus be out of the way for a time) and promised that he would look into every one of Thimayya's complaints after the meeting with Ayub. Convinced that Nehru sincerely meant to investigate the matter and take action to confine Menon's conduct to the proper scope of a Minister, Thimayya withdrew his resignation—a serious error, as quickly became apparent.

What might have transpired had the issue been kept from the public must remain conjectural. Nehru was certainly aware of Menon's arrogance and inability to work well with subordinates and his almost obsessive ambition to dominate those with whom he came into contact. He would have known that, at a time when China was threatening the northern frontiers, a first-class professional and nonpolitical soldier like Thimayya could be provoked to such drastic action only by the most serious reasons. Nehru could conceivably have cautioned Menon to avoid contentious actions, although Menon might have regarded even a mild caution as a rebuke and resigned. Extraneous factors entered into the entire matter, however, and probably affected Nehru's ultimate response. The existence of Thimayya's letter of resignation had been leaked by a member of Nehru's staff to a source at *The Statesman*, who secured confirmation from Thimayya himself in an accidental fashion. The reporter accosted the COAS outside his home with the query 'Have they accepted it?' and Thimayya replied 'No' before realising that the 'cat had been let out of the bag'. The matter was the subject of banner headlines the following morning, 1 September.

Menon's suitability for the Defence portfolio became the subject of extensive press comment. The *Manchester Guardian* declared (2 September) that, for all his talents, Menon's resignation 'can only strengthen the Indian Government'. Referring to Menon, the *News Chronicle* stated (3 September): 'However great his efficiency and his services to India when she was struggling for her independence, his reputation and record are a grave handicap to the Indian Government at this time'.

The actual extent to which Menon's position was threatened by public disclosure cannot be readily ascertained. A release by the semiofficial Press Trust of India (which generally accurately reflects official views) on the afternoon of 1 September stated that Menon had submitted his resignation to Nehru that morning, but an amended version issued that evening stated only that persistent lobby reports of Menon's resignation could not be confirmed from ministerial sources.[36] It is also understood that a PTI representative called at Thimayya's residence at 5 P.M. the same day with the information that the Cabinet was against Menon, who was going to be sacked; according to this source, only the venerable Home Minister, Pandit Pant, was believed to be in a position to save Menon—and he was regarded as not so inclined. Late in the afternoon, reports began to circulate that Menon had resigned, and lobby opinion tended to accept the view that his resignation would be accepted.

[36] Cited in *The Times*, 2 September 1959.

Press sources also speculated that Menon was to be removed from the Ministry. The *Manchester Guardian* felt that he might be sent off to the United Nations as Minister without Portfolio, with Nehru taking over Defence.[37] The *Hindustan Times* expressed the view on 3 September that Nehru would 'undoubtedly' relieve Menon of the Defence portfolio following the latter's return from the United Nations. An Associated Press despatch from New Delhi stated that 'sources close to the official residence of President Rajendra Prasad' had revealed that Nehru might announce a Cabinet shake-up that would oust Menon or give him another ministerial post.[38] With the advantage even of several weeks' hindsight, one Indian weekly stated that Nehru's handling of the issue (as against Menon's silence), and Menon's impending departure for New York at a time when border events required the closest attention of the Defence Ministry, 'seems to point to a kind of disengagement being pursued between the armed forces and the personality of Shri Menon. The process should lead to his ultimate departure from the Defence Ministry'.[39]

What passed between Nehru and Menon or among the Cabinet ministers concerning this isue is unclear, but it is improbable that Menon was ever in danger of losing his position; even if Nehru privately doubted the wisdom of some of his colleague's actions, his admiration for, and reliance upon, Menon were too strong. Also, Nehru had fiercely defended lesser colleagues on previous occasions even in the face of damning public evidence. The issue of civil authority had to be upheld, and shifting Menon from Defence at this time would undoubtedly have been widely interpreted as a concession to military pressure. Even a public rebuke of Menon's activities would have provoked such general delight among the Minister's legions of enemies, and have been such a blow to his stature, that Menon may well have warned the Prime Minister that he would have to resign if he was not strongly supported. It is most unlikely that, Pant excepted, any Cabinet Minister or collection of Ministers had sufficient influence with Nehru to sway his opinion on such an issue. The role of Pant in the matter is not known, but it would appear from the outcome either that he did not feel disposed to exert his influence for Menon's removal or that he intervened at Menon's request on his behalf—as one person interviewed by the writer alleged.

[37] 2 September 1959.
[38] Cited, *New York Times*, 3 September 1959.
[39] *Vigil*, 26 September 1959, p. 562.

Nehru's public rebuke of Thimayya caused the latter to consider submitting his resignation again—and finally—but there appeared to be no sense in taking such a step at this stage, as the matter had been publicly aired and had revealed strong public, press, and service support for the highly regarded and popular COAS. But as the *Daily Telegraph* noted (3 September), Nehru's attitude 'does credit to Mr Nehru's personal loyalty and it may cover up—for the present—the departmental row, but it perpetuates a dangerous state of affairs for India'.

AFTERMATH OF THE DISPUTE

The assignment to the Army, between August and November, of responsibility for securing the Himalayan frontier against Chinese intrusions appears to have removed that aspect of policy as a source of strain between the military and political arms of government, both sectors agreeing—albeit for somewhat different reasons—on the need for prudence while gradually developing communications in the region. However, the government remained unresponsive to Army requests for equipment and special mountain formations, nor did Menon show any signs of having been inhibited by the September furore as he continued to cultivate contacts with ambitious officers and strengthen his relationship with Kaul. He even attempted to have Thimayya take the eight months' leave due him preparatory to retirement and, although the COAS resisted such efforts and stayed on until two months short of retirement, the intervening period was one of minimal communication between the two. The September affair also resulted in cool relations between Thimayya on the one hand and Katari and Mukerjee on the other because of the manner in which the Navy and Air Force Chiefs of Staff had sought to disuade Thimayya from an action of which they had earlier pledged support, and the manner in which they publicly dissociated themselves from it—Mukerjee at a London press gathering and Katari in a radio message to the Fleet.

Thimayya's retirement in early 1961 was followed almost immediately by more controversial appointments, with Kaul again a central figure. About one week before Thimayya's departure from the top post, Menon informed him of his desire to assign Kaul to the post of Chief of General Staff—the third-ranking post behind the COAS and Deputy COAS. Thimayya refused to make such a recommendation on the grounds that Kaul, who was not considered to possess the requisite qualifications, would thereby become a virtual laughing-stock in the service and lower the prestige of the post. Furthermore, Thimayya recommended that his own successor be Lieutenant-General S. P. P. Thorat, then General Officer Commanding the Eastern Command and a former commander of the Korean Custodian Force. Thorat would thereby supersede Lieutenant-General P. N. Thapar, then GOC of Western Command and three months junior to Thimayya and two months senior to Thorat—Thimayya considering Thorat to be the more qualified and experienced. Menon proceeded to disregard completely Thimayya's recommendation and professional opinions, and arranged for Thapar's elevation to COAS and Kaul's appointment as CGS, thereby forcing Thorat—who had just completed his four-year term as Lieutenant-General—into retirement.

The elevation of Thapar and the retirement of Thorat left vacant both the Western and Eastern Commands, the aspirants for which, in order of seniority, were Lieutenant-Generals S. D. Verma, Daulat Singh, Lionel Protip Sen, Kumaramangalam, and Kaul. Singh (two and one-half years junior to Verma) was assigned Western Command, Sen was posted to Eastern Command, and the superseded Verma applied for premature retirement. The supersession of this experienced officer renewed suspicions that Menon aimed to clear the way for Kaul's appointment to COAS, and the suspicions were aired in a sensational letter, clearly written by a group of high-ranking Army officers, which appeared on the front page of the Bombay English-language weekly, *Current,* on 6 April 1961. The letter accused Menon of using promotions to create cliques in the Army personally loyal to him and aimed at an eventual *coup d'état.* The writers expressed the view that Menon proposed to have Kaul succeed, as COAS, either Thapar or Thapar's senior subordinate, Lieutenant-General J. N. Chaudhuri, after the latter served in the top post for a brief period; as Chaudhuri was due for retirement in May 1963 if not elevated in rank, the possibility that he would be superseded was very strong. Kaul would also have to supersede Kumaramangalam and Daulat Singh while Sen would be forced either to retire or accept the post of Deputy COAS (actually a demotion from Eastern Command in terms of prestige) when the incumbent, Lieutenant-General Mohinder Singh, retired in January 1963.

The promotional issue once again became the subject of heated debate in Parliament. Menon advanced statistics in defence of his argument that there was nothing unusual about supersessions, and noted that superseded officers had the right of appeal. He claimed the right to overrule recommendations of the COAS on promotions but stated that he had exercised this right only once and 'that one instance was an instance in which I had no other option'. Also, he declared that no officers had resigned over promotions and that there had been only one application for premature retirement.[40]

Having apparently cleared the way for Kaul's eventual elevation to COAS, Menon facilitated the placing of officers close to Kaul in the key posts of Director of Military Operations and Director of Military Intelligence. Menon and Kaul are also understood to have increased their long-standing effort to force from the service Major-General S. H. F. J. Manekshaw, the highly regarded and outspoken Parsee Commandant of the Defence Services Staff College (Wellington). Their previous efforts to have Manekshaw disciplined for making statements critical of themselves had been rebuffed by Thimayya,[41] but his successor, though undoubtedly a conscientious officer, was content to remain a somewhat passive bystander to the activities of his civilian superior and service subordinate.

Manekshaw made no effort to conceal his dislike of both men, of promotions policy in particular, or of military policy in general. He is believed to have been critical of the politically inspired external troop commitments, such as that in the Congo, at a time when the northern frontiers were so weakly manned. He apparently also regarded the official eschewal of atomic weapons as unrealistic and, under his direction, Staff College classes studied the implications of nuclear warfare on the premise that future staff officers must be familiar with the subject regardles of any moral objections.

His actions and statements were closely observed by officers close to Kaul and Menon, and several 'stooge' officers were persuaded to bring trumped-up accusations against him at a time when his third star had been announced but not yet awarded. The general charge was that he was impugning constituted authority, and the 'evidence'

[40] *LSD*, 2d sess., vol. 54 (26 April 1961), p. 10,540.
[41] Manekshaw apparently declared to an audience of service personnel in early 1960 that he would not permit Kaul or Menon to obtain publicity by opening installations in any area he commanded; news of his remarks had reached either Menon or Kaul. Thimayya also refused to act on a later report, tendered either by Menon or Kaul, that Manekshaw had been overheard in a mess hall to refer to him (Thimayya) as a 'bloody fool', as he was well aware of Manekshaw's bluntness and did not view the remark, if indeed it was made, as anything personal.

in support of this charge is understood to have included his taking a picture of Clive from the College basement and displaying it in a prominent position on his office wall. Manekshaw was prepared to resign in disgust but was presuaded by some of his colleagues (including Thimayya) to call his accusers' bluff. He was completely vindicated by a three-man service board of enquiry in New Delhi in December 1961, which recommended, furthermore, that his accusers be made to answer for their own conduct. The verdict did not, however, relieve the pressure brought to bear by Menon and Kaul, who sought to provoke Manekshaw into conduct which would warrant disciplinary action. Manekshaw refused to be goaded into such action, but it was generally believed that he would have been denied further promotion normally due in late 1962, at which time he would be retired.

The efforts of Menon and Kaul to manipulate Army promotions raises the question of motivation. Menon was politically ambitious but lacked popular support in the Congress party, and his intimate relationship with Nehru only served to increase the dislike which he provoked among other aspirants for power and influence. His leftist outlook also alienated him from the more conservative sector of Indian politics. It was widely felt that, through the Defence portfolio, Menon sought to acquire a favourable domestic image and a basis of support in the services foreseeing a possible scramble for power in Congress when Nehru passed from the scene. Indian publicists tended to dismiss the possibility of a military or military-backed coup almost out-of-hand,[42] but more impartial foreign observers did not share their view.[43]

[42] Writing in 1959, Taya Zinkin expressed the view that the idea of an army coup, either on its own initiative or in support of Menon, was absurd. The reasons she advanced in support of this contention were: the army was not a caste itself, with a separate outlook and interests; it had no heroes; and the middle class—which provides the military officers, technicians, administrators, and professional men running India—was predominantly Hindu, a religion which is 'much too vague and too individualistic to make it possible for one man to impose himself on others, except as a saint'. 'India and Military Dictatorship', *Pacific Affairs*, 32:1 (March 1959), pp. 89–90.

[43] See, for example, Robert Trumbull, *As I See India* (London: Cassell, 1957), p. 172. Hugh Tinker wrote in 1962 that, while the Indian Army was non-political, so was the Pakistan Army until 1958: 'The possibility of military intervention could not be ruled out, if public order ever seriously degenerated or if India was confronted by a grave external threat which was pusillanimously met by the politicians. Military governments in Hyderabad and Goa were of short duration; but in Kashmir the Army remains the real power

Menon's cultivation of Kaul was completely consistent with the political ambitions he may have aspired to advance with military support, whether implicit or explicit. In the event that chaos followed a sudden passing of Nehru, the Army would certainly be called upon to restore order in many parts of the country and perhaps impose martial law. In such an event, were it accompanied by a serious threat from Pakistan or China and ineffectual political leadership at the Union level, the Army in particular would be drawn into the political arena and its support would undoubtedly be crucial for any prospective head of government. The combination of two ambitious men—Menon and Kaul— heading the Defence Ministry and the Army respectively at such a crucial juncture could exercise decisive influence on developments. It would seem doubtful, however, if any such 'alliance of convenience' between two men of such sharply different backgrounds and political leanings could have long endured, particularly as Menon would have needed Kaul more than Kaul would have needed him. Whatever his political ambitions and susceptibilities Kaul was a Brahmin and by no means shared Menon's political orientation or passively acceded to Menon's will on policy issues. He favoured a strong line against China to the point of being dangerously provocative, opposed the purchase of Soviet An-12 transports, favoured serious consideration of Western aircraft before any decision was taken on the MIG's, generally preferred Western to Soviet arms, and may have dissuaded Menon from further purchases of Soviet equipment.[44] As COAS, Kaul may well have been far more independent of Menon's influence than was commonly supposed, and the relationship between them subject to considerable strain.

The conduct of the two men, however, had served to erode the professionalism of at least a segment of the Army officer cadre even as the country was moving almost inexorably towards a crisis in defence. Summing up the situation in May 1962, the well-informed Frank Moraes wrote:

There is no denying that a great deal of simmering discontent and frustration exists among the officers of our Armed Forces at various echelons . . . Individual ambition, prejudice and predeliction apart, the main

behind the State administration. The cry of Indian publicists "It can't happen here" has a shrill note: they know it could and might happen'. *India and Pakistan* (London: Pall Mall Press, 1962), p. 157.

[44] See Welles Hangen, *After Nehru, Who?* pp. 257-260.

grouse among the officers seems to be that promotions, particularly in the higher grades, often ignore merit and are not seldom dictated by personal or political likes and dislikes. Moreover, the present Defence Minister's habit of bypassing or ignoring senior commanders, of consorting with and counselling their juniors more susceptible to this influence and with a tendency to 'jee-hazoor' him makes for indiscipline and dissatisfaction.

He concluded that 'All is far from well with and within the Services and it is time the people of India knew it'.[45] It can only be speculated whether the professionalism and the nonpolitical tradition of the Indian armed forces could have escaped severe and even irreparable erosion given several more years of general apathy toward defence and Menon's apparent efforts to encourage political conformism and personal loyalties to his person among senior military officers. Developments in the Himalayas were, in the meantime, leading to a crisis which was to have far-reaching consequences for the civil–military relationship in India.

[45] *Indian Express*, 7 May 1962.

Chapter Ten

HIMALAYAN CONFLICT, 1962–1965

The cautious and limited deployment of Indian troops in Ladakh proved inadequate as either a deterrent to or a bulwark against further Chinese advances. In the autumn of 1960 China pushed a patrol within ten miles of Daulet Beg Oldi, to the south of Karakoram Pass, and in May of the following year the Chinese again pushed forward towards Chushul. Shortly thereafter Chinese troops occupied Dehra Compass, and their establishment of a post on the Chip Chap River 17 miles southeast of Daulet Beg Oldi in the late summer brought them to their 1960 claim line in this quarter. They established other posts at Niagzu and Dambur Guru and occupied Hot Springs.[1]

INDIA'S FORWARD POLICY

In response to these indications of Peking's intention to continue its advances in Ladakh, the Indian government took the momentous decision to challenge the Chinese actions by establishing small and generally isolated outposts in the disputed areas. The objectives of this 'forward policy' were apparently several: to block potential lines of Chinese advance; to undermine Chinese control of the disputed areas through the interposition of Indian posts and patrol activities between Chinese posts; and thereby to threaten Chinese lines of communication and supply.

It is still unclear to whom this policy can be attributed. It was attractive from a political viewpoint and it was practicable from the military viewpoint, although imposing a disproportionate burden upon the existing system of supply and communication. It was apparently based on the premise that the Chinese had been moving only where there was a vacuum and that they would not challenge

[1] See P. M. Jones, 'Passes and Impasses', *Far Eastern Economic Review*, 28 February 1963, p. 455.

169

Indian posts by force of arms. New Delhi may have hoped that such a modest display of its determination would make Peking amenable to some sort of negotiated settlement.

By April 1961 Indian patrols were probing forward around the long-established Chinese post on the Chip Chap River, setting up perhaps six posts in Ladakh by the end of the year. Several all-year barracks and supply posts were also established in forward areas to permit an Indian presence in the inhospitable area throughout the winter. The developments were viewed with optimism by the Indian Prime Minister. Speaking in the Lok Sabha on 28 November 1961, Nehru declared that 'progressively the situation had been changing from the military point of view and we shall continue to take steps to build up these things so that ultimately we may be in a position to take action to recover such territory as is in their possession'. He explained that the government regarded Ladakh as of greater immediate importance than NEFA, adding that Longju (evacuated in 1959) would be reoccupied when the time was appropriate. 'We cannot take adventurist actions which may lead us in greater military or other difficulties. It is not an easy matter to conduct warfare in these regions. But it may have to be done and therefore we have to prepare for it if necessary'. The despatch of an infantry brigade group to the Congo in March–April 1961 and the operation against Goa in December of the same year, however, suggest that no sharp deterioration of the situation in the Himalayan region was contemplated at that time.

In the spring of 1962, Nehru sanctioned a more provocative policy in Ladakh, involving direct attempts to cut Chinese lines of communications to their forward posts. According to one report, Menon ordered the spring advances in answer to election criticism that he was 'soft' towards China, but he let it be known discreetly that he was more realistic and tougher towards China than was Nehru—being neither optimistic about successful negotiations with China nor under any illusion about Soviet support in the event of a Sino-Indian clash.[2] In the view of another writer, it was Kaul who took the initiative to argue for such action with Nehru on the grounds that the Army needed to maintain its self-respect. 'Menon was hamstrung. He could not openly oppose a policy aimed at reclaiming lost Indian territory. Menon's long-standing orders that Indian patrols should not engage the Chinese under any circumstances were revoked. Indian troops were told to hold their ground and open fire if the Chinese sought to dislodge them from

[2] *Foreign Report*, 20 September 1962, p. 6.

any position on Indian soil'.³ The latter version would seem the more accurate; Kaul is known to have favoured a tough line against the Chinese, whereas Menon's career and excessively apologetic stand on the issue of Chinese actions in the Himalayas would have rendered problematical his political survival or diplomatic usefulness in the event that China was provoked too far and large-scale conflict ensued.

Several further Indian battalions were shifted into Ladakh to implement the new phase of the 'forward policy'. A number of new posts were established, including one at Spanggur Lake and one on both the north and south shores of Pangong Lake.⁴ With a confidence that indicated an increasingly firm attitude on the border question, Nehru claimed in the Lok Sabha on 29 June that India now had the military initiative and that new Indian posts were outflanking and endangering Chinese posts.

CHINESE REACTION

In furtherance of her previous policy and in response to the increasingly forceful Indian policy, Peking established more posts in the disputed area ⁵ while the Chinese press warned New Delhi of the possible consequences of its 'aggressive' actions. An editorial in *Jenmin Jihpao* in April hinted at a plot between Nehru, the Dalai Lama, Chiang-Kai-shek, and the United States to reinitiate 'interference' in Tibet ⁶—presumably by supplying arms to the rebels. The *Peking Review* warned India that, unless it withdrew its 'aggressive posts' and discontinued its provocations, Chinese frontier guards would be 'compelled to defend themselves'.⁷ Peking announced that it was resuming 'patrols' in the area between the Karakoram and Kongka passes and would commence patrolling the entire Sino-Indian frontier if India continued to invade and

---

³ Welles Hangen, *After Nehru, Who?* (London: Rupert Hart-Davis, 1963), p. 258.

⁴ A map published in the *Peking Review* on 20 July 1962 (no. 29, p. 15) showed fifteen Indian 'strongpoints' purportedly set up since the spring. It was subsequently charged in the same source (2 November 1962, no. 44, p. 23) that India had set up forty-three 'aggressive strongpoints' in Ladakh between May 1961 and October 1962.

⁵ Mrs. Lakshmi Menon, Minister of State for External Affairs, claimed in the Lok Sabha on 3 September 1962 that China had established thirty-four new posts in Ladakh since May 1962. *LSD*, 3rd sess., vol. 8, col. 5531.

⁶ Cited, *Peking Review*, no. 17 (27 April 1962), pp. 8-9.

⁷ *Ibid.*, no. 18 (4 May 1962), p. 17.

occupy Chinese territory.[8] A Chinese note dated 2 June 1962 warned that her frontier guards would not acquiesce in continuing Indian provocations,[9] and an editorial in *Renmin Ribao* on 9 July warned the Indian government to 'rein in on the brink of the precipice'.[10]

In a show of strength on 10 July, some four hundred Chinese troops encircled an Indian post which had been established a few days before astride the supply line to a forward Chinese post in the Galwan River valley; in accordance with Maoist tactics, a line of retreat was left open for the Indian personnel manning the post. After hurried discussions in New Delhi, the Indian troops were ordered to stand firm and to meet force with force. After several tense days the Chinese detachment withdrew, but Indian and Chinese troops exchanged fire on 16, 19, and 21 July.

In retrospect, this incident in the Galwan River valley appears to have been of great significance. To Peking, it must have indicated that the Indian government was now prepared to risk an armed clash to maintain its positions and that Chinese posts would either have to be abandoned as the supply lines to the individual forward posts were cut, or be secured through offensive action against the Indian forces. From the standpoint of New Delhi, the Chinese withdrawal was seemingly interpreted as confirming the view (hitherto held with less conviction) that China would not risk an open clash but would respect demonstrations of India's determination to maintain its territorial integrity by force of arms, if that was required. Thus emboldened, the Indian authorities decided on an even more resolute course of action in NEFA, where Chinese occupation of Longju remained an open challenge. The scope of the challenge was considerably broadened when Chinese forces seized the Dhola post and Thag La ridge in the Kameng Frontier Division on 8 September. As a former Chief of the Indian Army Staff, General Thimayya, aptly commented in retrospect, 'these actions in overrunning our post in Dhola Ridge and in occupying Thag La Ridge must have been with the specific aim of forcing us to react so as to give them a good excuse for launching an attack on us'.[11]

New Delhi's response could hardly have been more to Peking's

[8] *Ibid.*
[9] Cited *Peking Review*, no. 24 (15 June 1962), p. 9.
[10] Cited, *ibid.*, no. 28 (13 July 1962), p. 11.
[11] 'Chinese Aggression and After', *International Studies*, 5:1, 2 (July–October 1963), p. 51.

satisfaction, as it could later be argued that it was the 'aggressive' actions of India which necessitated the 'defensive' actions by the so-called Chinese frontier guards. Thus, Nehru stated in London on 10 September that the border dispute could 'develop suddenly into a conflict'.[12] In response to the establishment of another Chinese post ten miles inside the McMahon Line near Tawang on 12 September, troops from the 7th Brigade of India's 4th Infantry Division began to move from Tawang towards the Thag La–Dhola area. There were sporadic clashes between Indian and Chinese forces near Dhola on the night of 20–21 September and at the Che Jao bridge on 29 September. According to one press source, the decision to resort to direct action against the Chinese forces encamped on territory claimed by India was taken on 17 September.[13]

Nehru returned from his overseas trip on 1 October but made no immediate comment on the NEFA situation. On 5 October, however, the Defence Ministry announced that the Chief of the General Staff, Lieutenant-General B. M. Kaul, had been transferred to command of a new corps in NEFA and that he had already left for Tezpur.[14] Despite official efforts to represent the new command as merely a reorganization having no wider significance, its implications were correctly noted by sections of the press. The *Economist* (13 October) expressed the view that the move reflected a government decision 'to put Chinese intentions to the test especially in the McMahon Line Region'. The *Times of India* declared on 10 October that the Army was poised for an 'all-out effort to expel the Chinese intruders from the Thag La area'.

The drift to war quickened as Indian troops made a small probing attack northwest of Dhola on 10 October and it became fairly clear that they were preparing to eject the Chinese from the area. Official and unnecessarily dramatic confirmation of such an intention was given by Nehru in New Delhi on 12 October, when, just before leaving for a visit to Madras and then Ceylon, he declared to the press that the Army had been ordered to eject the Chinese from NEFA.[15] On 15 December Defence Minister Menon

---

[12] Cited, *The Times*, 11 September 1962.
[13] *Times of India*, 27 September 1962.
[14] Kaul's new command embraced the area of Uttar Pradesh, Sikkim, Bhutan, and NEFA and reduced Maj.-Gen. Umrao Singh's Eastern Command to the area south of the Brahmaputra River covering Nagaland and the border with East Pakistan.
[15] Cited, *Hindu*, 13 October 1962.

stated at Bangalore that the Chinese would be thrown from Indian soil.[16]

A temporary lull in the NEFA skirmishing was broken by an Indian claim on 16 October that their Dhola post had been fired upon. In reply, Peking charged that Indian troops had attacked on 17 October all along the Kechilang River, advancing northwards between Hatung Pass and Pangkangting and towards Sechang Lake.[17] The stage was appropriately set, and a leading Indian daily, the *Hindu*, reported on 19 October that there were elaborate Chinese preparations for an offensive along the borders of Sikkim, Bhutan, and NEFA.

BORDER CONFLICT WITH CHINA

The conflict erupted early on the morning of 20 October at both ends of the Sino-Indian frontier. Indian and Chinese reports differ as to the actual commencement of hostilities, but the preparedness of the Chinese forces was unmistakeable. The so-called 'defensive' actions by their 'frontier guards' were delivered in brilliant fashion by large numbers of infantry supported by artillery, mountain guns, mortars, and, on at least one occasion in Ladakh, by tanks.[18]

In Ladakh, Chinese infantry attacked south of the Karakoram Pass at the northwest extremity of the Aksai Chin plateau and in the Pangong Lake area some 100 miles to the southeast. Indian forces were speedily ejected from perhaps eleven posts in the vicinity of Karakoram Pass and from several in the Pangong Lake district but held firm at the vital posts of Daulet Beg Oldi (near the entrance to the pass) and Chushul (immediately south of Pangong Lake and at the head of the vital supply road to Leh). On 27 October other Chinese forces attacked in the vicinity of Demchok (100 miles southeast of Chushul) and quickly overran the Demchok and Jara La posts but were otherwise contained. In one instance, they conceded some ground to a counterattack by elements of the Jammu and Kashmir Militia.

In NEFA, the Chinese forces advanced almost at will despite

[16] Cited, *Daily Telegraph*, 15 October 1962.
[17] See *Survey of the Chinese Mainland Press* (SCMP), no. 2839 (16 October 1962), p. 27; no. 2840 (17 October 1962), p. 19; no. 2841 (23 October 1962), p. 23.
[18] The review of developments in the war has been collated from the daily reports of events in the Indian and foreign press and from informed individuals whom the writer interviewed in India.

Indian resistance at several key points. The Tsang Le post on the northern side of the Namka Chu River, the Khinzemane post, and the Indian brigade near Dhola were overrun on the first day, and the Chinese proceeded with a general offensive at both ends of the McMahon Line. In the western sector, Tsang Dar fell on 22 October, Bum La on the 23rd, and Tawang—headquarters of the 7th Infantry Brigade under Brigadier-General J. P. Dalvi—was lost to a three-pronged Chinese divisional assault on the 24th. In the centre, Chinese troops reoccupied the undefended frontier post at Longju (which they had evacuated during the summer because of the outbreak of an epidemic) and captured the Asafila border post 25 miles to the southwest. In the Lohit Frontier Division, a strong Chinese force captured the frontier post at Kibithoo on 22 October and advanced 15 miles down the Lohit Valley to Walong, reaching the vicinity of the town on 25 October. A Chinese offer of negotiations was advanced on 24 October and was rejected by the Indian government as it was undoubtedly expected to be [19]—and a lull set in on the battlefront as both sides prepared for the resumption of the next phase of hostilities.

The Indian Army made desperate efforts to strengthen its defensive positions in NEFA and Ladakh and to prepare against possible Chinese attacks through Sikkim and Bhutan. The measures were in general accordance with the contingency planning prepared in 1961, but their effectiveness was largely destroyed by the rapidity of events. Two brigades were withdrawn from Nagaland and sited at Rangiya (south of Bhutan), and a brigade of four battalions was rushed to defend Walong. The 5th Division from Jullundur–Ferozepore was shifted piecemeal to Misamari (near Tezpur), and three brigades drawn from the 4th and 5th divisions were hastily deployed into positions astride the Se La–Bomdila–Dirrang Dzong axis, supported by light Stuart tanks from Calcutta and paratroop artillery from Agra. The 17th Division was shifted from Ambala to Goyerkata (in northern Bengal between Bhutan and East Pakistan); two brigades were rushed to Siliguri from Amritsar and Khasali; and the Natu La–Gangtok–Siliguri–Kalimpong axis was further reinforced by two brigades drawn from Calcutta and Ranchi. A divisional organization was formed at Dibrugarh.

---

[19] China proposed a mutual withdrawal 20 kilometres behind the line of actual control as of 7 November 1959. For text see *Peking Review*, no. 43 (26 October 1962), pp. 5–6. The Indian government refused to enter into discussions unless Chinese forces withdrew behind the line of actual control as of 8 September 1962.

In Ladakh, in response to the initial Chinese attacks a divisional organization was created at Leh and Chushul was reinforced by air with several battalions of infantry, a battery of 25-pounders, and two troops (normally 32 units) of AMX light tanks which had been detached from the 5th and 17th Divisions. On 4 November the Daulet Beg Oldi post was abandoned as untenable, and its defenders were withdrawn over the 17,500-foot-high Sasar Brangsa Pass to more defensible positions.

India's armoured division at Jhansi and the independent armoured brigade at Patiala were not disturbed, and events appear to have developed too rapidly for other formations in south and southwest India to be disturbed. The Punjab was thus left almost denuded of combatant formations, suggesting that Army headquarters proceeded on the assumption that Pakistan would not take advantage of India's predicament. The Reserve was activated,[20] and one hundred units of the Territorial Army were embodied; most of the TA personnel were assigned to their previously designated anti-aircraft and coastal defence duties, but some were absorbed into technical units of the regular Army.[21]

The adjustments in Ladakh proved adequate to defend the Chushul perimeter against repeated shelling and assault, but the outlying posts at Rezang La and Gurung Hill and four posts in the Spanggur Lake area were overwhelmed by Chinese troops.

The situation in NEFA, however, quickly assumed the proportions of a debacle. Indian troops counterattacked in the Walong area on 13 November and captured a hill feature on a ridge northwest of the town, but were unable to hold it against determined Chinese attacks. With the loss of the vital Otter airstrip, the defending garrison had no choice but to commence a general retirement down the Lohit Valley to a new defensive position about twelve miles distant. The withdrawal on 16 November was made under heavy Chinese fire.

In the Kameng Frontier Division, a force of about six Chinese brigades thrust across the Tawang Chu River near Jang and advanced ten miles to the southeast to attack forward Indian positions at Nurang, eight miles below Se La, on the evening of 17 November.

[20] 26,144 JCO's and 110 officers were recalled and 8,989 JCO's and OR's remained with the colours as of 31 December 1962. Ministry of Defence, *Report*, 1963–64, pp. 29–30.

[21] Sixteen units were embodied before the declaration of emergency on 26 October, and a further 84 units thereafter.

At nightfall, the Indian force withdrew to the main defensive post at Se La which, although a strong physical position, was held by only about five battalions. The defences were frontally assaulted that same night by perhaps four Chinese brigades while simultaneous attacks were made against Dirrang and Bomdila by a Chinese force which, under cover of a heavy snowfall, had executed an undetected outflanking movement on 16-17 November over a mountain range 20 to 30 miles east of Se La. Both towns fell after some hard fighting in which up to a dozen Stuart tanks were destroyed. The force at Se La abandoned its positions on 18 November in an attempt to break out to the south but was dispersed before a strong Chinese roadblock north of Bomdila. Effective Indian resistance in the Kameng Division thereupon virtually ceased to exist, and Chinese troops swept south a further 30 to 40 miles to the vicinity of Foothills, a small town on the edge of the Assam Plains.

At this point, the Chinese were in possession of all the territory they claimed in Ladakh (Chushul being outside the Chinese claim line), and in NEFA they had advanced to within 40 miles of Tezpur and to within 100 miles of the important Digboi oil fields. Civilians and government officials were fleeing Tezpur, preparations were being made by British officials to evacuate their nationals from the areas north of the Brahmaputra River, and New Delhi seemed almost paralysed by the collapse of the NEFA defences and the fear that the Chinese meant to overrun all of Assam. Lieutenant-General Kaul had been replaced by a 'fighting general', Lieutenant-General Manekshaw, and had been posted to the Punjab, while the Chief of Army Staff, General P. N. Thapar, had gone on indefinite sick leave and the former GOC, Southern Command, J. N. Chaudhuri, had assumed the onerous task of directing the Army through the crisis.[22] The 4th Division had ceased to exist as a fighting formation, and the badly mauled 5th Division had been withdrawn from the line for reorganization under a new commander. The 2,500 troops in the Lohit Frontier Division were facing a desperate shortage of supplies, nearly 100 miles from the nearest roadhead. Over 10,000 troops were cut off in the Kameng Frontier Division, but in the south of Kameng other Indian forces were hastily

---

[22] Both Kaul and Thapar resigned shortly thereafter. According to an authoritative Indian military informant, Nehru had approached President Radhakrishnan with the suggestion that Kaul be appointed to succeed Thapar as COAS but the President had regarded the proposal as 'absurd' in the circumstances.

constructing new defensive positions north of Foothills. A fairly strong Indian force remained deployed against possible attacks in the Sikkim–Bhutan sector. In Ladakh, the former political deployment in small posts was being readjusted to a more realistic military position astride the highly defensible approaches to Leh.

India's unpreparedness in the military sphere was even more pronounced in the nonmilitary sphere, the confused response of the Prime Minister reflecting his bewilderment at the totally unexpected turn of events.[23] Though apparently not alarmed by the initial attacks, Nehru soon swung to the opposite extreme of acclaiming the Chinese actions as a 'major invasion' in which the fate of Asia and the world was at stake.[24] In an address to a conference of State Information Ministers on 25 October, he drew a parallel with Dunkirk, declaring that the Indian people must respond with the same determination as had the British people in the aftermath of that famous evacuation.[25]

A state of emergency was signed by the President on 25 October and proclaimed the following day. The Defence of India Ordinance of 1962 was promulgated, conferring special powers on the government for the duration of the emergency. Press censorship was invoked and a veil of secrecy was thrown over developments, with the result that both civilian and soldier alike were forced to reply upon Radio Peking for news of the fighting. Chinese nationals and pro-Peking members of the Indian Communist party were hustled into internment camps and jails. A National Defence Fund was established to which the public was invited to donate cash and valuables. Public appeals were also made for warm clothing to correct a shocking shortage which was forcing soldiers to endure unnecessary hardships through exposure and frostbite. The sudden increased demand for blood plasma could not be met from the only two existing plants in the country for freeze-drying of this

[23] He confessed in the Lok Sabha on 8 November 1962 that the government (i.e., himself) had felt that 'this type of aggression was almost a thing of the past'.

[24] See, for example, his statement in the Lok Sabha on 8 November 1962.

[25] Cited, *Hindu*, 26 October 1962. *Foreign Report* (8 November 1962, pp. 7–8) expressed the view that Nehru's broadcast to the nation on 22 October reflected his fear of alarming the country, while his subsequent swing to the other extreme evidenced his recognition of the need to meet the public mood and the prevailing attitude of the armed forces or be faced with an erosion of his own position.

vital requirement. In the absence of any production mobilization scheme, the sale of new cars, new jeeps, station wagons, trucks, steel products, and corporate stocks were frozen, with a consequent serious and quite unnecessary disorganization of the civilian economy.

The Chinese attacks provoked immediate demands from broad sections of Indian opinion for the removal of the controversial Defence Minister, V. K. Krishna Menon. A strong move developed within the Congress party itself, which crystallized around important persons.[26] Senior members of the party, including the deputy leader, Dr. Harekruchna Mahatab, U. N. Dhebar, Mahavir Tyagi, B. K. P. Singh, and the general secretary of the party, Raghunath Singh, met privately a fortnight before the scheduled session of Parliament and agreed upon the need for Nehru to dismiss Menon and assume the Defence portfolio himself. Dr. Mahatab conveyed the views of the group to the Prime Minister and was received coolly, but the group maintained its pressure. At a meeting of the Executive Committee several days later, Nehru was made completely aware of the strong feeling within the Party over Menon's failure as Defence Minister. The Prime Minister's effort to assume personal blame for the Himalayan situation was not greeted with the usual passive acquiescence. Faced with mounting public clamour and party pressure, Nehru had little choice but to take over the Defence post on 31 October. In an obvious attempt to lessen the significance of the demotion of his intimate friend, Nehru retained Menon in the Cabinet in the newly created post of Minister for Defence Production—but with limited responsibilities relating to inspection and organization of various factories and workshops and the research and development organization.[27]

The demotion, which undoubtedly dealt a deep personal blow to Menon, only appeared to increase his arrogance, as he proceeded

[26] Details of the developments within the Congress party pertaining to the ouster of Menon are taken from an article in *Thought,* 17 November 1962, p. 6. See also *Hindu,* 8 November 1962; *The Times,* 8 November 1962; and K. Rangaswami in *Hindu,* 9 November 1962.

[27] The *Times of India* (1 November 1962) expressed the view that Nehru had perhaps 'unnecessarily halted his journey at a half-way house'. In an editorial of the same date, the *New York Times* declared that Menon was still too highly placed and that his removal from the top list of officials 'would have been welcome evidence . . . that the Indian Government had completely turned away from the attitude of unrealistic trustfulness toward the Communist world that contributed to the present crisis on India's norhern frontier'.

to declare at Tezpur that really nothing had changed.[28] Although the claim was probably more of a defensive stratagem than a statement of fact, the remark added to his unpopularity both within and without the Congress party.[29] The next meeting of the Executive Committee, held on the morning of 7 November, was stormy. Members had resorted to the novel (by Indian standards) procedure of collecting signatures to a demand for Menon's complete dismissal from the government, and some of the members even made direct charges.

Nehru made an unsuccessful attempt to convince the members of Menon's sincerity by reading the latter's letter of resignation dated 30 October, and the meeting ended without any indication from the Prime Minister about his subsequent course of action. His attitude was undoubtedly based to some extent on the recognition that he himself was indirectly being attacked.[30] He could not ignore the plain fact, however, that his views could no longer command unquestioning support and that continued refusal on his part to meet the widespread demand (from all but the extreme political Left) for Menon's removal must inevitably weaken his own position and culminate in even more concerted actions leading to direct attacks upon himself. It is believed that he approached the President, Dr. S. S. Radhakrishnan, on the matter and that the latter, although personally friendly to Menon, advised that he would have to be dismissed for the good of the country.[31] Shortly before the general evening meeting of the Congress party on 7 November, Nehru announced in Parliament that he had accepted

[28] The *Hindu* (5 November 1962) reported that 'quarters close to Menon' denied that he had made any such statement. In view of Menon's well-known personality traits, however, it is very likely that he did make such a statement.

[29] Commenting on Menon's Tezpur statement, the *Times of India* (3 November 1962) stated: 'Perhaps too much importance should not be attached to this characteristic piece of egoism . . . Yet it needs to be said that a Union Minister capable of audaciously dismissing as "nothing" changes in a key portfolio which he formerly held invites the severest strictures. It also provokes the question whether the absence of anything resembling regretful admission of past errors does not disqualify him completely from holding a post of any consequence'.

[30] As the *Nation* commented on 1 December 1962: 'Menon was a scapegoat in one sense. He represented the era of vacillation, of half-heartedness, of uncertainty and confusion and bewilderment . . . He stood not for Nehru's policies and leadership, but for the lack of them. The politicians' revolt was not against what Nehru had decided, but against what he had not decided—then, and for so many years before'.

[31] *Foreign Report*, 29 November 1962, p. 4.

Menon's resignation: 'I feel that Mr Krishna Menon has done good work but the controversy will not rest until he quits and controversy is bad for the war effort'.[32]

The crisis had also led to the establishment of an Emergency Committee of Cabinet and of a variety of other emergency committees within the Defence Ministry. On 6 November, a thirty-member National Defence Council was set up to 'advise' the government on matters directly or indirectly affecting defence. As the crisis deepened, the Cabinet was reorganized in a manner designed to illustrate the government's determination to meet the challenge to the country's territorial integrity and prestige. The youthful and vigorous Chief Minister of Maharashtra, Y. B. Chavan, was appointed to the Defence portfolio on 14 November, and on the same day it was announced that K. Raghuramaiah had been shifted from Minister of State in the Defence Ministry to the post of Minister of Defence Production, that T. T. Krishnamachari, the Minister without Portfolio, had been transferred to the newly created post of Minister for Economic and Defence Co-ordination, and that V. R. P. Rao had replaced O. Pulla Reddy as Defence Secretary.[33] On 15 November retired Major-General Sardanand Singh was appointed to the newly created post of Director-General of Civil Defence.

The situation had, in the meantime, forced the government to appeal for immediate military support from Britain and the United States, the appeal being cloaked in a general appeal for support to all governments excepting Portugal and South Africa. (Relations with the latter country continued to be strained by

[32] Cited, *The Times*, 8 November 1962. The *Times of India* (8 November) felt that the removal of Menon was 'unquestionably the right one in a democracy' because of his loss of public confidence:

> Whenever a Minister, for whatever reason, forfeits the confidence of a substantial part of public opinion that is more than sufficient ground for a resignation and appropriate reshuffle of personnel. The principle of collective cabinet responsibility does not in any way negate the equally valid principle of individual responsibility and it is in relation to this that Mr Krishna Menon's earlier letter of resignation was most inadequate. Its failure to refer to the military setbacks in NEFA with which Mr Menon and his Ministry were directly concerned at that time is an astonishing and inexplicable omission.

[33] Reddy was widely considered to be a Menon protégé, but, though this may have contributed to his replacement at such a crucial juncture, it must be noted that his term was completed and that the situation favoured a 'new look' in a discredited Ministry.

India's abhorrence of its apartheid policy.) New Delhi sent an urgent request for military supplies to London and Washington on 26 October and received an immediate response from both these governments; the first consignment of British aid arrived in two Royal Air Force Britannias on 29 October, and the first American aid arrived from depots in Western Europe on 1 November. As the NEFA debacle grew, the Indian government on 19 November sent an urgent and specific request for American fighting air support.[34] Washington had not replied to the request when the Chinese announced their unilateral ceasefire.[35]

The surprise Chinese announcement was broadcast over the New China News Agency on 20 November. It declared that China would terminate the conflict at midnight of the following day and on 1 December would commence a withdrawal of her forces to 20 kilometres (12½ miles) north of the McMahon Line and to a similar distance behind the 'line of actual control' in existence in Ladakh as of 7 November 1959. The broadcast stated China's intention to proceed with her withdrawal regardless of the Indian reaction but warned that China reserved the right to strike back in the event that India attempted to reoccupy any of the territory taken by Chinese troops during their advance.[36] The withdrawal appears to have proceeded as planned and was completed in both sectors by about 15 January 1963.[37]

The official Indian reaction to the announcement was to declare that it was a unilateral action and that a precondition to Indian discussions with the Chinese government regarding the border dispute was restoration of the status quo as of 8 September 1962. However, New Delhi had little choice but to respect the Chinese warning against attempts to reoccupy with troops the areas lost to the advancing Chinese.

[34] According to an informed British observer on Indian affairs, Nehru made a desperate appeal to Britain and the United States on 19 November for fifteen bomber squadrons to attack the advancing Chinese troops. Michael Edwardes, 'Illusion and Reality in India's Foreign Policy', *International Affairs* (January 1965), p. 52.
[35] According to reports, the Indian Ministry of External Affairs repeated the request on 1 December and Nehru himself repeated it in reply to a query from President Kennedy in early January 1963. See Thomas Brady in *New York Times*, 25 January and 21 February 1963; *Times of India* leader, 29 January 1963.
[36] Text of announcement in *Peking Review*, vols. 47 and 48 (30 November 1962), pp. 5-7.
[37] For the timetable of the Chinese withdrawal, see *ibid.*, no. 49 (7 December 1962), p. 7; no. 50 (14 December 1962), p. 15; no. 1 (4 January 1963), p. 26.

Immediate attention had necessarily to be given to preparations against renewed fighting in the following spring, with the aid of emergency shipments of military equipment and stores offered, ironically enough, only by the countries of the Western bloc whose approach to the 'Chinese problem' had been subject to such heavy criticisms by the Indian government. The Soviet bloc, whose friendship India had so assiduously cultivated, remained studiously noncommittal, and India's nonaligned colleagues chose to treat the issue in accordance with the well-known 'Indian approach', from the viewpoint of practical politics that aimed at 'reducing tension' rather than at legal or moral niceties.[88]

The brief and limited conflict had exposed many deficiencies in India's defences. The performance of many of the senior Army officers charged with NEFA defences was marked by confusion, uncertainty, and lack of initiative. Kaul had attempted to direct operations from the front instead of from his headquarters, with the result that operations proceeded without coordination; the removal of corps headquarters from Tezpur to Gauhati and then back to Tezpur aggravated an already confused situation. Officers were generally left to their own devices—a situation for which many were not equipped. The commander of the Indian force at Se La made only a half-hearted attempt to break through a Chinese roadblock south of Dirrang Dzong but chose to abandon his road-bound equipment and by-pass the roadblock; the result was that the approximately two brigades comprising his force lost any effectiveness as a fighting formation. The attempt to hold both principal Chinese thrusts as far forward as Se La and Walong in the face of poor logistics disregarded the prudent contingency planning prepared as early as 1961 and enabled the Chinese to destroy two divisions in almost piecemeal fashion. A nervous brigade commander is understood to have contributed to the Bomdila debacle when he effected a disorderly withdrawal of his command (believed to be the 48th Brigade of the 4th Division), thereby exposing two other brigades.

Tactics were too conventional, forces tending to be roadbound both in tactical and logistical movement and unable to cope with the unorthodox procedures so skilfully employed by the Chinese. Officers, many of whom had shown little interest in unorthodox warfare right up to the outbreak of the war, were unable to provide

---

[88] For a discussion of the reaction of the various countries and 'blocs' to India's difficulties, see *International Studies*, 5:1, 2 (July–October 1963).

the necessary leadership at company and platoon level and were, furthermore, totally unfamiliar with Chinese tactics, equipment, and capabilities. The troops under their command were deficient in battle training and in training required for operations in the jungles and mountains in which they found themselves, and were also not acclimatized to fight at the heights to which many of them were exposed. Many of the initial reinforcements for NEFA were Madrassis from the warm tropical south of India. Patrolling was poor, permitting the Chinese to retain the initiative throughout.

There was an overall shortage of equipment; much of what was in existence was obsolete. Although the .303 bolt-action rifle was an effective weapon in the hands of a trained soldier, it was incapable of offsetting Chinese automatics, superior artillery support, and a longer-range mortar. The almost total absence of mines and wire in the forward positions precluded any chance of holding positions against 'human sea' tactics. Stock of upplies in forward areas were inadequate for augmented forces. The absence of a well-thought-out logistics plan for Himalayan operations prevented the rapid despatch of stores and equipment from depots to front-line areas.[39] The communications equipment proved almost completely useless under the conditions to which it was subjected, since certain key components generally failed. The extensive shortage of high-altitude clothing caused hundreds of cases of exposure.

The inability of the Army to cope with limited attacks attest to the complacency which affected Indian military preparations in the Himalayan region. Committed to secure the Himalayan frontiers and the Himalayan kingdoms against Chinese attacks, the Indian Army had not been allocated the additional resources to meet its new commitments, nor had the government felt the need to seek some sort of understanding with Pakistan for co-operative action to meet the challenge posed by China. The contingency of war with China was regarded as so remote that New Delhi continued to base military strategy against her weaker neighbour. Her actual planning for the Tibetan frontier allowed for little more than local intrusions, notwithstanding contingency planning against possible divisional attacks which amounted to little more than staff exercises.

*For example, rifles urgently needed in NEFA were reportedly flown to Calcutta from depots elsewhere in India in a matter of hours but then took six

The decision to challenge the Chinese in the forward areas of Ladakh in the spring of 1962 and in NEFA in September 1962 was clearly based on the assumption that the Chinese would not risk a major conflict with a country of India's size and international stature merely for the sake of a few square miles of frontier territory. It tended to ignore the fact that Chinese as well as Indian prestige was at stake and that Nehru's public announcement that he had ordered the Army to clear the Chinese from Indian territory merely ensured that, if only for the sake of prestige, Peking could not passively retire. As a London newspaper expressed it, Nehru's determination may well have been 'the accumulated result of affronted pride, reflected in the clamour to do something, and real concern about the possible effect of failure to maintain Indian sovereignty in the north-east frontier'.[40] However, his determination revealed itself too late to have the desired effect but in a fashion that ensured the very occurrence that Indian diplomacy had counselled other nations against, placing China in a situation where she could feel that there was no credible recourse but to force of arms.

The extent to which the military (essentially Army) leadership must share the blame for the debacle is difficult to ascertain. Nehru claimed that decisions relating to Himalayan defence 'were taken by Government in full consultation with the Chiefs of Staff and other senior Army officers concerned and in the light of their expert advice. This applies particularly to the decision that the Army should not withdraw in October–November 1962 from its forward position in NEFA'.[41] He also claimed that his public statement that the Army had been ordered to eject the Chinese was 'not my decision alone; it was the viewpoint of the military people too. They wanted to do it. Otherwise I would not have dared to say anything like that'.[42] Although some senior officers regarded the 'forward policy' with some concern, in view of the Army's inability to counter any substantial military reaction by China in these forward areas, other high-ranking officers—perhaps even a majority—shared the opinion noted by the *New York Times* writer, A. M. Rosenthal: 'Everyone knew it could not happen.

days to reach their destinations in the forward areas. See *Times of India*, 30 January 1960.

[40] *Daily Telegraph*, 15 October 1962.
[41] *LSD*, 3rd sess., vol. 13, col. 1331.
[42] *Ibid.*, 5th sess., vol. 19, col. 2213.

Prime Minister Jawaharlal Nehru knew it, his recently dismissed Defence Minister, V. K. Krishna Menon knew it, and even Indian generals knew it. "We thought it was a sort of game", said one officer of high rank recently. "They would stick up a post and we would stick up a post and we did not think it would come to much more" '.[43]

This smugness did not extend, however, to the proposal apparently advanced by the somewhat impetuous Kaul that the Army eject the Chinese from the Thag La–Dhola area. The proposal was regarded with dismay by more responsible officers, including Lieutenant-General Sen (GOC, Eastern Command) and the luckless brigadier assigned to effect the dislodgement with a brigade of poorly acclimatized and ill-equipped troops at the end of long and primitive communications with nothing in reserve to provide support. Even Kaul began to doubt the feasibility of the operation after the 10 October clash, which revealed that the Chinese were in the area in far greater strength than was hitherto believed—evidencing poor intelligence up to this point. According to an informed Indian military source, Kaul thereupon returned to New Delhi to stress the need for a far stronger force if the plan was to be carried out. Thapar, the COAS, called in Sen (Kaul's superior in theory although not in practice) [44] for consultations, and the three generals discussed the matter with Defence Minister Menon. The decision as to the course of action in the Thag La–Dhola area in the light of the altered situation was referred to Nehru, who declined to interfere in what he clearly felt to be a 'military' problem. The decision was then taken, in Nehru's presence and with his concurrence, to 'sit tight' until spring, at which time the entire situation could be reviewed. For some unexplained reason, however, probing actions continued and the public remained of the belief that the government was proceeding with its preparations to force the Chinese out of NEFA.[45] It was,

[43] *New York Times*, 11 November 1962.
[44] It is understood that Kaul tended to by-pass Sen and deal directly with Thapar and Menon, Thapar himself being a passive bystander to direct dealings between Kaul and Menon and primarily desirous, as one informant stated, 'of finishing his term with the minimum of fuss'. It is also understood that the official enquiry on the NEFA debacle was critical of Sen for not exercising his authority over his subordinate, Kaul, in professional matters.
[45] Such probing actions may well have been decided upon by Menon and Kaul to maintain public belief that the Army was preparing to eject the Chinese—and therefore escape the probable hostile reaction to cessation of all

in any case, undoubtedly too late to revert to a more prudent policy.

The conflict dispelled any lingering illusions in official Indian circles regarding Chinese inhibitions about employing force against India. It brought into focus a grave threat in a quarter where geography had been regarded as an almost insurmountable barrier to serious attack by land. It confirmed India's dependence upon external help against attack by a major power and the availability of Western military aid in a crisis involving Communist China. It showed that the balance of power thesis did not preclude a limited conflict in which an aggressor could initiate hostilities and terminate action after achieving the desired objectives—and then resume his pre-conflict military posture without interference. The Chinese advance in NEFA was a reminder that the absence of the necessary strategic depth in the corridor between Bhutan–Sikkim and East Pakistan rendered most problematical any defence of the area against a sustained assault from the north. There had been an unreal obsession with the supposed military threat posed by Muslim Pakistan—the 'historical ghost'—to the detriment of suitable and phased adjustments in defence strategy and foreign policy to accord with the changing geopolitics in the Himalayan region. The result for India was traumatic—militarily, politically, and diplomatically.

INDIA'S DEFENCE PROBLEMS IN THE HIMALAYAN REGION

The problems of Himalayan defence are momentous. Along a 2,800-mile border broken only by several powerless kingdoms, India faces a powerful and militant China which is antagonistic to her social and political system, disdainful of her 'pretensions' to equal status on the Asian scene, appears determined to retain possession of the Aksai Chin region of Kashmir, and has stated claims to 32,000 square miles of NEFA and to parts of Ladakh, the 'middle sector', and Bhutan. Peking continues to advance such proposals as a Confederation of Himalayan States that would include Nepal, Bhutan, Sikkim, Nagaland, and an 'Eastern Hills State' in what is now NEFA; and seemingly alternative possibilities such as 'regional autonomy' for a 'Darjeeling–Duars district'; a Federation of Bhutan and Sikkim; and a Gurkhistan which would

activities by a public which had been led to expect dramatic results. The onset of winter would thereby have enabled both men to ease out of a predicament in which their actions and public statements had placed them.

include all Nepalis in North Bengal and Assam.[46] The threat is both immediate and long-term, overt and covert, diplomatic, economic, and ideological as well as military.

Indian influence in Nepal is being progressively eroded, although Indian technicians continue to help man some border checkposts on the Nepal–Tibet border and Kathmandu has permitted increased Gurkha recruitment by the Indian Army in the face of Chinese pressure to terminate the practice altogether. China has warned that she would regard any Indian intervention in Nepal as a *casus belli*,[47] is rushing construction of the strategic Kathmandu–Koderi road and is aiding the construction of another road to link Bhadrapur with Olangchung in eastern Nepal which, in a crisis, could possibly be used by Chinese troops to outflank Sikkim to the west. Nepal's weakening ties with India are further evidenced by a marked improvement in her relations with Pakistan,[48] her adoption of a neutral position on the Indo-Pakistan conflict in 1965, and her acquisition of military equipment and stores from Britain and the United States—as against her complete dependence upon India for such material during the 1947–62 period.[49]

Bhutan poses a major military problem, as its integrity is a vital prerequisite to the defence of NEFA–Assam and Sikkim. Construction of the desired defence works within the kingdom is precluded by Peking's threat to regard any such activity as a *casus belli*. Sikkim appears content to be a 'protectorate' of India for the present, but Maharaja Palden Thondup Namgyal has given New Delhi notice that Sikkimese confidence in their official 'protector' is grounded upon the presumed readiness of Britain and the United States to assist India in any crisis [50]—with the implication that India

---

[46] See, for example, G. F. Hudson, 'What Does China Want in the Himalayas', *Financial Times*, 18 February 1963.

[47] Speaking in Peking on 5 October 1962, on the first anniversary of the Sino-Nepalese boundary treaty, the Chinese Foreign Minister, Marshal Chen Yi, warned that 'should any foreign power dare to attack Nepal, the Chinese Government and people . . . will forever stand by Nepal'. Cited in *SCMP*, no. 2836 (10 October 1962), p. 32. As India stated a similar policy as early as 1949, both powers have thus declared Nepal's integrity to be a basic goal of policy.

[48] A Pakistan–Nepal trade agreement was signed in October 1962, a transit agreement in January 1963, and an air agreement in the same year. Pakistan is training aircraft engineers, mechanics, and pilots for the Royal Nepal Air Line.

[49] See *Hindu*, 27 October 1964.

[50] The Maharaja indicated in Gangtok on 23 June 1963 that he was confident

should not take Sikkim for granted. The security of the Northeast is complicated by an increasingly onerous tribal problem; the Naga revolt flickers on, and the eruption of a minor insurrection among the 260,000 Mizos in western Assam in early 1966 bodes ill for the future tranquillity of these strategic areas. Chinese aid to the dissident tribes would aggravate the situation—and cannot be discounted.

Indo-Pakistan War

The appearance of a recognizable Chinese threat to India's Himalayan frontiers and vital interests was accompanied by a marked deterioration in Indo-Pakistan relations. Neither country made serious efforts to improve relations in the immediate aftermath of the Sino-Indian border conflict, and tension was heightened by an increasing number of violations of the ceasefire line in Kashmir, by clashes between Indian and Pakistani troops in the disputed Rann of Kutch and in the Kargil area in April and May 1965, respectively, and by the 22-day undeclared 'war' between the two countries in September of the same year.

The outbreak of general conflict followed provocative and reckless actions by both governments. On 5 August, some 3,000 Muslim 'freedom-fighters'-cum-'infiltrators' began a series of small-scale actions in Indian Kashmir seemingly designed to stir up the local Muslim majority and to focus world attention once more on the Kashmir issue. Indian troops retaliated by crossing the ceasefire line to seize a number of suspected staging areas used by the so-called 'infiltrators' and, when this action was not immediately contested, proceeded to capture two important Pakistani outposts and to 'liberate' much of the Uri–Poonch salient. These actions left Pakistan President Ayub Khan with little choice but to demonstrate equal firmness by a localized punitive action launched across the Chhamb sector of the ceasefire line on the morning of 1 September by a force comprised of an infantry brigade and about 70 Patton tanks. The Indian government reacted by invoking the long-standing contingency plan designed to cripple Pakistan's military capability—and thereby the sanction for her 'hard line' toward India—by a 'war of attrition' in the Lahore–Sialkot sector of West Punjab.

of India's ability to defend Sikkim *because* Britain and the United States would come to India's aid. Cited in *The Nation*, 25 June 1963.

The resulting 'war', however, does not appear to have been particularly decisive inasmuch as ground actions were confined to the Sialkot–Lahore area (with secondary activity around Gadra, in Sind); air activity was restricted to support operations and strikes against military airfields and installations, with only sporadic air combat; and naval activity was limited to a brief and militarily insignificant bombardment of the west coast Hindu centre of Dwarka by units of the Pakistan Navy, which thereupon retired to the security of their Karachi base. At the time of the United Nations-sponsored ceasefire at 3 A.M. on September 23 (Indian time), therefore, India's policy of 'attrition' had achieved only limited success. The Pakistan Army had suffered considerable tank losses, but it was nonetheless containing stronger Indian forces before Sialkot and Kasur, on the Icchogil canal—Lahore's inner defence line—and beyond Gadra. The Pakistan Air Force was effectively exploiting its qualitative superiority to counter the quantitative advantage enjoyed by the IAF. The Pakistan Navy was intact and secure in its Karachi base. There were no indications that a breakdown of Pakistani civilian or service morale was imminent.

The conflict illustrated the absence of a military solution to the Kashmir impasse and the shortcomings of an Indian policy on the issue which sought to substitute an expedient and admittedly stop-gap military solution for a courageous long-term political compromise. It provided vivid evidence of Peking's readiness to exploit Indo-Pakistan antagonisms to her own advantage in the form of a threat to take action if India refused her demand to dismantle her military works on the Sikkim–Tibet border. Implied and explicit criticisms of the resort to force from Moscow and the Western powers—and the suspension of American and British economic and military aid pending a rapprochement between India and Pakistan—were pointed reminders of India's acute vulnerability to sanctions and of a shift in the Soviet position from a pro-Indian to a neutral one.

Recognition in both Delhi and Rawalpindi of the existence of a military stalemate, of widespread international criticism of their actions and demands for a peaceful solution of their problems, and of the urgent need to secure the resumption of American economic and military aid resulted in acceptance by both governments of a Soviet offer of Tashkent as the venue for bilateral discussions aimed as reaching a settlement of the conflict. It quickly became apparent, however, that while President Ayub and Prime Minister Shastri (who succeeded Nehru following the latter's death in May 1964) recognized the need to disengage their military forces and effect a resumption in normal relations, neither was prepared to make any concessions on the question of Kashmir. The untimely death of Shastri hours after conclusion of the agreement on these issues terminated any 'understanding' that may have developed between Ayub and Shastri at Tashkent, and the relationship between the two countries quickly reverted to the traditional pattern, including hundreds of alleged violations of the agreement by both governments in succeeding months.

In their assessment of the country's defence requirements, therefore, Indian defence planners must consider possible contingencies ranging from tribal unrest to limited conflict with a major power, China, and including attempts by both Pakistan and China to seek to capitalize upon India's involvement with the other to advance its own ends. India's leaders cannot ignore the increasing threat to internal stability posed by linguistic and communal issues and by discontent among the masses because of a flagging economy, a soaring population, and persistent food shortages which appear to be increasing in severity. What is the nature of the official reaction to the country's altered defence needs?

Chapter Eleven

THE NEW INDIAN DEFENCE PROGRAMME

The Indian government of Prime Minister Nehru concluded, in the aftermath of the conflict with China, that 'military weakness has been a temptation, and a little military strength may be a deterrent'.[1] As the Union Minister for Planning, Gulzaril Nanda, declared in a broadcast over All-India Radio on 6 February 1963:

We can safeguard peace only when we have the strength to make aggression a costly and profitless adventure. The greater our economic and defence potential, the less will be the danger from across our borders. The bare truth is that our faith in our neighbour in the north has been shattered and it cannot soon be restored. India has henceforward to remain on a constant vigil and in a state of complete readiness for every eventuality . . . From now on, defence and development must be regarded as integral and related parts of the national economic plan.[2]

In accordance with its assessment of the altered strategic situation, the Indian government has undertaken a considerable expansion of the armed forces, the production base, and the operational infrastructure. The blueprint for this expansion is a five-year plan sanctioned in early 1964, which appears to be a revision of a three-year plan hastily drawn up shortly after the 1962 border war. The plan has six major objectives for the period April 1964– March 1969:

1. Creation of a 825,000-man Army and the modernisation of its weapons and equipment.
2. Stabilisation of the Air Force at forty-five squadrons, its re-equipment with modern aircraft, and the provision of suitable ancillary facilities.
3. Maintenance of the Navy at approximately its present strength,

---

[1] Statement by the President of India, Dr. S. S. Radhakrishnan, in a Washington television interview, 9 June 1963. Cited in *Dawn*, 10 June 1963.
[2] Cited, *Hindu*, 8 February 1963.

replacing obsolete vessels with new foreign or Indian ships.
4. Establishment of production facilities so as to materially reduce dependence on external sources of supply.
5. Construction and improvement of communications in the border areas, aimed at creation of an operational infrastructure.
6. Expansion of the research organization.[3]

According to one press source, the Army is expected to constitute the main 'bastion' of defence until 1970 or 1975, by which time it is expected that the Air Force will have developed its own production base and be capable of assuming some of the Army's present deterrent functions.[4]

The financial burden of this defence plan is expected to total Rs 5,000 crores, including a foreign exchange component valued at about Rs 680 crores.[5] Projected defence expenditure for the Fourth Plan period (1966–71) has been placed by the Planning Commission at Rs 5,500 crores, involving an outlay that is expected to rise from Rs 920 crores in 1966–67 to Rs 1110 crores in 1971–72.[6] Although economies will no doubt be effected wherever practicable,[7] it is understood from a high-ranking Indian military informant that the Indian Cabinet agreed in early March 1964 to make available for defence a minimum of Rs 800 crores a year over the subsequent decade irrespective of a level of foreign economic and military aid or of the domestic or external situations.

ARMY PROGRAMME

In view of India's chronic shortage of foreign exchange even for nonmilitary purposes, the government has been forced to do a complete about-face on the issue of military aid.[8] India is relying

[3] Details of the plan have been collated from press reports, statements by Indian official spokesmen, and interviews with informed sources.

[4] H. R. Vohra, *Times of India*, 29 May 1964.

[5] See statement by Defence Minister Y. B. Chavan in London on 19 November 1964, cited in *Times of India*, 20 November 1964.

[6] *Hindu*, 19 June 1964. This compares with the tentative estimated outlay for the entire Plan of Rs 24,000 crores.

[7] For fiscal 1965 an economy cut of about Rs 20 crores in allocations for defence was carried out by postponing or phasing of construction schemes that included family quarters for officers.

[8] Nehru shifted to the view that receipt of military aid was compatible with nonalignment so long as no formal alliance war involved. See his statement cited in *The Times*, 12 November 1962.

upon 'friendly' countries to make available the desired foreign exchange funds for the military in the form of outright grant aid or long-term credits on easy terms, while at the same time requesting increased general economic aid on better terms than hitherto and also concessions regarding repayment on previous aid. Aid-seeking missions have been despatched to various countries, but reliance is being placed upon the United States, Britain and the 'old Commonwealth' (Canada, Australia, and New Zealand), and the Soviet Union.[9]

The Army is being expanded to a well-equipped force of twenty-one divisions, including four or five formations (with smaller establishments) capable of expansion in an emergency. Ten of these divisions will be mountain units comprised of ten infantry battalions (14,000 personnel) and about 300 vehicles and specially organized, trained, and equipped for operations in the Himalayan region.[10] A concerted effort is being made to recruit the hill peoples, Nagas and other frontier peoples, and Gurkhas, the strength of the latter group having been already increased to at least thirty-four battalions.

Training has been reoriented for warfare in jungle and mountain terrain. The capacity of the High Altitude Warfare School has been greatly increased, and a mobile Army Headquarters Training Team is giving instruction in jungle warfare to units at their particular stations. The first course in a programme aimed at toughening young officers mentally and physically for patrol activity over long periods in the Himalayan terrain began in March 1964 at the Infantry School (Mhow). Simulated battle training, discontinued after independence so as to avoid casualties, has been reintroduced, and the organizational structure of infantry, artillery, and service corps units is being revised to improve operational capacity in mountainous areas.

[9] H. R. Vohra reported in the *Times of India* (8 June 1964) that the Indian government hoped for about $550 million in military aid from the United States and $150 million from Britain and the Commonwealth for the five-year defence plan. He reported in the same paper on 23 May 1964 that, during Chavan's visit to Washington in that month, the Indian Defence Minister had submitted a list of defence needs totalling $550 million over a five-year period, including $60 million in grants and $50 million in credits for each of the five years.

[10] Defence Minister Chavan informed the Lok Sabha on 23 March 1964 that each of the four mountain and two regular infantry divisions raised by that date cost Rs 25 crores to equip and required about Rs 7.5 crores for ammunition and other supplies for a three-month operation.

A new Directorate of Combat Development has been set up in the General Staff Branch to develop new weapons and tactical concepts, and a series of decisions have been made to supply the Army with modern weapons, equipment, and stores adequate until the early 1970's. The .303 Lee-Enfield British rifle is being replaced by the semi-automatic Ishapore model, and all .303's are being converted to the new 7.62 bore, which has been adopted as the new standard small-arms bore. The Sten machine carbine is being replaced by the more modern Sterling, also of British manufacture. The 4.2-inch mortar is to be replaced by a lighter type of local design. The French-built Brandt heavy mortar has been acquired in quantity and is now being produced under license. A mountain howitzer is being developed in Ordnance. New types of communications equipment are to be acquired both locally and abroad. The armoured formations began receiving medium tanks from the Avadi Heavy Vehicles factory in early 1965, and some seventy light tanks were purchased from the Soviet Union under a loan agreement concluded in September 1964. Light tanks of British design may be produced at Avadi.

A long-deferred programme to replace the Army's worn vehicle fleet is in progress. As the production schemes underway in the ordnance factories are unable to meet the increased needs of the Army, large orders have been placed with local automobile manufactures for Mercedes-Benz three-ton trucks, Dodge one-ton power wagons, and Willys jeeps. Henceforth, trucks will be disposed of after 35,000 miles or seven years' service—whichever is later—and before the required first major overhaul, and jeeps will be discarded after 30,000 miles or five years' service—whichever is later.

A new Central Command was created out of the unwieldy Eastern Command on 1 May 1963, the NEFA Corps remaining separate. A new organization was set up under the Master-General of Ordnance for the procurement of equipment and stores from foreign countries. To ensure better collation, evaluation, and assessment of intelligence, the number of officers in the Military Intelligence Directorate were increased by about 50 per cent. The 7th and 14th Battalions of the Jammu and Kashmir Militia were merged with the Army, and the remainder of the militia passed under the administrative and operational control of the regular service in an agreement signed in early 1964. One Scout Battalion was raised for service on the Uttar Pradesh–Tibet border and another for service on the Punjab and Himachal Pradesh borders with Tibet. Additional police forces were raised by the Union, Kashmir, and Madras authorities, the last for employment on the NEFA border.

AIR FORCE PROGRAMME

The Air Force is being developed into a force of forty-five squadrons, conceived to meet the requirements of air defence, ground attack, communications, and logistics support to the Army, the Border Roads Development Organization, the NEFA and Nagaland administrations, and engineers constructing airfields in border areas.

The air defence organization has been strengthened by the creation in June 1963 of a new Eastern Command with headquarters at Shillong, Assam. Ground-to-air guided missiles are to be employed for the protection of certain vital areas, and an early warning system is under construction across northern India with American aid.[11] The border war spurred the long-proposed shift of Maintenance Command from Kanpur to the more centrally located Nagpur. Works projects have been implemented for the construction, extension, or improvement of a number of airfields, including a new IAF field at Hindan (near Ghaziabad) which is designed to relieve congestion at Palam. Policy and procedures for the provisioning and procurement of stores has been streamlined.

The transport capacity of the Air Force has been strengthened. After the first Chinese attacks the Indian government contracted with an American firm for the augmentation of the standard two Wright R-3350 piston engines on 27 of their fleet of 53 C-119's. The United States provided 24 C-119 Packets and two Caribou I's in emergency military aid, and Canada gave eight C-47's and five Otters as emergency grant aid, with India purchasing 16 Caribou I's under a loan agreement concluded in July 1963. Thirty more An-12's were acquired from the Soviet Union under a loan agreement signed in July 1963, and the decision has been taken to employ this type as the standard heavy transport. An order for 29 Avro-748's has been placed. But no decision appears to have been made regarding the suitability of this British type as the future standard medium

[11] Mobile radar units provided by the United States in 1963 were sited at Amritsar and to the north of Calcutta. The ultimate fixed radar system will probably comprise small advance radar posts sited as far forward in the Himalayas as possible and backed by perhaps fifteen larger radar centres located at the edge of the plains.

transport. The project was severely criticised in the report of the Public Accounts Committee submitted to the Indian Parliament on 28 February 1966, which referred to 'grossly unrealistic' production schedules resulting in the diversion of technical personnel from maintenance duties.

Orders were placed in 1963–64 for about 50 helicopters, but a Soviet offer to establish a plant in India to produce them under licence from Avaiaexport [12] was declined by New Delhi for the stated reason that 'the number of Mi-4 helicopters required by the IAF do not justify the establishment of manufacture in India'.[13] Although it appears that French credit terms were not attractive from the Indian viewpoint, a number of Alouette III's were purchased in 1963, and India proposes to meet its future service requirements for helicopters by manufacturing about 150 additional units of this model. The first units were assembled in late 1965, with production beginning in early 1966.

India's Krishak Mk 2 was accepted for the air observation post duties formerly performed by the Auster, A.O.P. 9 and 30 units were ordered for late 1965. The sharply increased requirements for training aircraft were alleviated by 36 Harvards provided by Canada as emergency grant aid and a small number of Vampires purchased from Indonesia in November 1962.[14] Efforts were made to acquire more Harvards from other countries, but they are ultimately to be replaced by the HJT-16 jet trainer Kiran, a model of which will possess a ground attack capability. The conflict with China caused most of the project's design team to be transferred to priority work on the HF-24 fighter, but major assembly of the prototype Kiran was begun in November 1963 and the first flight took place on 4 September 1964. The first 24 preproduction models were produced before the end of 1966.

The Vampires and the French Ouragans and Mysteres are to be phased out of front-line service as the HF-24 Mk 1 Marut fighter becomes available. The first four Mk 1's were handed over to the IAF at Bangalore on 10 May 1964, and a three-squadron 'batch' of the supersonic MK 1A version is being produced, which is

[12] *Flight*, 27 December 1962, p. 998.
[13] Minister of Defence Production K. Raghuramaiah, *LSD*, 3d Series, vol. 12, 21 January 1963, col. 5427.
[14] *Hindu*, 11 November 1962. Indonesia's sale of these aircraft was probably motivated by a desire to dispose of obsolete equipment rather than by any sympathy with India's difficulties.

powered by the HAL-made Bristol Orpheus 703 Reheat engine.[15] As an apparent interim measure pending the availability of the Mk 1A's in quantity, India acquired additional Hunters from Britain.

More Canberra light bombers and reconnaissance aircraft were also obtained from Britain. No decision seems to have been made to date, however, regarding the future of this arm.

The manner in which the fighter arm was to be re-equipped was for some time the subject of apparent indecision by Indian officials and speculation by foreign observers. During the border war, IAF officers reportedly sounded out United States authorities on the possibility of obtaining aircraft with a performance roughly comparable to the F-104G.[16] Feelers were also put out to Britain and France.[17] A plan to purchase a 'lot' of Mirages was not pursued because the price demanded by France was 'obviously' too much.[18] Indian officials were also reported to be looking for an aircraft suitable for close support work like the McDonnell F-101 Voodoo.[19]

India's major interest was in the supersonic F-104's, however, and the government persisted in its efforts to acquire such aircraft despite Western convictions that India had no immediate need for this high-performance weapons system. From 'an early date' the IAF and Indian Defence Ministry reportedly regarded the joint Indian–Commonwealth–United States air exercises held in India in November 1963 'as an opportunity to show that without supersonic fighters the problems of Indian defence against air attack are insoluble'.[20] Speculation on the progress of their efforts continued into mid-1964 and included the possibility that India would receive all-weather F-102 interceptors simultaneously with American provision of these aircraft to Pakistan.[21] The United States was also

---

[15] *Flight*, 6 August 1964, p. 235.
[16] Cecil Brownlow, *Aviation Week*, 19 November 1962, p. 38.
[17] K. C. Khanna, *Times of India*, 1 August 1964.
[18] See statement by T. T. Krishnamachari at a Washington press conference. 23 May 1964, cited in *The Nation*, 24 May 1964.
[19] *Aviation Week*, 26 November 1962, p. 31.
[20] Delhi correspondent in *The Times*, 20 November 1963. India argues that supersonic fighters are needed, since an early warning system cannot be completely effective because of the interference from the Himalayas. The United States and Britain are of the view that several squadrons would be of little value, that the creation of an effective force is prohibitively expensive, and that, in any event, India would ultimately depend upon Western air support.
[21] H. R. Vohra, *Times of India*, 2 February 1964.

believed to be willing to make available three to five squadrons of F-5I Skyray or F-5B Freedom Fighters equipped with Sidewinder missiles.[22]

Possible direct Indian purchase of some F-104's or the establishment of a F-104 assembly or production plant in India was also reported. With the apparent concurrence of the U.S. State Department, Lockheed representatives reportedly took the initiative to hold talks with senior officials of the Indian ministries of Defence, Finance, and Defence Production in New Delhi in late February 1964. Lockheed, according to the report, proposed to establish a production unit in India for the F-104 or a comparable aircraft; if that was not acceptable to the Indian government, an alternative was the sale to India of a certain number of F-104's on a commercial basis.[23] In May 1964 it was reported that India had proposed a $200 million American-built plant to manufacture F-104's in India, the project being preferred by 'some' Indian ministers to the MIG project. Although the report stated that Washington was unlikely to extend grants for such a project, American authorities ostensibly had under consideration an assembly plant to be financed with a 20-year credit from the Export–Import Bank in the event the MIG project failed.[24]

That particular project had made little real headway, and there were sufficient grounds for pessimism concerning its future. An American correspondent had reported from New Delhi on 17 December 1963 'the impending abandonment' of the project for the reason that cost estimates had jumped from the initial estimate of $143 million to a 'current working figure of $336 million' and that Moscow had to date proved unwilling to make the MIG-21 an all-weather aircraft with an expanded radius of action.[25]

The Indian Defence Ministry had issued an immediate denial, claiming that 'the project is proceeding according to plan',[26] but it

[22] See Jack Raymond in *New York Times*, 12 May 1964; Easwar Sagar in *Hindu*, 20 May 1964; Press Trust of India report in *Times of India*, 12 May 1964; H. R. Vohra in *ibid.*, 8 June 1964. India also apparently made enquiries about, but no specific requests for, Britain's Firestreak missile and America's Sidewinder.

[23] Political correspondent in *Hindustan Times*, 4 March 1964. Lockheed had reportedly made similar approaches in 1961 and 1962; see K. Rangaswami in *Hindu*, 7 July 1962, and George Wilson in *Aviation Week*, 5 November 1962, p. 26.

[24] *Washington Post*, 19 May 1964.

[25] Selig Harrison in *ibid.*, 18 December 1963.

[26] Cited, *Hindu Weekly Rview*, 23 December 1963.

was reported in a leading Indian daily on 26 January 1964 that India was not going to acquire MIG's because the cost of establishing the complex of factories was prohibitive and American aircraft were preferred by the IAF.[27] The same paper reported on 5 March, however, that Anglo-American reluctance to give India high-performance aircraft had caused even the Air Force to veer around to the view that the MIG project, despite its obvious shortcomings, was the only political and military solution. Defence Minister Chavan included three squadrons of F-104's in the list of defence requirements he submitted to the United States government in May 1964, while India made what would seem to have been final efforts to obtain a favourable arrangement with Moscow to enable the MIG project to proceed. The six MIG-21's which arrived during the spring of 1964 under a thick cloak of Soviet-inspired secrecy were devoid of such essential equipment as fire-control radar and had meagre armament and a severly limited combat radius. Russian technical experts assigned to the project apparently showed indifference to Indian pressure for speed, and New Delhi was unsuccessful in its efforts to persuade the Soviet government to agree to certain modifications in the design.

Sometime during the summer, for reasons known only to senior Soviet leaders but probably related to the virtually irrevocable split with Peking, Moscow indicated its willingness to be much more co-operative on the MIG project. When an Indian defence mission visited Moscow in September, an agreement was signed several hours before President Radhakrishnan arrived to begin his state visit. Russia agreed to provide: technical aid and plant to facilitate the establishment of MIG factories by the end of 1965; 38 more MIG-21's (in addition to the six promised in 1962 but as yet undelivered) incorporating the modifications requested by India; and components for the initial assembly scheme in India which would presumably include some of the 44 planes promised. The Soviet authorities also agreed to keep India informed of subsequent improvements in the design and equipment of the MIG-21.[28] According to one report, a total of 450 MIG-21's were planned for India.[29]

[27] H. R. Vohra, *Times of India*.

[28] See statement by Defence Minister Chavan in the Lok Sabha on 21 September 1964.

[29] The *Sunday Telegraph* (London) cited in *The Australian*, 28 September 1964.

The MIG-21 is conceived as the standard interceptor for the IAF through the 1970's, but production of the economical Gnat is being continued for operational squadrons. The future of the HF-24 Mk 2 remains uncertain.

NAVAL PROGRAMME

Financial stringency and priorities limit the present naval programme largely to replacement of obsolete vessels. After the border conflict, the Indian government indicated an interest in possible Swedish or Japanese collaboration in the construction of frigates at Mazagon Docks, but the 'interest' would appear to have been little more than a bargaining counter designed to stimulate the British government into responding to Indian requests for long-term credits to cover the external costs of the desired 'Leander' class frigate project. During his visit to Britain in November 1964, Defence Minister Chavan accepted the British government's offer of a special defence credit totalling £4,700,000 ($13,160,000) to cover the external costs over the next four years of the construction of three 'Leander' class frigates and to consider further aid for the project. The keel of the first frigate was laid down in mid-1966, and the vessel is expected to be completed by 1971.[30]

During his visit, Chavan expressed the hope that at least two frigates could be made available immediately. He requested the loan of three Daring class destroyers on the understanding that they would be returned in any emergency affecting Britain. A British counteroffer of three 'Weapon' class destroyers from its mothball fleet [31] was declined, the Indian government evidently still hopeful that London would prove more accommodating in future. The United States is understood to have been unresponsive to an Indian request for three destroyer replacements. In the face of these Anglo-American attitudes, and with some reluctance, based on technical factors, India accepted a Soviet offer of frigates in an agreement signed in 1965.

The Indian government accepted the long-standing Naval proposal for a submarine arm, to be started by acquiring a training submarine. Although the British government was initially cautious,

[30] See Navy Day message, 15 December 1964, by Vice-Admiral B. S. Soman, cited in the *Times of India*, 15 December.
[31] Britain only had seven Daring class types in service, and all were fully operational.

it later agreed in principle to provide a submarine for training purposes. In November 1964 Britain offered Chavan a World War II model—the only one it had available for immediate transfer—but the Indian Defence Minister declined such an obsolete unit and accepted instead an alternative offer whereby a Royal Navy submarine would be loaned to India for several months each year. New Delhi took under consideration a British offer of facilities for the construction of an 'Oberon' class type but British terms do not appear to have met with Indian approval. Chavan informed the Lok Sabha on 6 September 1965 that an agreement had been concluded with the Soviet government for the provision of submarines, but he declined to give further details.

Three seaward patrol boats and two minesweepers are under construction locally, and a modern fleet replenishment tanker is to be obtained—seemingly by external purchase. The shipboard air complement of the carrier *Vikrant* has been augmented by ten more Sea Hawk jet fighter-bombers and by several additional Alouette III helicopters. Further base facilities are being developed to extend the operational capabilities of the fleet: a naval base at Marmagoa (which includes a naval air station at Dabolim), a major naval base and dockyard at Vizakhapatnam, and a naval establishment at Port Blair in the Andaman Islands. A British military correspondent has been cited as stating that additional naval facilities may also be developed in the Nicobar Islands, another Indian-owned group about 250 miles south of the Andamans on which there is already an all-weather airstrip.[32]

Adjustments have been made in the scope and nature of the various paramilitary organizations, which involve the cancellation or severe restriction of the military aspects of the schemes. The Territorial Army has been reorganized to correct deficiencies revealed during the border conflict with China. A million-strong Home Guard has been set up to serve as an auxiliary to the police and to aid local communities in emergencies; the Lok Sahayak Sena scheme was rendered superfluous by the Home Guards and was thereupon dissolved. The Auxiliary Cadet Corps was abolished in April 1965, but the National Cadet Corps has been expanded and NCC training was introduced as a compulsory subject in the curriculum for male college students in the academic session beginning July–October 1963. Defence Minister Chavan informed

---

[32] Anthony Mann in the *Daily Telegraph*, cited in *Dawn*, 22 March 1964.

the Lok Sabha on 10 December 1965 that the government was also considering a scheme of selective conscription to the armed forces, designed to discipline the younger generation and make it conscious of its responsibilities for defence.

DEFENCE INDUSTRIES

The border war caused a marked upsurge in the nature and scope of production in the ordnance factories.[33] Contracts for certain items were allocated to civil and private manufacturers for the first time. New lines of production included Ishapore semi-automatic rifles, a three-inch pack howitzer of Indian design, the Brandt heavy mortar from France, 7.62 mm. ammunition, ammunition for the Brandt mortar and the three-inch pack howitzer, 75 mm. light tank shells and light tank high-explosive shells, 3.5-inch anti-tank rockets, anti-aircraft guns, and improved Sterling carbines. Bulk manufacture of electrically fired ammunition began in India for the first time in 1964–65.

A plant for the manufacture of 30 mm. aircraft ammunition was set up with British technical assistance at Khamaria (near Jabalpore) in March 1964, and a clothing factory, first conceived in 1961, was established at Avadi and began the production of parachutes in October 1963. The Chandigarh field cable factory commenced mass production in February 1964. The capacity of Praga Tools at Secunderabad to manufacture small arms was increased, and the cordite factory at Aruvankadu was augmented by a new plant, commissioned in March 1964, to produce semi-solvent propellants for rockets. It is also proposed to establish a vehicle factory for the manufacture of one-ton and three-ton trucks for the Army.

The prototype of the first medium tank was completed in early 1963, and the first unit rolled off the Avadi heavy-vehicles assembly line on 29 December 1965. Despite rumours of possible French or Russian collaboration in a light tank project at Avadi, an offer by Vickers–Armstrong to design a light tank to Indian specifications appears to have the 'inside track' and may be taken up in the near future.

---

[*] The Minister for Defence Production, A. M. Thomas, stated in a written reply, tabled in the Lok Sabha on 14 September 1964, that there were then 31 ordnance factories and other production establishments employing 172,000 personnel.

India's aircraft production facilities were subjected to the scrutiny of a special committee appointed in March 1963 under the chairmanship of J. R. D. Tata, head of Air India International and a prominent industrialist.[34] The committee surveyed the requirements of aircraft and ancillary electronic equipment required by the armed forces and submitted its recommendations to the government in April. Details of the report were not made public, but they are believed to have included a proposal to scrap the MIG project and purchase Western supersonic fighters and to replace the Avro project with a production line for the Caribou II turboprop transport.[35] After some consideration of the Caribou, the government apparently concluded that it was too deeply committed to the Avro project, since it announced that production facilities were actually to be expanded.[36] The government likewise appears to have regarded itself as too firmly committed to the MIG project, both financially and politically, to terminate it on purely practical grounds. In apparent accord with the committee's recommendation, however, the government amalgamated all the aircraft manufacturing units in India into a single state-owned undertaking, called Hindustan Aeronautics India Limited, designed to streamline production and effect economy in the utilization of men and material.

There is no indication that the government at any time seriously considered terminating the HF-24 Mk 2 project, but little progress has been made because of the lack of a firm decision regarding a power plant. Efforts to produce a suitable engine in India have continued,[37] and, after much speculation, a collaboration agreement was signed with the United Arab Republic in Cairo on 2 November 1964 whereby Egypt was to provide the engine and India the airframe of a Mach 2 fighter. The issue was confused, however, by

---

[34] The committee, which included senior representatives of the Army, IAF, and Defence Science Establishment, was reportedly set up by the Ministry of Economic and Defence Co-ordination without prior consultation with the Defence Ministry and to the latter's consternation. See Prem Chopra in *The Statesman*, 7 and 21 July 1963.

[35] *Aviation Week*, 17 June 1963, p. 39.

[36] *Ibid.*, 5 August 1963, p. 26. Clearly contradicting official claims of an expanded scheme, however, is the fact that, whereas the original plan was for 130 units, the IAF had ordered only 29 by May 1966.

[37] It is understood that Bristol Siddeley is co-operating with the Indian government in modifying the Orpheus 703 power plant by adding boosters from the Soviet VK-7 to achieve a substantial increase in thrust and a barely supersonic version of the HF-24 designated the HF-24 Mk 1B.

apparent Indian hopes that the United States and Britain would provide aid for the HF-24 project. Experts from the USAF research and development centre at Dayton, Ohio, and representatives of Rolls Royce visited India in July 1964 to investigate ways and means of improving the performance and rate of production of the HF-24 but apparently concluded that the project would require some years and considerable Western aid in design, tooling and finance to mature into a supersonic weapons system.[38] With Indo-Soviet agreement on the MIG project in September 1964, the likelihood of Western aid for the HF-24 project virtually ended, given the Western view that two supersonic aircraft projects were greatly beyond poverty-striken India's needs and resources.

India's future ordnance requirements have been assessed by the Directorate of Planning and Co-ordination, with the assistance of an American consulting firm, D. Little, Inc. Modernization of the existing ordnance factories is scheduled for the 1964–69 period at an estimated cost of Rs 30 crores, which includes a foreign exchange component of Rs 15 crores.

The first phase of the expansion scheme was intended to establish six new factories, but the plan was heavily dependent upon foreign assistance, which to date (May 1967) has been offered for only three of the factories. The United States provided a complete small arms ammunition plant (the St. Louis Ammunition Factory), which was formally opened at Varangaon, near Bhusawal, on 15 October 1964, and assisted in the establishment of the Ambajahari Engineering Factory, which will produce heavy artillery shells. Britain provided aid for the Rs 16 crore Bhandara Filling Factory, which began production in January 1965. To date, however, India has received no offers of aid for the Panvel Propellants Factory, the Burla Explosives Factory, or the small arms factory at Tiruchirapalli. The Indian government decided to go ahead with the Tiruchirapalli project despite the consequent pressure on the country's chronically weak foreign exchange reserves, and the plant went into production in 1966. It has, however, accepted the advice of American experts that the Panvel and Burla plants were impractical as their 'investment–output' ratio was high and their civilian use in times of general peace was very limited. New Delhi plans to stockpile the necessary explosives and propellants by importing Rs 8 crores of these items and increasing production at the Bhanadara factory—an eco-

[38] *Times of India*, 17 August 1964.

nomical policy, given the estimated Rs 60 crore cost of the Panvel and Burla projects, of which Rs 21 crores would have had to be found in foreign exchange.

No details of the second phase of the ordnance expansion scheme are known to the writer, but it is understood that self-sufficiency for the Army is proposed.

India's defence research organization is being further expanded. New laboratories of Instruments Research and Development Establishment and an Armament Research Laboratory have been established.

COMMUNICATIONS

Border communications are being substantially extended. In mid-1963, the BRDO approved a programme to construct 3,000 miles of new roads and improve 3,000 miles of existing roads.[39] A long-deferred Rs 25 crore project to link the Leh-Srinagar road (itself being improved with American aid) with another connecting Manali to Upshi and Kulu in eastern Ladakh was sanctioned in late 1963. A 700-mile road is being constructed at a cost of about Rs 100 crores from Bareilly in western Uttar Pradesh to Amingaon in Assam along the Himalayan foothills. The main road connecting Manali to Keylong across Rohtang Pass has been widened for use by trucks, and a new motorable road to link Leh and Chushul has been built some distance back from the old lateral road, which, though still in use, is very vulnerable to Chinese activity in the event of renewed hostilities. New airfields are being constructed in the border areas, the United States having assisted in the construction of a military airfield at Leh. The Tezpur–North Lakhimpur road has been improved for heavy traffic, and the Hindustan–Tibet road is nearing completion. By January 1965, the first phase of the North Sikkim highway, a 47-mile road linking Gangtok and Sinhik, had been completed by the CPWD and opened to traffic. An intensive development programme has been launched in the far-flung and sparsely populated areas of Uttar Pradesh, Himachal Pradesh, Punjab, Assam, and NEFA; the latter area was transferred from the External Affairs Ministry to the Home Ministry in July 1965. India is meeting the entire estimated Rs 9 crore cost of the

---

[39] See statement by Defence Minister Chavan in the Lok Sabha on 9 September 1963.

128-mile Sounauli-Pokhara road project in Nepal, scheduled for completion in late 1968.

Significance of Defence Programme

India's post-1962 defence programme was based upon four main presumptions: the People's Republic of China posed the major threat to Indian security; a Pakistani threat could materialize at any time; Sino-Pakistan collusion against India was conceivable;. and India required a credible military sanction for her diplomacy. The limited 1965 conflict with Pakistan did not unduly affect any of these presumptions, but the Indian government can be expected to pursue its military goals with even greater vigour than before, given Pakistan's willingness to engage India's far more powerful military forces and China's attempts to capitalize on the war (p. 190). The timetable for the various parts of India's defence programme may, however, be set back by the heavy cost of the war and the expense of replacing equipment damaged or destroyed during the conflict, by the American suspension of 'nonlethal' military aid between September 1965 and March 1966, and by her continued suspension of 'lethal' military aid, imposed on 8 September 1965. In view of India's economic afflictions, aggravated by severe drought in 1966–67, her ultimate attainment in defence may well depend upon the extent to which the developed countries of the Western and Soviet blocs are prepared to help India achieve her ambitious economic and military aspirations.

CONCLUSIONS

There is no basis for the view that the policies of a sovereign India during the 1947–62 period constituted a unique approach to national security distinct from the traditional one of power politics. Given India's geographical contiguity to the Soviet Union and China and her need for the greatest number of sources from which economic aid might be obtained, India's leaders opted for a policy of nonalignment toward the two power blocs. Such a posture was designed to avoid giving provocation to the Communist powers and to preclude India's automatic involvement in any East–West conflict. It was also regarded as the best contribution that a weak, but supposedly potentially powerful, India could make towards maintaining the balance of power between the Soviet and Western blocs. Panch sheel and the 'peace area' were natural corollaries to this stance—all designed to protect India against the rivalries of the major powers.

With the country's financial limitations, India's military liabilities were confined to what may be called the domestic military requirement of defending the frontiers against a minor power with added provision for aid to the civil power in maintaining law and order. In the event of an attack by a major power, the Indian government proceeded on the premise that external aid would be rendered well-nigh axiomatic by the desire of each of the power blocs to prevent India's vast resources from falling under the control of the opposing bloc. The only serious military problem appeared to be Pakistan in the northwest and her subordinate authorities in Azad Kashmir. The assessment of this threat and the operational plan conceived to meet it were basically similar to the 'Outline Plan of Operations 1938', which had been prepared to meet a possible Afghan and tribal threat. The contingency of a serious Chinese attack in the Himalayan region was virtually dismissed even after 1959, but the orientation of strategy against Pakistan remained largely unchanged up to the eve of the Sino-Indian border conflict in October 1962.

India's response to the Chinese occupation of Tibet in 1950–51 bore some resemblance to the policy adopted by Britain towards China's attempt to reassert her control in Tibet in 1906–11. India recognized the legality of the Chinese action, but, though she granted asylum to the Dalai Lama and other Tibetan refugees, she did not permit them to carry on political activities while resident in India. While good relations were desired with China, prudence dictated that India would have to strengthen her position in the Himalayan kingdoms and along the Indo-Tibetan frontier against possible Chinese aggrandisement. Nepal, Bhutan, and Sikkim were accordingly brought into intimate treaty relationship with India, and measures were undertaken to promote social, economic and political progress in these kingdoms. India undertook more comprehensive policing and administration of the border areas contiguous to Tibet.

The similarities between the Himalayan policies of Britain and a sovereign India should not, however, be overdrawn. Britain's modest and economical response to the Chinese re-entry into Tibet in 1906–11 was sufficient to preserve her position in the area, but Indian power and influence in the Himalayan region suffered progressive erosion during the early 1950's. There were several reasons. Britain faced a militarily impotent and decadent Manchu China which collapsed from internal stresses, while the Nehru government had to contend with a resurgent Chinese state of some permanency and possessed of a large, if ill-equipped, military machine. In the first decade of the century, with the prevailing state of military technology, the British rulers of India were able to draw comfort from the Himalayan mountain mass; by 1950, technological developments had rendered the Himalayas of doubtful value as a barrier against an attack from the north or northeast. The armed forces of imperial Britain had posed a deterrent to Chinese aggression, while those of independent India were relatively much less significant and were, moreover, deployed against Pakistan in the northwest.

In formulating his country's policies towards China's Himalayan postures, Nehru failed to fully appreciate the fact that the policies of the former British government would no longer suffice in the radically altered geopolitics. This failure was compounded by other errors of judgment. Nehru mistakenly persisted in the view that China valued Indian goodwill too much to risk losing it for a few square miles of Himalayan territory; Chinese inroads in the Himalayan region thus went without serious challenge until the point had been reached at which neither government could make real concessions, unilateral or bilateral, without loss of prestige and, in India's case at least, serious internal repercussions. Nehru relinquished India's inherited treaty rights in Tibet without even seeking to acquire some sort of equivalent. He hesitated to take firm countermeasures in the Himalayas for fear of provoking Peking, even though Peking appeared to act without any similar inhibition. Nehru's actual measures, once undertaken, were so cloaked in secrecy as to have minimal deterrent effects; his generally passive response to China appeared to have the effect of encouraging, rather than deterring, that country's rulers.

For the Nehru government, as for all governments, the primacy of the national self-interest was a central determinant of policy. While urging others to settle disputes by negotiation, the Indian government showed no similar willingness to subject its claims to mediation or arbitration. Hugh Tinker has written that Gandhi induced the government to pay Pakistan a large sum owing to it after partition, 'have been utterly barren of any act of Gandhian compromise and reconciliation on the part of the Government of India'.[1] On India's attitude towards Kashmir, Goa, and the border dispute with China, a leading Irish newspaper commented with insight in mid-1962:

On the subject of Kashmir, to which Pakistan has an arguable claim, Mr Nehru refuses both a plebiscite and a conference. On Goa, where India has a good case if not a watertight one, he chose the unilateral decision of military occupation. On the Chinese border dispute, where India is one hundred per cent in the right, he is ready to grasp at any straw to bring the aggressor to the negotiating table. It is difficult to avoid the conclusion that what Mr Nehru has he holds, what he can obtain without trouble he takes and what he has taken from him by superior force he considers negotiable even when it is his in all justice.[2]

The ambivalence underlying India's entire approach to disputes is further evidenced by the statement offered by an official Indian publication in defence of the Goa action: 'A nation has the ultimate right to use force in situations where methods of peace and persuasion have failed and where justice and one's own rights de-

---

[1] 'Magnificent Failure? The Gandhian Ideal in India After Sixteen Years', *International Affairs*, April 1964, p. 274.
[2] *Irish Independent* (Dublin), 9 August 1962.

manded positive action'.³ Peking could use the same argument to even greater effect.

Indian military policy was one of continual and usually unsatisfactory compromises between what was politically desirable, financially possible, and militarily prudent.

The Indian Navy represented a compromise between self-reliance and explicit dependence upon friendly powers. A navy powerful enough to dominate the Indian Ocean against a major power was beyond India's financial capacities, but her continued explicit reliance upon the Royal Navy for naval defence was neither politically possible nor wise, as India and Australia both learned to their regret at the fall of Singapore in 1942. Independent India developed a small task force large enough to give her local superiority against any neighbouring country in the strategic arc from Suez to Singapore and so constituted as to facilitate co-operation with Western navies to defend their mutual interests in the Indian Ocean against Soviet-bloc submarines in any general war. To some extent, the Indian Navy assumed the functions of the former East Indies squadron of the Royal Navy. Its development programme was considerably affected by financial stringency, but to no apparent extent by Pakistani or Chinese postures.

The Indian Air Force was developed as a balanced tactical air force having local superiority against any neighbouring country save China. The prestige attached to modern aircraft clearly placed the service in a very favourable position for budgetary allocations. The Hunter acquisition and the MIG scheme attest to the primacy of prestige over the objections by the Finance Ministry and the budget-starved Army and Navy.

The Army's role during the 1947–62 period was consistent with its pre-World War II responsibilities of internal security, watch and ward on the frontiers (primarily in Kashmir but also in Nagaland from 1955 and in NEFA and Ladakh from 1959), and defence against a minor power. The regular professional standing Army was retained, together with conventional armaments; contrary to sound military policy—but consistent with financial stringency—effectiveness tended to be subordinated to size.

In view of the complacency with which India's political leaders viewed their country's security during most of the 1947–62 period

³ *Goa Regains Freedom* (Sydney: Information Service of India, December 1961).

and in the context of acute poverty, the military programme seemed to reflect a belief that a sizeable military establishment was required for reasons of prestige and prudence in a power-conscious world. A *Round Table* commentator charged in 1957 that 'India is doing what all others do, nothing worse and nothing better. Only persistent claims to be doing better make the affair look worse. And the fact that India is so poor makes it much more painful too'.[4] The *Times* wrote in 1961 that 'India's growing military strength may be as much a symbol of desire for international status as a reaction to any specific threat'.[5] Also, as John Maddox and Leonard Beaton observed, referring to the Nehru government's stern anti-nuclear line:

> The skeptic about Indian sincerity in these protestations may point to two tendencies of Indian policy: the high priority given to the atomic energy programme based on complete self-sufficiency in all the related technologies, and the consistent opposition of the Indian Government in the International Atomic Energy Agency to safeguards in peaceful nuclear sharing. These certainly suggest an anxiety to have the option on producing a bomb.[6]

Noting further that the Indian atomic energy programme proceeded at heavy cost in scarce money and scientific and technical personnel, Beaton and Maddox concluded that 'the most reasonable inference is that Mr Nehru, advised by Dr Bhabha, has decided to give the country the option to produce a nuclear device in 1963 in case this should become politically or militarily necessary'.[7]

In the aftermath of the border conflict with China, the creation and maintenance of an imposing military establishment has become an obsession in India—a feeling heightened by the minor 'war' waged against Pakistan in September 1965. The Defence ministry has been catapulted from relative obscurity to become perhaps the most attractive post in government next to that of the Prime Minister. The position of the armed forces has changed dramatically. The Indian peoples' growing awareness of the feelings and needs of the military make them and their elected representatives more solicitous of military (particularly Army) views. The manner in

[4] Vol. 47 (1956-57), p. 393.
[5] 29 August 1961.
[6] *The Spread of Nuclear Weapons* (London: Chatto and Windus for the Institute for Strategic Studies, 1962), p. 136.
[7] *Ibid.*, p. 141. Dr. H. J. Bhabha, an outstanding physicist, was killed in the crash of an Air India jet liner in 1966.

which India has responded to the altered strategic situation is apparent in the prominence now being accorded to military views. A useful comparison can be made of current Indian policy and the course adopted by Pakistan in 1947.

In 1947, Pakistani military planners were faced with an uneasy ceasefire in Kashmir, a fairly long and exposed frontier in the Punjab and Rajasthan (not to speak of East Bengal), an historical problem on the North–West Frontier with restless tribals, and an Afghan neighbour with stated claims to territories beyond the Durand Line. In the Pakistani view, their larger Indian neighbour had seized territory that rightfully belonged to Pakistan and such a seizure could not be accorded legitimacy. Pakistan's relative weakness and vulnerability precluded any attempt to eject Indian forces from the portions of Kashmir under their occupation, but military preparations had to be undertaken both to deter further 'aggression' and to permit Pakistan to negotiate outstanding disputes with India from a position of at least reasonable strength. Pakistan accordingly deployed its army and air force to face India, taking the risk of leaving light semi-military forces to police her North–West Frontier and relying upon diplomacy and a stronger military stance to deter overt aggression from that quarter. To reduce the military imbalance with India while proceeding with her economic development, Pakistan was able to secure massive economic and military aid and a formal military alliance with the United States.

After the 1962 border conflict with China, Indian military planners faced a similar predicament—an uneasy ceasefire in Ladakh and NEFA, a long and vulnerable frontier with a more powerful neighbour with stated designs on Indian territory, and the 'historical' problem posed by Pakistan. India could not contend with a simultaneous attack from both these states, as a maximum effort would be required to contain even a limited Chinese assault, but such collusion was not, in any case, seriously entertained by India's military leadership. It was felt that Pakistan's leaders would not sacrifice their country's military and economic ties with the West for any short-term gains obtained in collusion with China at India's expense. Defence planning was therefore focused upon the threat posed by China, although the strategic situation resulted in a convenient deployment of forces which permitted of an adequate defence of the country's borders with Pakistan against any threat from that quarter. Developing and maintaining sizeable military forces, however, required larger doses of economic aid from external sources and maximum amounts of military aid. Fortunately for India, both the Soviet and Western blocs were prepared to advance such aid without demanding any realignment of India's internal or external policies. Contrary to popular Indian views, this achievement was due primarily to favorable extraneous factors and only superficially to India's particular form of nonalignment and diplomatic expertise.

The brief 'war' with Pakistan in September 1965 did not result in any fundamental change in policies decided upon during the 1962–65 period. It confirmed Pakistan's vulnerability to Indian military pressure and the relative security of Indian territory in any isolated and limited conflict with the neighbouring Muslim state. The declaration of the American government that it would intervene if China sought to exploit Indo-Pakistan hostilities to further its own ambitions provides India with reasonable security against a two-front war. Far from causing Indian defence planners to revert to their pre-1962 obsession with Pakistani intentions, the 'war' with Pakistan in September 1965 quite possibly eased the concern with Pakistan's military capabilities and resulted in a more confident and realistic assessment of the supposed 'threat' from the northwest, thereby focusing attention on the only real military threat to India —that from China. While Indian politicians will undoubtedly continue to profess serious concern regarding Pakistani intentions, the Indian military will focus their attention on Himalayan defences. Notwithstanding efforts by the Indian government to utilise the spectre of a massive Chinese onslaught on India to lever increased economic and military aid from the United States—efforts that have not met with a sympathetic hearing in Washington—the Indian military conceive of, and are planning for, at most another limited conflict.

India's current defence planning is not, however, limited to protecting herself against China and Pakistan but indicates a deliberate intention to provide a credible military sanction for the country's ambitious, but previously 'toothless', diplomacy. For this reason, the Indian military programme will probably not be unduly influenced by the state of relations with either of her two unfriendly neighbours in the foreseeable future. Thus, the defence plan was described in 1964 as having 'little or nothing to do with the [Chinese] border dispute as such and will be primarily concerned with India's larger role in South-East Asia in relation particularly [but not exclusively] with Communist China'.[8] In obvious reference to the balance of power thesis, the Indian High Commissioner to Britain, M. C. Chagla, argued in early 1963 that India's decision to expand her Army was 'not only in our interests but in the interests of the whole of South-East Asia and, ultimately, of democracy and peace'.[9] The decision to construct air and naval facilities in the Andaman and Nicobar islands was interpreted by one leading Indian daily as indicating that 'a decision has been taken to play a bigger role in the defence of South-East Asia'.[10] The same decision was defended by Rear Admiral S. G. Karmakar (Flag Officer, Bombay) as due to the need to guard the Indian Ocean and its approaches against all eventualities in view of China's [alleged] ability to cripple Indian trade by a surprise submarine attack from a single base in Southeast Asia.[11] Although the location of such a base was not stated, it is understood that Indian officials were at this time alive to the possibilities of Sino-Indonesian collusion at some future date. Also noteworthy is the declaration by the Chief of Naval Staff, Vice-Admiral A. K. Chatterji, in August 1966 that the Indian Navy is to be doubled in strength within ten years, and his accompanying emphasis upon the need for a second aircraft carrier —and for a fleet for each of India's coasts.[12]

Doubts about the adequacy of India's current conventional defence programme have been expressed in some quarters, however, in the context of Peking's concerted efforts to develop a nuclear bomb, as attested by the explosion of a series of nuclear devices, the first on 16 October 1964. One section of Indian opinion argues that India must develop an independent nuclear deterrent regardless of cost. Another section views the cost of such a programme as prohibitive and favours securing guarantees of protection against nuclear attack from the established nuclear powers—the United States, Britain, France, and the Soviet Union. A third school of thought, which includes Krishna Menon, is promoting the view that the situation requires neither Indian possession of the 'bomb' nor attempts to secure specific guarantees against Chinese nuclear blackmail from the established nuclear powers, but that efforts should be concen-

[8] *Times of India*, 29 April 1964. See also *Hindu*, 25 May 1963.
[9] Statement at a Bombay press conference, 2 January 1963. Cited, *Times of India*, 3 January 1963.
[10] *Hindu*, 6 April 1963.
[11] Cited, *Times of India*, 1 April 1964.
[12] Cited, *ibid.*, 20 August 1966.

trated on mobilizing world opinion against nuclear proliferation and for disarmament.

The question poses a dilemma for Indian leaders which, though common to most states having similar aspirations, is particularly painful for a country plagued by severe poverty and inhibited by the adamant and self-righteous stand against nuclear weaponry that has hitherto characterized Indian policy.

At the present stage, India's development of a nuclear device would require use of the Trombay reactor, installed on an island in Bombay harbor. The donor country, Canada, could not consent to such use of the installation without compromising her policy on reactors, and a unilateral Indian decision would seriously strain not only Indo-Canadian relations but also India's relations with other countries of the West and, quite likely, the Soviet Union. Such a decision would require India to renounce her adherence to the test-ban treaty, which would raise doubts about India's bona fides on any matter. Furthermore, such a programme would impose a heavy burden on the country's available technical and financial resources and would probably result in a refusal by the developed countries to cover the required diversion of resources through increased aid allotments, and even a possible cutback in current aid, with serious consequences for India's economic plans.

The mere explosion of several nuclear devices would not have nearly the impact of China's first nuclear detonation, nor would it necessarily enhance Indian prestige among the increasingly more sophisticated nations of Afro-Asia, several of which could probably develop a similar capability with less strain on their economies. The most likely effect of an Indian nuclear blast would be to provoke other Afro-Asian states into undertaking at least symbolic nuclear programmes, either to demonstrate their own technical competence or, as in Pakistan's case, out of fear of being subjected to Indian nuclear blackmail over disputed Kashmir.

The next logical step of the Indian government would be to develop a tactical nuclear capability, a costly undertaking. Although the IAF's small force of Canberra Mk 8's could carry a small atomic bomb, their vulnerability to attack from a modern air defence system would require Indian acquisition of aircraft with at least a limited supersonic performance. India could push the development of the HF-24 Mk 2 or purchase a foreign-made Mach 2 platform, but either would be very costly. The former would probably require extensive foreign technical assistance, and the expense of the latter might be prohibitive, even if countries possessing such aircraft were prepared to make sales, which is by no means certain.

Even if India were able to create a tactical nuclear force, the usefulness of such an independent force would be marginal against the only real military threat, that of China in the Himalayan region. The Chinese heartland is virtually out of reach of aircraft based in India, whereas India's major cities and industrial complexes are acutely vulnerable to air power based in Tibet. Strikes against Chinese bases and communications in Tibet would not compensate for the devastation that would accompany a Chinese nuclear response. In any case it seems unlikely that Chinese leaders would employ nuclear weapons against a neighbour over which its strategic and conventional superiority is so marked. China's main strength for the foreseeable future will be in her reserves of disciplined manpower, and Indian military planners must formulate their policy accordingly, relating it to the country's capabilities. In view of the increasingly chauvinistic tendencies of Indian public opinion, which seems strangely insensitive to the country's severe nonmilitary problems and meagre financial resources, a heavy responsibility devolves upon the political, military, and civil hierarchies to maintain a proper perspective on current and future needs and to establish sensible priorities in the allocation of available resources. A nuclear weapons programme now or in the immediate future would be a serious distortion of the country's needs. Strategy is always a choice between alternatives, and security can never be absolute; like many nations before her, India must learn to live with insecurity. The adjustment will not be easy, but at stake is the very survival of the multi-ethnic state, whose disintegration would have grave consequences for the subcontinent, Asia, and the world at large.

APPENDIXES

Indian Currency

The rupee is divided into 100 equivalent units called naye paise. One lakh equals 100,000 rupees (written Rs 1,00,000). One hundred lakhs equals Rs 10 million or one crore (written Rs 1,00,00,000).

From 1947 until early 1966, the rupee was officially valued at about $0.21 American, or about 4.78 to the dollar. In early June 1966 the rupee was devalued from 4.76 to the dollar to 7.5.

APPENDIX I

a. Indian Central Government Revenue and Expenditure [a]
(in 1,000 million rupees)

	1950	1951	1952	1953	1954	1955	1956	1957	1958	1959	1960	1961	1962
1. Current revenue	8.03	9.17	8.44	8.51	9.09	10.28	11.66	13.22	13.90	15.20	16.83	18.71	20.75
2. Current expenditure	6.59	6.89	7.11	7.35	7.76	8.58	9.58	11.20	12.00	12.87	14.09	15.63	19.12
Civil	3.71	3.88	4.06	4.35	4.62	5.12	5.61	6.27	6.99	7.60	8.59	9.27	10.49
Defence	1.88	1.97	1.98	2.09	2.10	2.03	2.26	2.93	2.92	2.83	2.97	3.31	5.21
3. Defence as a percentage of current expenditure	29.0	28.6	27.9	28.5	25.8	23.7	23.6	26.2	24.3	22.0	21.1	21.1	27.7

[a] The figures represent 1,000 million rupees and were obtained from the United Nations' *Year Book of National Statistics*.

b. Defence as a Percentage of Expenditure for 1957–59 [a]

United States	9.8	Communist China	4.4	Pakistan	3.0
Yugoslavia	9.0	West Germany	3.7	Turkey	2.6
Burma	7.3	Norway	3.4	INDIA	2.4
Soviet Union	6.9	Thailand	3.2	New Zealand	2.2
Britain	6.5	Belgium	3.1	Finland	1.7
France	6.2	Switzerland	3.0	Japan	1.6
Sweden	4.7	Australia	3.0	Philippines	1.6
Canada	4.6	Malaya	3.0	Ceylon	1.0
Indonesia	4.6				

[a] Figures represent the average official military expenditure as a percentage of the gross domestic product for the period 1957–59, with several exceptions: the figure for Malaya is for 1957; the figure for Pakistan represents the ratio to net national product, and that for India represents the net domestic product at factor cost.

SOURCE FOR BOTH: *Economic and Social Consequences of Disarmament;* Report of the Secretary-General Transmitting the Study of his Consultative Group (United Nations, New York: Department of Economic and Social Affairs, 1962), E/3593/Rev. 1, annex 2, tables 2–1, 2–2 and 2–3.

APPENDIX II

a. ACTUAL GROSS EXPENDITURE OF EFFECTIVE ARMY AND NONEFFECTIVE ARMY, 1949-50 TO 1962-63
(in lakhs of rupees)

Details	1949-50	1950-51	1951-52	1952-53	1953-54	1954-55	1955-56	1956-57	1957-58
Effective Army									
Main Head 1—Pay and allowances of the Army	32,56	37,71	42,15	44,75	44,89	45,46	44,73	45,11	49,07
Main Head 2—Pay and allowances and miscellaneous expenses of Territorial Army, National Cadet Corps, State Forces, etc.	2,78	8,71	1,28	40	45	64	1,24	1,44	1,54
Main Head 3—Pay and allowances of civilians	23,05	21,74	22,36	22,48	22,96	22,53	22,75	23,04	24,64
Main Head 4—Transportation and miscellaneous	13,76	11,07	12,59	11,93	11,40	12,23	11,67	12,31	14,03
Main Head 5—Expenditure on manufacturing and research establishment	15,27	17,20	20,14	20,43	17,55	16,99	16,74	16,46	17,78
Main Head 6—Purchase and sale of stores	30,06	28,14	33,15	35,65	31,41	29,39	19,95	25,22	37,97
Main Head 7—Expenditure on works	11,42	11,02	15,66	14,94	14,13	13,53	12,90	12,75	11,54
Main Head 8—Charges in England	4,81	11,72	6,30	7,06	5,34	9,71	7,31	16,52	22,88
Main Head 9—Loss or gain by exchange	—	2	1	1	1	2	1	3	4
Total, Effective Army	1,33,71	1,47,33	1,53,64	1,57,65	1,48,14	1,50,50	1,37,30	1,52,88	1,79,49
Noneffective Army, Rewards and Pensions (including State Forces)	7,72	9,06	9,43	9,44	9,62	10,16	13,64	13,76	13,82
Grand Total, Effective and Noneffective	1,41,43	1,56,39	1,63,07	1,67,09	1,57,76	1,60,66	1,50,94	1,66,64	1,93,31

Details	1958-59	1959-60	1960-61	1961-62	1962-63	Revised Estimates 1963-64	Budget Estimates 1964-65
Effective Army							
Main Head 1—Pay and allowances of the Army	52,61	53,50	65,75	69,42	84,84	1,21,52	1,35,99
Main Head 2—Pay and allowances and miscellaneous expenses of Territorial Army, National Cadet Corps, State Forces, etc.	1,84	2,16	3,57	3,84	4,53	9,26	6,15
Main Head 3—Pay and allowances of civilians	25,40	25,92	29,41	25,77	30,59	37,20	40,00
Main Head 4—Transportation and miscellaneous	16,43	15,49	17,76	20,75	30,13	36,03	35,20
Main Head 5—Expenditure on manufacturing and research establishment	19,09	25,56	28,79	43,73	80,65	1,42,50	1,54,40
Main Head 6—Purchase and sale of stores	36,00	29,92	29,51	39,57	83,70	1,71,49	1,77,94
Main Head 7—Expenditure on works	11,65	12,48	13,73	11,96	17,44	26,18	22,76
Main Head 8—Charges in England	4,65	2,22	1,91	2,92	6,59	6,78	10,45
Main Head 9—Loss or gain by exchange	1	—	—	1	1	1	—
Total, Effective Army	1,67,68	1,67,25	1,90,43	2,17,97	3,38,48	5,50,77	5,82,89
Noneffective Army, Rewards and Pensions (including State Force)	13,84	14,69	14,84	18,67	17,94	18,40	21,36
Grand Total, Effective and Noneffective	1,81,52	1,81,94	2,05,27	2,36,64	3,56,42	5,69,17	6,04,25

SOURCE: India, Ministry of Defence, Adjutant General's Branch (Budget).

b. Expenditure of the Navy and Air Force, 1951-52 to 1962-63
(in lakhs of rupees)

Year	Navy			Air Force		
	Revenue	Capital	Total	Revenue	Capital	Total
1951-52	7,66.18	1,27.21	8,93.39	16,02.50	1,11.91	17,14.41
1952-53	8,68.69	1,77.27	10,45.96	15,62.74	1,87.82	17,50.56
1953-54	10,42.62	2,16.18	12,58.80	28,56.61	1,64.26	30,20.87
1954-55	11,08.24	3,94.77	15,03.01	29,73.78	2,02.99	31,76.77
1955-56	12,04.67	7,33.52	19,38.19	30,05.63	2,71.23	32,76.86
1956-57	12,46.61	8,10.87	20,57.48	38,58.50	3,68.14	42,26.64
1957-58	14,16.80	13,31.85	27,48.65	72,74.68	4,32.26	77,06.94
1958-59	16,37.66	15,50.41	31,88.07	77,35.04	3,34.80	80,69.84
1959-60	15,11.12	19,25.50	34,36.62	60,91.20	3,34.47	64,25.67
1960-61	17,66.96	15,24.01	32,90.97	53,19.17	3,87.51	57,06.68
1961-62	20,66.45	4,41.34	25,07.79	54,07.97	4,53.61	58,61.58
1962-63	16,58.16	5,01.95	21,60.11	77,88.10	16,65.09	94,53.19
Total	162,94.16	97,34.88	260,29.04	554,75.92	49,14.09	603,90.01

SOURCE: India, Ministry of Defence.

APPENDIX III

DEFENCE EXPENDITURE OF BRITISH INDIA: SELECTED YEARS [a]
(in crores of rupees)

Year	Expenditures	Year	Expenditures	Defence as Percentage of Total Expenditure
1891	24.1	1937	47.4	54.5
1911	29.3	1938	46.18	54.3
1914	30.7	1939	49.54	52.4
1915	33.4	1940	73.61	64.5
1916	37.5	1941	1103.93	70.6
1917	43.6	1942	214.62	74.3
1918	66.7	1943	358.40	81.5
1919	87.0	1944	395.49	79.7
1920	87.4	1945	360.23	74.3
1921	69.8	1946	207.37	60.4
1923	56.2	1947	86.63	46.8
1931	51.8	1948	146.05	45.5
1932	46.7	1949	148.86	46.9
1936	45.5	1950	164.13	46.7

SOURCES: P. J. Thomas, *The Growth of Federal Finance in India* (Madras: Oxford University Press, 1939), p. 502, for period 1891–1936; R. N. Poduval, *Finance of the Government of India Since 1935* (Delhi: Premier Publishing, 1951), pp. 36–37 for period 1937–50. See also R. N. Bhargava, *The Theory and Working of Union Finance in India* (London: Allen and Unwin), pp. 279–288.

[a] Refers to GOI up to 1921 and to central government thereafter. Because of the changes in financial policy from 1921 comparisons between periods before and after are misleading. Figures after 1947 refer to Indian Union.

APPENDIX IV

NOTES ON BRITISH HIMALAYAN POLICY

British policy in the Himalayan region was directed towards asserting such forms of control as were deemed necessary to maintain tranquillity on the frontiers of the areas over which the Crown exercised paramountcy, and to deny power in, or control of, these areas to any other power.

The expanding Gurkha kingdom in Nepal was defeated in 1814–15. The question of annexation arose but was rejected, and the Treaty of Sagauli signed on 2 December 1815 provided only for Gurkha withdrawal from Sikkim, Kumaon, Garhwal, and the Terai to the west of the Gandak River; acceptance of a British Resident; and agreement to British recruiting of Gurkhas for the army in India. Britain's subsequent strict adherence to a policy of noninterference in Nepali affairs and acceptance of almost total exclusion of Europeans helped maintain a friendly relationship, to the mutual advantage of both governments. Nepalese aid during the Indian Mutiny in 1857 was rewarded by the restoration to Nepal of a large part of the Terai annexed in 1816; Nepal's support to the Younghusband military expedition to Lhasa (Tibet) in 1904 was at least balanced by the support received by Kathmandu in countering Chinese demands during the period 1906–11; generous Nepalese aid during the First World War led Britain to make a token annual grant of Rs 1 million in perpetuity. This was capitalised in 1947 with a gift of £1.75 million (approximately $8.4 million). Nepal's complete independence was formally recognized by a treaty of peace and friendship signed in 1925, which provided for mutual consultation on problems involving a third party. Nepal's subsequent relationship up to the British withdrawal from the Indian subcontinent in 1947 was close and friendly, attested to by the generous aid which Nepal provided to Britain during the Second World War.

British political contact with Sikkim began in the spring of 1815, when a British force entered Morung during actions against the Gurkhas. Under the terms of the Treaty of Titalia, signed in February 1817, the East India Company guaranteed to protect Sikkim against renewed Gurkha aggression in return for a measure of control over the foreign relations of the state. In 1835 the Sikkimese ruler was induced to cede Darjeeling to India under a deed of grant in return for an annual allowance. Fiction persisted over the issue of slavery (which was legal in Sikkim) and the maltreatment of British officials and subjects, leading to further British territorial annexations and a military action against the kingdom in 1860–61, which resulted in a treaty concluded on 28 March 1861 providing for an annual subsidy to Sikkim on condition that its ruling authorities maintain the peace.

The British ejection of a Tibetan force from Sikkim in 1886 led to an Anglo-Chinese convention in March 1890 in which the watershed of the Tista was stipulated as the Sikkim–Tibet boundary and Sikkim was recognized as a British protectorate, with Britain having direct and exclusive control over the internal administration and foreign relations of the state. Tibetan refusal to recognize this treaty and a supplementary trade agreement were contributing causes for the Younghusband expedition in 1904. The Lhasa Convention concluded between Tibet and Britain provided for Tibetan acceptance of the Anglo-Sikkimese treaties.

British relations with Sikkim after 1890 were described by a former Political Officer in the state as being characterized by 'too little tact and sympathy, too much of the hobnailed boot';[1] a Political Agent appointed in 1888 introduced various reforms into the kingdom and progressively reduced the authority of the Maharaja. In April 1918, however, Maharaja Tashi Namgyal was invested with full administrative powers, and the subsequent period up to British withdrawal from India in 1947 was one of tranquillity within Sikkim and of close and cordial Anglo-Sikkimese relations. In both world wars, the Sikkimese gave loyal support to British efforts, and Tashi's eldest son died in service with the Royal Air Force in 1941.

British contact with Bhutan began when the British ejected a Bhutanese force from Cooch Behar in 1792 in response to a request for help from the principality's ruler. Subsequent misunderstandings, missed Bhutanese payments for their use of the Assam Duars, and Bhutanese depredations caused the British to annex certain territories in 1841 and 1864 and to fight a brief war with Bhutan in 1865, which resulted in the Treaty of Sinchula on 11 November 1865. The British government agreed to pay compensation for the annexed territory, on condition that Bhutan maintained the peace. The ensuing good Anglo-Bhutanese relations were not appreciably

[1] Sir Charles Bell, *Tibet Past and Present* (Oxford: Clarendon Press, 1924), p. 170.

affected by minor disputes in 1868 and 1880. Bhutan refused aid to Tibet in the Anglo-Tibetan conflict in 1888 and despatched a mission to accompany General Macdonald in his march to Lhasa in 1904. In 1907 British support enabled the penlop (governor) of the Tongaa District to establish himself as the hereditary king and thereby promoted a measure of political stability in the previously strife-torn state.

Tibetan developments led Britain to seek an amendment of the Treaty of Sinchula in 1910. Bhutan agreed to accept the guidance of the British government in its external relations, and Britain increased the annual subsidy to Rs 100,000 and agreed not to interfere in the kingdom's internal administration. A political crisis in the state in 1929, however, led to the creation of the post of dewan or chief minister in an effort to modernize the Bhutanese administration and maintain law and order. In 1942, for reasons clearly related to the Japanese threat to Assam, the British increased the subsidy to Rs 200,000 per annum.

British contact with the tribals in the northeast began with the occupation of Assam in 1826. Varying degrees of British 'authority' were asserted in treaties and agreements with the various tribes between 1835 and 1888, excepting the Mishmis, with whom no written agreements were concluded. The Naga Hills District of about 4,000 square miles was administered by the government of India through its agent, the Governor of Assam, as an 'Excluded Area'. Its inhabitants were extensively evangelised by Christian missionaries, especially by American Baptists. The Naga areas lying to the east of this administered district were collectively classed as an 'Unadministered Area'.

To check tribal depredations, British authority largely continued the policy of earlier Assamese rulers—suspension of their subsidies, blockade (thereby denying the particular tribe access to the goods and markets of Assam, which they required), and, in the last resort, punitive expeditions.[2] To lessen the chances of friction with the tribes, the Bengal Frontier Regulation of 1873 created an 'inner line' beyond which certain tribesmen could not pass without special permits. This line served as an administrative boundary beyond which no taxes were collected. Though the tribal areas of Assam

---

[2] Such expeditions were sent against the Miris and Abors in 1859, the Abors in 1860, the Daflas in 1874–75, the Akas in 1883, the Abors in 1894, the Mishmis in 1899, and the Abors in 1911. A revolt in the Naga Hills was put down in 1877–80.

Himalaya were not directly administered, they were nonetheless regarded as falling within the British sphere of influence.

By the beginning of the twentieth century, there were persons like Noel Williamson (Assistant Political Officer of Sadiya) who argued the need for greater control of the areas beyond the foothills in Assam. A case for such a policy had meanwhile been building up as a result of the interest the Chinese were showing in the regions adjoining Assam Himalaya after their forceful re-entry into Tibet in 1909–10. The death of Williamson at the hands of Abor tribesmen in the Lohit Valley in early 1911 provided the British with an immediate occasion for a forward move, despite the fear of the Viceroy and the British Cabinet of thereby provoking reprisals from Russia in Central Asia and trade reprisals from China. The British plan of action had, as its ultimate objective, 'to define a border more or less along the mountain crests and main watersheds, to exercise British control "of a loose political nature" up to that boundary, and, if the circumstances seemed propitious, to inform China of the new limits of British sovereignty'.[3] A military expedition punished the Abors, missions were sent to the Miris and Mishmis, and a host of surveys were undertaken which greatly increased British knowledge about Assam Himalaya. The hills were divided into Western, Central, and Eastern Sections (subsequently modified and given new names) under the supervision of Political Officers. The construction of a road up the Lohit Valley commenced in 1912 but made slow progress and came to a halt in 1914, long before it had even reached the boundary area. A recommendation by T. P. M. O'Callaghan (Assistant Political Officer of the Eastern Section) in early 1914 that work should continue on the road and that a military post be constructed near Walong was ignored.

Little attention was paid to the tribal areas during the period between the two world wars. No attention was given to a warning from one Political Officer in 1928 that the Tibetan frontier would become of great political importance once normalcy returned to the Chinese internal scene. In 1936, the Tibetans were still administering and taxing the Tawang Tract, east of Bhutan. The publication of Chinese maps, which showed all of Assam Himalaya as part of Tibet (i.e., China), caused the Governor of Assam to despatch a Political Officer in 1938 to demonstrate British sovereignty in Tawang by collecting a tax, but the Indian government was unwilling

[3] Cited, Alistair Lamb, *The India–China Border* (London: Oxford University Press, 1964), p. 139.

to accept the additional administrative responsibility and expense involved in the officer's proposal that British officials be permanently stationed in Tawang and Dirrang Dzong. In response to Tibetan efforts to collect taxes and utilize labour in the Dihang Valley as far as Karko, however, British Political Officers began to tour up the Dihang deep into Abor country.

The Japanese threat and the appearance of further Chinese maps prompted the British to establish armed posts at Karko and Riga in the Dihang Valley in 1940–41, to extend armed posts up the Lohit to the McMahon Line in 1943, to plan a motor road from Sadiya to Rima, and to make concerted efforts to cultivate tribal loyalties. During the military operations against the Japanese, tribals were employed as porters, and the Nagas were armed and revealed an ability to conduct skillful guerilla operations. In 1942 the Tirap Frontier Tract was created from the Sadiya Frontier Tract, and in 1946 the Balipara Frontier Tract was bifurcated into two divisions, the Abor Hills and the Mishmi Hills.

APPENDIX V

SUMMARY OF THE CHATFIELD COMMITTEE REPORT, 1938-39

The problems of Indian defence were assessed in late 1938 by an expert committee appointed by His Majesty's Government at the request of the government of India and presided over by Admiral of the Fleet, Lord Chatfield.[1]

The Committee advanced the view that the 'Major' and 'Minor' divisions of responsibility for Indian defence had been rendered obsolete by international developments. It declared that 'The arena of India's defence against external aggressions should therefore now be regarded as covering not only primarily her North-Western land frontier but also to an increasing extent her sea communications in Eastern waters and the strategic points which are vital to their security'. The Committee noted that this principle had been embodied in the British-Indian naval agreement concluded in January 1938, and it recommended that India acknowledge her external defence responsibilities and bear the ordinary maintenance costs of units designated for service beyond her borders in an emergency affecting her external security. It favoured a policy whereby units designated for foreign service would be an integral part of the forces in India as a whole, but would receive better equipment.

The Committee made specific proposals regarding the modernization of the Army. It expressed the belief that the increased efficiency and mobility would permit a shift of an approximate 25 per cent of the British troops in India to the Home Establishment (while remaining in India) and a proportionately smaller, but absolute, reduction in the Indian component. It proposed re-equipment of the RAF squadrons in India with the aid of a grant of about £1,700,000 (approximately $8.2 million). Measures were recommended to bring the stocks of stores for war requirements up to the requisite scale. The Committee largely accepted the Nine Year Plan prepared by the Royal Indian Navy, endorsed the proposal of the Auchinleck (Modernization) Committee that two bomber squadrons be equipped for the dual role of frontier and coast defence, confirmed the proposals of the General Staff regarding the requirements of coast defence and anti-aircraft artillery, and suggested the raising

[1] Source: *Chatfield Committee Report, 1938-39.*

of five flights of aircraft on a voluntary basis to assist in the defence of the major ports. The Committee proposed that, to the greatest possible extent, India should be made self-sufficient in munitions required for war, with initial reliance upon government factories for defence items.

It was estimated that the net capital cost of the measures proposed would total £34.33 millions ($165 million). As such funds were not available in India, the Committee noted that the British government was prepared to obtain Parliamentary sanction for this sum from the Home Exchequer over a five-year period, the estimated time for the non-naval aspects of the plan. Three-quarters of the sum would be provided as a free grant, and the remaining one-quarter as a loan.

APPENDIX VI

SIZE AND COMPOSITION OF THE INDIAN ARMED FORCES,
AUGUST 1939

1. *Army* [1]
    22 cavalry and armoured regiments, including 4 Bodyguard units
    4 batteries of field artillery
    28 sapper and miner companies including field troops and divisional headquarter companies
    113 infantry battalions including 17 training battalions and Gurkha battalions but excluding 20 trainer companies of Gurkha Rifles
    Personnel: 194,373 in India and overseas excluding Indian State Forces, auxiliary and reserve forces, all British officers and men in British service.

2. *Navy* [2]
    5 sloops (2 of pre-1922 commission)
    1 survey vessel
    1 patrol vessel
    1 steam trawler
    Personnel: 19 Indian and 95 British commissioned officers, 25 Indian and 30 British warrant officers, and 1,677 Indian seamen.

3. *Air Force* [3]
    1 (incomplete) army co-operation squadron equipped with Wapiti aircraft
    Personnel: 16 commissioned officers, 1 warrant officer, 268 other ranks, and 1,343 persons in other categories.

[1] Nandan Prasad, *Expansion of the Armed Forces and Defence Organisation, 1939–45*, Combined Inter-Services Historical Section, India and Pakistan (London: Orient Longmans, 1956), Appendix I, p. 393.
[2] *Ibid.*, p. 399 and pp. 408–409.
[3] *Ibid.*, pp. 398–399 and 408–409.

APPENDIX VII

SIZE AND COMPOSITION OF THE INDIAN ARMED FORCES, 1945

1. *Army* (August 1945)[1]
    19 cavalry and armoured regiments including 2 Indian States Forces Regiments serving under the Crown
    207 batteries of artillery of all types
    107 companies of Indian Engineers including field companies, field park companies, and field squadrons but excluding all laundry, pipeline companies, etc.
    268 battalions of infantry including 32 Indian States Forces and 8 Gurkha battalions serving under the Crown but excluding independent and garrison companies, etc.
    Personnel: 2,065,554 including 16,351 of Indian State Forces serving overseas but excluding all British units as of 1 July 1945.
2. *Navy* (1 July 1945)[2]—includes ships in service and those about to be commissioned.
    6 modern sloops
    3 frigates
    4 corvettes
    4 Bathurst class minesweepers
    13 Bangor class minesweepers
    18 trawlers
    4 motor minesweepers
    1 landing ship infantry (large)
    1 coastal force depot ship
    4 old sloops
    2 store ships
    1 salvage vessel
    4 old gunboats
    1 mobile wiping and deperming unit (for demagnetizing ships' hulls)
    11 vessels of coastal forces organised in 3 flotillas
    2 detached boats for anti-submarine and torpedo training

[1] Nandan Prasad, *Expansion of the Armed Forces and Defence Organisation, 1939–45*, Combined Inter-Services Historical Section, India and Pakistan (London: Orient Longmans, 1956), Appendix I, p. 399.
[2] *Ibid.*

    41 craft in the landing craft wing
    4 LCA (Landing Craft Assault) flotillas
    3 LCW (Landing Craft Weapons) formations
  Personnel: 30,478 excluding civilians and noncombatants.
3. *Air Force* (1 July 1945)[3]
    3 fighter reconnaissance squadrons
    2 ground attack squadrons
    2 light bomber squadrons
    2 fighter squadrons
  Personnel: 29,201 officers, airmen, and enrolled followers, excluding civilians and temporary followers.

[3] *Ibid.*, pp. 398–399.

APPENDIX VIII

a. British Planning for India's Postwar Defense Forces [1]

The first major step in fixing demobilization targets was taken in January 1944, at which time the Commander-in-Chief directed the Chiefs of Staff Committee to prepare a paper defining the size and composition of the defence forces required for India after cessation of the war with the Axis powers.

The Chiefs of Staff Committee submitted its report in March 1944. It based its recommendations on the following appraisal of the postwar situation:

1. A threat from Afghanistan was unlikely if India maintained adequate forces, but the border tribals would create trouble if conditions in India were unsettled.
2. Relations with the Soviet Union and China were likely to be generally friendly. However, after a few years, when their shattered economies had been rehabilitated, aggression from them could not be ruled out.
3. India would remain responsible for internal security, for defence against a minor power, and for defence against a major power until imperial reinforcements could arrive.
4. India would provide the greater part of the garrisons for Southeast Asia Command areas (Burma, Malaya, and Siam), and Indian forces might be needed for some time in the Persia and Iraq Command and in the Middle East area.
5. Internal security would be a difficult problem.

The Committee concluded that, in the immediate postwar period, army requirements would total 9 infantry divisions, 5 infantry brigade groups, 113 infantry battalions, and 22 garrison companies. The required naval establishment was estimated at 3 cruisers, 9 destroyers, and the necessary support vessels, plus a nucleus of assault ships and craft. The needs of the Indian Air Force were estimated as: 7 squadrons for tribal control, 5 squadrons for internal security, 3 squadrons for the North–East Frontier, and 21 squadrons to form the nucleus for expansion in case of a major threat of war.

[1] Source: S. V. Desika Char, "Planning for the Post-War Defence Forces" in Nandan Prasad, *Expansion of the Armed Forces and Defence Organisation, 1939–45*, Combined Inter-Services Historical Section, India and Pakistan (London: Orient Longmans, 1956), pp. 196–206.

The report of the Committee was accepted by the Indian government as a useful foundation for further detailed study of the question.

In a further report submitted in April 1945, the Chiefs of Staff proposed force levels for the immediate postwar period (designated the 'upper limit'), and for the ultimate postwar military establishment in India (the 'lower limit'). The cost of the 'lower limit' was estimated by the Financial Adviser at Rs 130 crores for 'effective charges' and Rs 15 crores for 'noneffective charges'. However, a rough estimate of India's stabilised postwar budget prepared by the Financial Adviser, the Finance Member, and the Finance Department had allotted only Rs 70 to 75 crores for defence; the Financial Adviser accordingly recommended a drastic cut in the 'lower limit'. Acting on this proposal, the Commander-in-Chief issued a directive to the Chiefs of Staff on 24 April 1945 to ascertain the minimum needs required by India for local defence: to maintain law and order in India, to maintain order among the tribes and peoples of the North-West and North-East frontiers, to conduct war with Afghanistan (neither side having allies), and to protect India's coasts, coastal merchant shipping, and fisheries.

The Chiefs of Staff effected further reductions, and their proposals for this 'lowest limit' were accepted by the Commander-in-Chief's War Committee on 12 June 1945. It was generally realized, however, that this 'lowest limit' was based largely upon financial considerations and was in no sense a military recommendation. The cost estimates of the three levels ('effective expenditure') were (in crores of rupees):

	RIN	Army	RIAF	Total
Upper limit	10	120	54	184
Lower limit	6	80	42	128
Lowest limit	5	62	23	98

b. POSTWAR PLANNING (as of 12 June 1945)

	Upper Limit	Lower Limit	Lowest Limit
1. Army			
Frontier defence	50 battalions in brigade groups	11 battalions in 4 brigade groups	11 battalions in 4 brigade groups
Frontier defence reserve	5 brigade groups and armoured element	++ ᵃ	++
Internal security	6⅔ battalions	++	++
Corps HQ troops	2	2	2
Infantry divisions	10	9 and 12 battalions	6 and 12 battalions
Armoured divisions	1	1	1
Armoured brigades	1	2	1
Airbourne divisions	1	—	—
Parachute brigade groups	—	1	1
2. Navy			
Cruisers	—	3	3
Sloops	7	8	6
Frigates (incl. survey ships)	9	8 (4) ᵇ	8 (5)
Corvettes	3	—	—
Minesweepers	16	16 (8)	16 (8)
Trawlers	20	11 (6)	11 (6)
Motor minesweepers	10	8 (4)	8 (8)
Hulks for reserve training	2	2	—

ᵃ ++ denotes frontier defence reserve and internal security troops included in formations.
ᵇ Figures in parentheses show the number of vessels included in totals but to be held in reserve.

SOURCE: S.V. Desika Char, 'Planning for The Post-War Defence Forces' in Nandan Prasad, *Expansion of the Armed Forces and Defence Organisation 1939–45*, Combined Inter-Services Historical Section, India and Pakistan (London: Orient Longmans, 1956). Appendix 17, p. 464 (Navy); p. 465 (Air Force); p. 464 (Army).

Harbour Defence Motor Launches	27	8
Motor Launches	27	—
Depot ship	1	—
Sea-going training ships	6	1
Landing ships (all types)	19¹	7¹
Landing ships	3	2

3. *Air Force*

Transport	15	7	7
Tactical reconnaissance, fighter reconnaissance, or ground-to-air	13	8	6
Fighter	12	12	2
Photoreconnaissance flight	2	1	—
Light or fighter-bomber	3	3	2
Heavy bomber	4	4	—
Long-range general reconnaissance	2	2	2
Total squadrons and flights	51	37	19 (later 19½)

APPENDIX IX

THE INDIAN ARMED FORCES, POST-PARTITION (1947)[1]

1. *Army*
   Personnel: about 280,000 of all categories.
   Divisional organizations: 4th, 5th, and 10th.
   Infantry regiments (15): Punjab, Madras, Mahratta Light Infantry, Rajputana Rifles, Rajput, Jat, Sikh, Dogra, Garhwal Rifles, Kumaon, Assam, Sikh Light Infantry, Bihar, Mahar. The Gurkha Rifles consisted of the 1st, 3rd, 4th, 5th, 8th, and 9th regiments totalling 16 battalions.
   Armoured units (12): Skinner's Horse, 2nd Lancers, 3d Cavalry, Hodsons' Horse, 7th Light Cavalry, 8th Light Cavalry, Deccan Horse, Scinde Horse, 16th Light Cavalry, Poona Horse, 18th Cavalry, and Central India Horse.
   Artillery regiments (18½)
   Engineers: 61 units organized into the Madras, Bengal, and Bombay Engineer Groups.
2. *Navy*
   Personnel: 1,000 officers and 10,000 ratings.
   Vessels:
   - 4 sloops
   - 2 frigates
   - 1 corvette
   - 12 fleet minesweepers
   - 4 trawlers
   - 4 motor minesweepers
   - 4 motor launches
   - 1 survey ship
3. *Air Force*
   7 fighter squadrons (Tempest 2's and Spitfires).
   1 transport-communication squadron (C-47's and Devons).
   1 artillery observation post flight (Auster 5's).
   Miscellaneous Tiger Moth, Percival Prentice, and Spitfire training aircraft.

[1] The information was compiled by the writer from official and unofficial sources.

APPENDIX X

THE INDIAN ARMED FORCES, 1962

1. *Army*

   Three Commands embracing 550,000 personnel organized into the 2d, 4th, 5th, 10th, 17th, 19th, 26th, and 27th Infantry Divisions; 1st Armoured Division; 1st Independent Armoured Brigade; 50th Paratroop Brigade; miscellaneous unattached units. Redeployment since 1953 consisted of about two brigades in Ladakh; a squadron of Stuart light tanks in the Vale of Kashmir; one regiment of AMX light tanks with each of the two infantry divisions in Punjab Force; 4th Infantry Division in NEFA; one infantry brigade covering Sikkim; 14 infantry battalions in Nagaland and immediately contiguous parts of Assam; one infantry brigade at Ranchi; a 5,000-man brigade group with the United Nations in the Congo; one infantry battalion with United Nations Emergency Force (*UNEF*) in Gaza.

2. *Navy*

   Fleet: 1 'Majestic' class light fleet aircraft carrier
   1 'Leander' class light cruiser
   1 'Mauritius' class light cruiser
   3 'R' class fleet destroyers
   3 'Hunt' class type 2 frigates
   2 'Whitby' class anti-submarine frigates
   3 'Blackwood' class anti-submarine frigates
   3 'Leopard' class anti-aircraft frigates
   2 'Kistna' class frigates
   2 'River' class frigates employed for training and survey
   2 'Sutlej' class frigates employed as survey vessels
   1 'Bangor' class fleet minesweeper
   4 'Ton' class coastal minesweepers
   2 'Ham' class inshore minesweepers
   miscellaneous craft

   Fleet Requirements Unit (squadron 550): 10 Sealand light amphibians, 5 Fairey Firefly T.T.1's, 5 T.T.4's, and several HT-2 trainers.

   Miscellaneous: Vampire jet flight (INS *Hansa*) at Sulur.

3. *Air Force*
    Regular: fighter: four squadron of Mysteres and two squadrons of Gnats.
       fighter-bomber: six squadrons of Hunters, two squadrons of Ouragans, and one squadron of Vampires.
       light bomber: three or four squadrons of Canberra B (1) .58's.
       reconnaissance: one squadron of Canberra P.R.57's.
       transport: about six squadrons comprised of C-119's, DC-3's, Devons, Il–14's, Otters, and An-12's.
       helicopters: about 60 units comprised of Bell 47G-2's and -3's, Sikorsky S-55's and -62's, and Mi-4's.
       trainers: Hunters, Canberras, Vampires, Texans, HT-2's, Ouragans, DC-3's, and Prentices.
       air observation post: Auster Mk 9's.
       miscellaneous: B-24's, Viscount 730's and Harvards.
    Auxiliary: squadron nos. 51 (Delhi), 52 (Bombay), 53 (Madras), 54 (Allahabad), 55 (Calcutta), 56 (Bhubandeshwar), and 57 (Chandigarh).

APPENDIX XI

THE POLICY-MAKING MACHINERY

The executive management of Indian defence is characterized by a hierarchical structure of committees arranged in the classic pyramid based on the three Services, with the Cabinet at the apex. A superimposed conciliar structure provides a formal means for lateral communication among officials at similar levels in different hierarchies, but the vertical 'superior-subordinate' relationship constitutes the 'skeleton'. It is within this system that the three Services struggle concurrently against each other and against budgetary pressures from Finance and an economy-minded administration.

This committee system of policy management evolved largely *ad hoc* after independence, but the system afforded, in theory, a co-ordinated approach with a measure of consistency being ensured by all branches being served by the Military Wing of the Cabinet Secretariat. Proposals relating to the annual defence grants are initiated by the respective services, and the estimates are studied by the appropriate division of the individual service branch under the scrutiny of Deputy Financial Advisers. The revised estimates are then discussed in the Defence Minister's Army, Navy, and Air Force Committees and in the Defence Minister's (inter-services) Committee, after which they are examined by the Defence Ministry. The resulting estimates are then sent to the Defence Committee of the Cabinet for consideration, and the conclusions of this body are forwarded to the full Cabinet for approval. The assessment of military need that emerges from this process is presented in the form of defence estimates to Parliament for discussion and approval. The funds are thereupon expended under the constant observation of the Deputy Financial Advisers, who are responsible for checking the progress of expenditure against budgetary grants and allotments and examining irregularities.

Financial controls are thus pervasive, inside the defence organization and yet independent of it. Annual and supplementary estimates cannot be submitted to Parliament without the prior approval of the Ministry of Finance; audit supervision of expenditure is exercised through the Comptroller, the Auditor-General, and the Public Accounts Committee.

The Financial Adviser to the Defence Services—the origins of which office date to a resolution inspired by Lord Kitchener in 1906—has a triple responsibility. He must scrutinize all proposals involving defence expenditure and advise whether they should be accepted. He has direct access to the Finance Minister for this purpose. He also has direct access to the Defence Minister and may, at his discretion, require that any case in which he thinks a decision contravenes financial principles be submitted to the Finance Minister direct or via the Defence Minister. He is also responsible to internal audit and accounting for all monies voted by Parliament for defence purposes and prepares the annual appropriation accounts.

SELECTED BIBLIOGRAPHY

PRIMARY SOURCES

GENERAL SOURCES

Indian Parliamentary Debates, *Official Records*, 1945-1964.
Indian Ministry of Defence, *Annual Reports*, 1945-1964.
Indian Ministry of External Affairs, *Annual Reports*, 1945-1964.

COLLECTED DOCUMENTS

The Background of India's Foreign Policy: Resolutions of the Indian National Congress on Foreign Policy, 1885-1952 (New Delhi: All-India Congress Committee, 1952).
Foreign Policy of India: Texts of Documents, 1947-59 (New Delhi: Lok Sabha Secretariat, 2d edition, December 1959).
The Question of Tibet and the Rule of Law (Geneva: International Commission of Jurists, 1959).
Report of the Officials of the Governments of India and the People's Republic of China on the Boundary Question (New Delhi, Ministry of External Affairs, February 1961).
Resolutions on Foreign Policy, 1947-1957 (New Delhi: All-India Congress Committee, 1958).
Select Documents on the History of India and Pakistan, vol. IV, *The Evolution of India and Pakistan, 1858-1947*, ed. by C. H. Phillips (London: Oxford University Press, 1962).
White Papers: Notes, Memoranda, and Letters Exchanged Between the Governments of India and China, 1954-1963 (New Delhi: Ministry of External Affairs), nos. I-VIII.

BIOGRAPHIES, AUTOBIOGRAPHIES, AND COLLECTED SPEECHES

Bose, D. R. (ed.). *New India Speaks* (Calcutta: A. Mukerjee, 1949).
Bright, Jagat S. (ed.). *Important Speeches of Jawaharlal Nehru* (Lahore: Indian Printing Works, n.d.).
Cousins, Norman. *Talks with Nehru*, recorded interview (New York: John Day, 1951).
Narain, S. K. (ed.). *Jawaharlal Nehru: Selections* (London: Oxford University Press, 1956).
Nehru, Jawaharlal. *An Autobiography* (London: Bodley Head, 1942).
———. *The Unity of India: Collected Writings, 1937-1940* (New York: Lindsay Drummond, 1942).
———. *The Discovery of India* (London: Meridian Books, 1945).
———. *Soviet Russia: Some Random Sketches and Impressions* (Bombay: Chetna, 1949).

———. *Independence and After: A Collection of Speeches, 1946–1949* (New York: John Day, 1950).
———. *Before and After Independence: A Collection of Speeches, 1922–1950* (New Delhi: Indian Printing Works, 1951).
———. *Speeches, 1946–1949* (New Delhi: Publications Division, GOI, 1954).
———. *Speeches, 1949–1953* (New Delhi: Publications Division, GOI, 1958).
———. *Speeches, 1953–1957* (New Delhi: Publications Division, GOI, 1958).
Panikkar, K. M. *In Two Chinas: Memoirs of a Diplomat* (London: Allen & Unwin, 1955).
Prabhu, R. K. (ed.). *The India of My Dreams: Statements and Writings of M. K. Gandhi* (Bombay: Hind Kitabs, 1947).
Prime Minister on Chinese Aggression (New Delhi: Ministry of External Affairs, n.d.).
Prime Minister on Sino-Indian Relations, vol. II, *Press Conferences* (New Delhi: Ministry of External Affairs, 1961).

NEWSPAPERS AND MAGAZINES

Indian
Asian Recorder (New Delhi).
Eastern Economist (New Delhi).
Economic Weekly (Bombay).
Hindu (Madras).
Hindustan Times (New Delhi).
Indian Express (Delhi).
Link (New Delhi).
Organiser (Delhi).
Statesman (New Delhi).
Thought (New Delhi).
Times of India (New Delhi).

Foreign
Aeroplane and Astronautics (London).
Aviation Week (New York).
Daily Telegraph (London).
Dawn (Karachi).
Economist (London).
Flight (London).
Keesings Contemporary Archives (London).
Manchester Guardian.
Naval Review (London).
New York Times.
Observer (London).
Peking Review.
Round Table (London).
Survey of the Chinese Mainland Press (Hong Kong: American Consulate General).
Time and Tide (London).
The Times (London).

SECONDARY SOURCES

BOOKS

Appadorai, A. et al. *Bases of India's Title on the North-East Frontier* International Studies, 1:4 (April 1960).
Barton, Sir William P. *India's North-West Frontier* (London: John Murray, 1939).
Beaton, Leonard, and John Maddox. *The Spread of Nuclear Weapons* (London: Chatto & Windus for the Institute of Strategic Studies, 1962).
Bell, Sir Charles. *Tibet, Past and Present* (Oxford: Clarendon Press, 1924).
Bhargava, G. S. *The Battle of NEFA* (Bombay: Allied Publishers Private, 1964).
Brecher, Michael. *India's Foreign Policy: An Interpretation* (New York: Institute of Pacific Relations, 1957).
———. *Nehru: A Political Biography* (London: Oxford University Press, 1959).
Campbell-Johnson, Alan. *Mission with Mountbatten* (London: Robert Hale, 1951).
Chakravarti, P. C. *India's China Policy* (Bloomington: Indiana University Press, 1962).
Das, M. N. *The Political Philosophy of Jawaharlal Nehru* (London: Allen & Unwin, 1961).
Das Gupta, J. B. *Indo-Pakistan Relations, 1947-1955* (Amsterdam: Djambatan, 1958).
Dodwell, H. H. (ed.). *The Cambridge History of the British Empire*, vol. V, *The Indian Empire, 1858-1918* (London: Cambridge University Press, 1932).
Evans, Humphrey. *Thimayya of India: A Soldier's Life* (New York: Harcourt Brace, 1960).
Fisher, M. W., Leo E. Rose, and Robert A. Huttenback. *Himalayan Battleground: Sino-Indian Rivalry in Ladakh* (New York: Praeger, 1963).
Hangen, Welles. *After Nehru, Who?* (London: Rupert Hart-Davis, 1963).
Indian Council of World Affairs. *Defence and Security in the Indian Ocean Area* (New York: Asia Publishing House, 1958).
Jain, Girilal. *India Meets China in Nepal* (New York: Asia Publishing House, 1959).
———. *Panch Sheel and After: A Reappraisal of Sino-Indian Relations in the Context of the Tibetan Insurrection* (London: Asia Publishing House, 1960).
Karan, Pradyumma P., and William M. Jenkins, Jr. *The Himalayan Kingdoms: Bhutan, Sikkim, and Nepal* (New York: D. Van Nostrand, 1963).
Lamb, Alastair. *The India-China Border* (London: Oxford University Press, 1964).
Menon, V. P. *The Transfer of Power in India* (Princeton: Princeton University Press, 1957).
Military Handbook of General Information on India (Simla: Government

Press, 1908).
Moraes, Frank. *Jawaharlal Nehru: A Biography* (New York: Macmillan, 1956).
——. *India Today* (New York: Macmillan, 1960).
Nehru, Jawaharlal. *India and the World* (London: Allen & Unwin, 1936).
Noorani, A. G. *Our Credulity and Negligence* (Bombay: Bhatkal, 1963).
Panikkar, K. M. *The Future of South-East Asia* (London: Allen & Unwin, 1943).
——. *India and the Indian Ocean* (London: Allen & Unwin, 1945).
——. *Geographical Factors in Indian History* (Bombay: Bharataiva Vidya Bhavan, 1955).
——. *Problems of Indian Defence* (New York: Asia Publishing House, 1960).
Patel, H. M. *The Defence of India*, R. R. Kale Memorial Lecture, 1963, Gorkhale Institute of Politics and Economics (Bombay: Asia Publishing House, 1963).
Prasad, Bimla. *The Origins of Indian Foreign Policy* (Calcutta: Book lands Private, 1960).
Prasad, Bisheshwar. *Defence of India: Policy and Plans*, Combined Inter-Services Historical Section, India and Pakistan (London: Orient Longmans, 1963).
Prasad, Nandan. *Expansion of the Armed Forces and Defence Organisation, 1939–45*, Combined Inter-Services Historical Section, India and Pakistan (London: Orient Longmans, 1956).
Richardson, H. E. *Tibet and Its History* (London: Oxford University Press, 1961).
Sharma, Ram. *India's Foreign Policy: The British Interpretation, 1947–57* (Gwalier: Gyan Mandir, 1961).
Singh, Rajendra. *Organisation and Administration in the Indian Army* (London: Gale and Polden, 1952).
Tuker, Lt.-Gen. Sir Francis. *While Memory Serves* (London: Cassell, 1950).
Wint, Guy. *The British in Asia* (New York: Institute of Pacific Relations, 1954).

ARTICLES

Alston, Brig. W. L. 'Reliance on U.N.O.: Some Questions on the Defence of India,' *USI Journal*, 78:328 (July 1947).
Anonymous. 'The Indian Army', *Round Table*, no. 211 (June 1963).
Armstrong, Lt.-Col. G. L. W. 'The Defence of the Indian Ocean and Far East', *USI Journal*, 77:326 (1947). Gold Medal, 1945–46.
Auchinleck, Sir Claude. 'Planning India's Post-War Armed Forces', *USI Journal*, 76:325 (October 1946).
——. 'The British-Indian Army', *Geographical Magazine* (April 1952).
'Auspex'. 'India's Strategical Future', *USI Journal*, 75:319 (April 1945).
Barton, Sir William P. 'The Defence of India', *Fortnightly* (July 1947).
Bhagat, Brig. B. S. 'Can the Defence Forces of India Undertake Nation-Building Activities and Revenue-Earning Activities?' *USI Journal*, 81:342–343 (January–April 1951). Gold Medal, 1950.

——. 'The Recent Korean Campaign . . .', *USI Journal*, 82:346–347 (January–April 1952). Gold Medal, 1951.
——. 'Officer Recruitment in the Armed Forces of India', *USI Journal*, 83:350–351 (January–April 1953). Gold Medal, 1952.
——. 'Reorganisation of Defence Services', *USI Journal*, 89:375 (April–June 1959).
Caroe, Sir Olaf. 'The Geography and Ethnics of India's Northern Frontier', *Geographical Journal*, 126:3 (1960).
Chaphekar, Lt.-Col. S. G. 'A Frank Survey of India's Defence Problems', part I, *USI Journal*, 78:327 (April 1947); part 2, 78:328 (July 1947).
Chaudhuri, Brig. J. N. 'The Indian Army', *Asiatic Review* (October 1947).
Chaudhuri, Nirad C. 'The Indian Navy', part 1, *Thought*, 22 January 1955.
Datta, Lt.-Com. Narapati. 'An Aircraft Carrier for the Indian Navy', *USI Journal*, 87:367 (April–June 1957).
'E.F.' 'India's Post-War Navy', 75:321 (October 1945).
Edwardes, Michael. 'Illusion and Reality in India's Foreign Policy', *International Affairs* (January 1965).
——. 'Tashkent and After'. International Affairs (July 1966).
Foucar, Col. C. Rebuilding a Navy, *USI Journal*, 86:324 (July 1946).
Graham, Ian C. C. 'The Indo-Soviet MIG Deal and Its International Repercussions', *Asian Survey* (May 1964).
Gutteridge, William. 'The Indianisation of the Indian Army, 1918–45', *Race*, 4 (May 1963).
Halladay, E. 'The Indian Army Since 1947', *Army Quarterly*, 137:2 (January 1964).
Hessler, William H. 'India as a Prospective Partner', *United States Naval Institute, Proceedings*, 90:2 (February 1964).
Jones, P. M. 'Passes and Impasses: The Sino-Indian Border Conflict', *Far Eastern Economic Review*, 28 February 1963.
Knox, Rawle. 'Updating the Indian Army', *Reporter*, 8 October 1964.
Krishnan, Comm. N. 'Strategic Concepts of Indian Naval Expansion', *USI Journal*, 88:327 (July–September 1958).
Martin, Lt.-Gen. H. G. 'India's Army in the New Era', *Daily Telegraph*, 20 November 1946.
——. 'India's New National Army', *Daily Telegraph*, 22 November 1946.
Mills, J. P. 'Problems of the Assam–Tibet Frontier', *Journal of the Royal Central Asian Society*, 37:2 (1949).
Moore, Maj.-Gen. F. M. 'Post-War Indian Army', *USI Journal*, 74:317 (October 1944).
Naib, Maj. V. P. 'National Planning for Defence', *USI Journal*, 86:362 (January–March 1956).
——. Lt. Colonel V. P. 'Unity Through Diversity', *USI Journal*, 87:366 January–March 1957). Gold Medal, 1956.
Narayan, Brij, 'Post-War Planning of Defence Services', *USI Journal*, 75:319 (April 1945).
Nehru, Jawaharlal. 'Changing India', *Foreign Affairs*, 41:3 (April 1963).
O'Ballance, Major Edgar. 'The Strength of India', *Military Review*, 42:1 (January 1962).
Paine, Com. H. E. Felser (RN), 'An Indian Ocean Pact', *RUSI Journal*

(February 1950).

Palit, Lt.-Col. D. K. 'The Military Lessons of the Korean War', *USI Journal*, 82:348-349 (July-October 1952).

Panikkar, K. M. 'Defence and National Efficiency', *Asiatic Review* (July 1945).

Parry, Vice-Adm. W. E. 'India and Sea Power', *USI Journal*, 79:334-335 (January-April 1949).

Patel, H. M. 'Balance of Hopes and Fears: A Review of the Past Five Years', *USI Journal*, 82:352-353 (July-October 1953).

——. 'Realities of the Situation', *Seminar* (July 1962).

——. 'Self-Preservation', *Seminar* (April 1964).

Patterson, George. 'Recent Chinese Policies in Tibet and Towards the Himalayan States', *China Quarterly* (October–December 1962).

Pizey, Adm. Sir Mark. 'The Indian Navy Today', *Asian Review*, 52:189 (January 1956).

Ponappa, Lt.-Col. C. B. 'My Views on India's Post-War Forces', *USI Journal*, 77:326 (January 1947).

Pringsheim, Klaus H. 'China, India, and their Himalayan Border, 1961-63', *Asian Survey*, 3:10 (October 1963).

Pugh, Alistair, 'The Indian Air Force', *Flight*, 29 May 1959; 5 June 1959; 28 August 1959.

Reid, Sir Robert: 'The Excluded Areas of Assam', *Geographical Review*, 103 (January–February 1944).

Rose, Leo E. 'Conflict in the Himalayas', *Military Review*, 43:2 (February 1963).

Rudolf, Lloyd I., and Susanne Heober. 'Generals and Politicians in India', *Pacific Affairs*, 37:8 (Spring 1964).

Satyanarayana, Wing Comm. C. 'The Origin and Growth of the Royal Indian Air Force', *USI Journal*, 79:334,335 (January–April 1949).

Sen, Chanakya. 'India and China: Response to Challenge', *World Today* (June 1964).

Singh, Batuk. 'Finance and the AFHQ', *USI Journal*, 86:363 (April–June 1956).

Singh, Lt.-Col. Rajendra. 'A New Conception of the Defence of India', *USI Journal*, 79:334, 335 (January–April 1949).

Strachey, Anthony. 'Some Aspects of the Future Defence of the New India', *Asiatic Review* (April 1947).

Thimayya, Gen. K. S. 'Adequate Insurance', *Seminar* (July 1962)

Tinker, Hugh. '1857 and 1957: The Indian Mutiny and Modern India', *International Affairs* (January 1958).

——. 'Magnificent Failure? The Gandhian Ideal in India After Sixteen Years', *International Affairs* (April 1964).

'Tughlak'. 'The Birth of the Indian Navy', *Naval Review*, 44:2 (April 1956).

Tuker, Gen. Sir Francis. 'Defence of India and Pakistan', *Manchester Guardian*, 15 December 1949.

Varma, Maj. M. R. P. 'The Foundations of National Defence in India', 86:363 (April–June 1956).

Zinkin, Taya. 'India and Military Dictatorship', *Pacific Affairs*, 32:1 (March 1959).

INDEX

Abbottabad, 34
Abdullah, Sheikh Mohammad, 157
Abyssinia, 14
Aden, 123
Admiralty, British, 116, 118. *See also* Britain
Afghanistan, 9-40 *passim*, 208, 213; Amir of, 16
Africa, 18, 26
Ahmedabad, 100
Aircraft industry, 17. *See also* Hindustan Aircraft Limited
Aircraft Maintenance Depot, 132, 137
Aircraft Manufacturing Depot, 135
Air Force: size and composition, 4, 20, 102, 108; creation, 12, 17; expansion, 20, 30, 102-108, 192, 196-201; operations, 32, 35, 190; British personnel in, 103; Auxiliary Air Force, 108; Air Defence Reserve, 108; Regular Reserve, 108; equipment policy, 109-113; effectiveness, 113-115; operational role, 114-115; as sanction of civilian authority, 142; character and outlook of officer corps, 152; inferiority complex, 157; general policy, 211; nuclear delivery capabilities, 216
Air India International, 204
Akhnur, 34
Aksai Chin, 51, 62, 63, 154, 158, 174, 187
Ali, Asaf, 26
Ali, Saiyad Fazl, 71
All India Congress Committee, 22, 25n., 26. *See also* Congress party
All India Radio, 192
Along, 48, 73
Ambajahari Engineering Factory, 205. *See also* Defence industries
Ambala, 85, 87, 157, 175
Ambarnath, 127
Amingaon, 206
Amlekganj, 57
Amritsar, 34, 85, 175
Andaman Islands, 202, 215

Anglo-Indian Auxiliary Force, 12. *See also* British India
Anti-Comintern pact, 14
Ao, Dr Imkengliba, 72
Arab bloc, 92
Arabian Sea, 117
Armed forces. *See* Air Force; Army; Navy
Armed Forces Academy, 92
Armed Police, 46, 97
Army: size and composition, 4, 30, 83-86 *passim*, 97, 192, 194; operations, 32-34, 51, 52, 100-101, 170-178, 189-190; deployment, 35, 47-51 *passim*, 84, 85-86, 98-100, 171, 175-176; operational role, 37, 67, 68; demobilization, 84-85; Central Command, 86, 195; contingency plans, 87-88, 98-100; expansion, 89, 192, 193-196; equipment policy, 89-92; officer corps, 92-93, 151-153; recruitment policy, 93-94; organization and character, 94-95, 97-98; views on Himalayan defence, 95-96, 158-159, 167, 170-171, 185-186; promotions policy, 154-168 *passim;* Southern Command, 177; deficiencies exposed in conflict with China, 183-187; Eastern Command, 195; NEFA Corps, 195; Military Intelligence Directorate, 195; general policy, 211-212
Army Cadet College, 93
Asafila, 175
Asia, 21, 28, 29, 40, 41, 65, 178
Asian Federation, 28
Asian Relations Conference, 28, 43
Assam, 9, 17n., 19, 48-88 *passim*, 115, 177, 188, 189, 206
Assam Rifles, 46-49 *passim*, 66, 67, 71, 87, 97, 99, 158
Atomic bombs, 27, 27-28n.
Auchinleck, Field Marshal Sir Claude, 30
Australia, 26, 111, 194, 211

Auxiliary Cadet Corps, 202
Avadi, 130, 131, 195, 203
Avaiaexport, 197
Ayyangar, Gopalaswami, 120, 147
Azad Kashmir, 208
Azad Kashmir forces, 33, 34, 36, 98

Babariawad, 32
Bagh, 34
Bajpai, G. S., 39, 148n.
Baltal, 74
Bangalore, 18, 86, 131, 133, 134, 174
Bara Lacha Pass, 51
Baramula, 32-33
Beaton, Leonard, 212
Belfast, 121
Bellauri, 57
Bengal, 19; Bay of, 19, 117
Berlin blockade, 118
Bezwada, 32
Bhabha, Dr H. J., 212
Bhadrapur, 188
Bhainse Dhoban, 57
Bhalja, G. S., 29
Bhandara, 130, 205
Bharat Electronics, 127
Bhatia, Prem, 113n.
Bhutan, 52, 66, 69, 88, 174, 187, 209; as part of British India's 'inner ring', 9; Chinese claims to, 42, 187; India's relations with, 53-54, 76-78; road construction in, 73, 74; Indian contingency military planning for, 77, 87, 98, 175, 178
Bhutias, 75
Bombay, 18, 26, 27, 102, 116-123 *passim*
Bombay Province, 32
Bomdila, 49, 88, 99, 175, 177, 183
Border Roads Development Board, 73, 74, 196, 206
Brahmaputra River, 177
Brecher, Michael, 6
Britain, 13-56 *passim*, 107-142 *passim*; personnel in Indian armed forces, 34, 92, 103, 122; Himalayan policy, 52, 209; tanks, 90, 97; military 'tie' with Indian armed services, 97, 152; aircraft in Indian service, 102-105 *passim*, 107, 111, 120, 131, 132, 137, 198; Indian enquiry about guided missiles, 106n.; Menon preference for equipment from, 112; conception of Indian naval requirements, 116; as source of naval vessels for Indian Navy, 118-123 *passim*, 201-202; as source of military aid to India, 181, 194, 201-202, 205; military aid to Nepal, 188; suspends aid to India, 190; Indian desire for nuclear guarantee from, 215
British India: British military liability, 8; defence and foreign policy, 8-20 *passim*; Army, 10-14 *passim*, 17, 18; British troops in, 10, 11, 16, 17n.; Navy, 10, 16, 17, 18; subvention to Royal Navy, 10n., 16; ordnance, 11, 17, 18; defence expenditure, 11, 16, 17; Anglo-Indian Auxiliary Force, 11; Indian Territorial Force, 11; Air Forces, 11, 12, 17, 18; contribution in World War I, 12; Army Reserve, 12, 17; British subsidy to defence of, 16; State Forces, 17n.; contribution in World War II, 18; lessons of World War II for, 19; contingency plans for postwar defence of, 20
Bum La, 175
Burla, 205, 206
Burma, 26, 38, 42, 62, 108, 110, 156

Cabinet, 110, 146-162 *passim*, 193; Secretariat of, 72; Defence Committee of, 89, 127, 144, 146; Ministers of, 159; Emergency Committee of, 181
Cairo, 204
Calcutta, 18, 77, 86, 88, 108, 114, 120, 129, 175
Campbell-Johnson, Alan, 20
Canada, 17, 194, 216; aircraft in IAF, 104, 111; military aid to India, 196, 197
Cariappa, Gen K. M., support for joint Indo-Pakistan defence, 69; Nehru's views on, 70
CENTO (Central Treaty Organization), 38, 69
Central Provinces, 32
Central Public Works Department, 74, 206
Central Reserve Police, 87, 97
Ceylon, 26, 173
Chagla, M. C., 215
Chaman, 15
Chandigarh, 99, 130, 203
Chatfield Committee, 16, 18
Chatfield, Lord, 16
Chatra Canal project, 79n.
Chatterji, Vice Adm A. K., 215

INDEX

Chaudhuri, Lt.-Gen. J. N., 164, 177
Chavan, Y. B., 181, 200, 201, 202
Chhamb, 189
Chiang Kai-shek, 171
Chibber, S. L., 75
China, Manchu, 209
China, Nationalist, 14, 22-27 *passim*, 31
China, People's Republic of, 5, 6, 38-217 *passim;* military forces of, 1, 3, 47-217 *passim;* Indian view of, 5, 26, 27, 40-45 *passim,* 47, 62-69 *passim,* 70, 71; entry into Tibet, 5, 38, 47, 51, 54, 84, 95; territorial claims against India, 41-42, 63-64, 187; claims against Bhutan, 42, 54, 187; relations with Nepal, 59-60, 79-81, 188; intrusions into territory claimed by India, 62-68 *passim,* 169-174 *passim;* seizure of Bhutanese enclaves in Tibet, 76; India's response to intrusion by, 169-179 *passim,* 182-188 *passim*
China Pictorial, 64
Chini, 50
Chip Chap River, 169, 170
Chittagong, 124
Chou En-lai, 47, 63, 64, 68, 80
Chushul, 51, 74, 87, 99, 169, 174, 175, 177
Civilian-military relations, 141-168
Cochin, 116, 120, 123, 124
Coimbatore, 122
Colemn, 101
Commonwealth, 19, 31n., 116, 123, 152, 194; Third Unofficial Relations Conference, 26
Commonwealth Aircraft Corporation (Australia), 111n.
Communications. *See* Strategic roads
Communism and communists, 2, 39-43 *passim,* 83, 153-157 *passim,* 208
Compagnie de Telegraphie sans Fils, 127
Confederation of Himalayan States, proposed by China, 187
Congo, 3, 142, 170
Congress party: attitude toward World War I, 21; attitude toward British Indian defence and foreign policies, 21-25; adopts Gandhi's policy of non-co-operation with British, 22; Working Committee of, 22; Kerala Provincial Conference, 22; seeks to capitalize upon Japanese threat, 25; views of leadership on role of free India, 26; change in view of Gurkha Rifles, 94; leadership view of Thimayya proposals for Himalayan defence, 96; Parliamentary Party of, 130; attitude towards Indian National Army, 142; prejudice against armed forces, 148n.; hostility to Menon, 150, 166; demands for dismissal of Menon, 179-180
Constitution, Article 53 (2) of, 144
Cook, Hope, 76
Criminal Law Amendment Act (1961), 72
Current (Bombay), 164
Curzon, Lord, 10, 25

Dabolim, 202
Dacca, 14
Daily Express (London), 149
Daily Telegraph (London), 149, 163
Daimler-Benz, 128, 130
Dalai Lama, 43, 171; flight from Lhasa to asylum in India, 64, 66; symbolic importance of, 65; Indian attitude towards, 81, 209
Dalvi, Brig.-Gen. J. P., 175
Dambur Guru, 169
Darjeeling, 53
Darjeeling-Duars district, proposed by China, 187
Daulet Beg Oldi, 87, 169, 174, 176
Defence: expenditure, 4, 5, 30, 39, 61, 84n., 193; planning, 5, 8-20 *passim,* 29-38 *passim,* 68-69, 187-189, 192-193; industries, 28-29, 126-140, 193, 203-207. *See also* Air Force; Army; Navy
Defence Department, 145n., 150n.
Defence Minister's (Research and Development) Committee, 127
Defence, Ministry of, 35, 46-49 *passim,* 82-96 *passim,* 100-107 *passim,* 127-132 *passim,* 139, 140, 145-148 *passim,* 162, 167, 173, 181, 198, 199, 212
Defence of India Ordinance, 178
Defence Production, Ministry of, 179, 199
Defence Production Board, 128
Defence Research and Development Organization (DRDO), 127
Defence Research Policy Board, 127
Defence Science Advisory Committee, 127
Defence Science Organization, 127, 137

Defence Science Service, 127
Defence Services Staff College, 165
Dehra Compass, 169
Dehra Dun, 12, 13, 96
Delhi, 75, 78, 86, 105, 114, 119, 132, 190
Demchok, 51, 99
Desai, Morarji, 148
Dhantok, 73
Dhebar, U. N., 179
Dhola, 99, 172, 173, 174, 186
Dibrugarh, 175
Digboi oil fields, 177
Directorate of Combat Development, 195
Directorate of Planning and Co-ordination, 205
Dogra, 32, 94
Dorji, Prime Minister, of Bhutan, 76–77
Dras, 33, 99
Dum Dum, 11
Dungti, 74
Dunkirk, 178
Durand Line, 16, 213
Dwarka, 190

East Bengal, 213
Eastern Hills State, proposed by China, 187
East India Company, 10
East Pakistan, 36, 37, 69, 84, 87, 98, 108, 187. *See also* Pakistan
East Punjab, 51, 86. *See also* Punjab
Economist (London), 173
Elmhirst, Air Marshall Sir Thomas, 109n.
English Electric, 104
English language, 103
Estimates Committee, 145
Executive Council, 144
Expert Committee on Ordnance Factories, 28
External Affairs, Ministry of, 39, 43, 47–53 *passim*, 62

Fairchild Aircraft Company transports, 103, 105, 111
Fairey Firefly target-tug aircraft, 120
Federation of Bhutan and Sikkim, proposed by China, 187
Ferozepore, 85, 175
Finance, Ministry of, 199, 211
Finland, 91
Five Principles. *See* Panch sheel

Five Year Plans, 46; Second, 72, 120; Third, 72, 73, 90, 130; Fourth, 193
Focke–Wulf, 133
Folland Aircraft, 131
Foothills (town), 48, 177, 178
France, 23, 127; Brandt mortar purchased from, 89n., 91, 203; AMX tanks purchased from, 90; aircraft types in IAF, 102–104 *passim*, 108, 111; possible source of jet aircraft, 107, 112, 198; Indian interest in nuclear guarantee from, 215

Gadra, 190
Gallen, 67
Galwan River, 172
Gandak Irrigation Project, 79
Gandhi, Mohandas K., 22, 25n., 143, 210; precepts of, 152
Gangtok, 52, 53, 74, 75, 87, 99, 175
Garden Reach Workshops Ltd., 135, 136
Garhwalis, 94
Garubhada, 54
Gauchar, 57
Gauhati, 183
Gaza Strip, 3, 142, 158
Gazette of India, 72
General Reserve Engineering Force, 73
General Staff Branch, 195
Germany, 13, 14, 23, 90, 129, 130, 133
Ghatage, Dr V. M., 132, 133
Ghaziabad, 196
Goa, 3, 123, 142, 170, 210; crisis over, 100–101
Gorakjpur, 50
Government College, 13
Government of India Act, 13
Grampjoo, 50
Gurdaspur, 85
Gurkha Rifles, 82, 94
Gurkhas, 54, 188, 194
Gurkhistan, proposed by China, 187
Gurung Hill, 176
Gwalior, 86
Gyani, Maj.-Gen. P. S., 157, 158

Hatisar, 54
Hatung Pass, 174
Hawker Siddeley Aircraft Company, 105, 132
Helmand River, 11
High Altitude Warfare School, 96, 194. *See also* Army

Himalayan kingdoms. *See* Bhutan; Nepal; and Sikkim
Himalayas, 24, 42, 56, 87, 111, 171, 209, 210
Himachal Pradesh, 49, 68; border district established in, 71, 72; road project in, 73; development scheme in, 206
Hindan, 196
Hindi language, 97
Hindu (Madras), 174
Hindus and Hinduism, 69, 142
Hindustan Aeronautics India Ltd., 204
Hindustan Aircraft Limited, 18, 102, 104, 131–137 *passim*, 198
Hindustani language, 97
Hindustan Machine Tools, 137
Hindustan Motors, 129
Hindustan Shipyard Ltd., 120
Hindustan–Tibet Road, 50
Home Affairs, Ministry of, 46, 206
Home Guard, 202
Hot Springs, 169
Hughes missiles, 106
Hungarian revolution, 62
Hyderabad, 3, 31, 82, 142; Nizam of, 32

Ilyushin aircraft, 104, 105, 112, 113
Imperial Defence College, 152
Imperial Defence Committee, 13
Imperial Reserve, 16, 17
India. *See* Air Force; Army: Defence; Navy; etc.
India Sandhurst Committee, 13
Indian Communist Party, 39, 178; insurrection by, 83. *See also* Communism and communists
Indian Conciliation Group, 23
Indian Frontier Administrative Service, 47, 71
Indian Institute of Science, 133
Indian Military Academy, 13, 93
Indian National Army, 142
Indian Ocean, 4, 9, 26, 27, 38, 117, 122, 123, 125, 211, 215
Indian Territorial Force, 12
Indian Tibet Boundary Force, 68
Indo-China, 142
Indonesia, 26, 123, 125, 197, 215
Industrial Resolution Policy, 126
Infantry School, 96, 194. *See also* Army
Institute of Armament Studies, 127
Intelligence Bureau, 48 and n.
Irish Independent (Dublin), 210

Ishapore, 11
Israel, 79, 92
Italy, 14, 18, 23, 119, 123

Jaipur, 86
Jalalabad, 14, 15
Jaldhaka River, 78
Jalpaiguri, 74
Jammu, 33
Jammu (town), 34
Jammu and Kashmir (Ladakh), 68
Jammu and Kashmir State Militia, 97, 174
Jang, 176
Jan Sangh, 69
Japan, 13–25 *passim*, 128, 130, 201
Jara La, 174
Jayanti, 54
Jenmin Jihpao, 171
Jhangar, 33
Jhansi, 86, 176
Jodhpur, 86
Joint Defence Council, 31
Jorhat, 87
Jubbulpore, 129
Jullundur, 85, 175
Junagadh, 3, 31, 32, 142
Jungle Warfare School, 96

Kabul, 11, 13, 15
Kalimpong, 75, 87, 175
Kandahar, 13, 14, 15
Kandaiwala, 50
Kanpur, 11, 102, 114, 132, 196
Karachi, 18, 27, 36, 37, 102, 124, 190
Karakoram Pass, 87, 99, 169, 171, 174
Karmakar, Rear Adm S. G., 215
Kashmir, 31, 32–37, 50, 51, 60, 69, 82–86 *passim*, 90, 98, 106, 113, 114, 138, 142, 150–157 *passim*, 187–191 *passim*, 196, 210–216 *passim*
Kasur, 190
Katanga, 4
Katari, Vice Adm R. D., 121, 122, 159, 160, 163
Kathmandu, 55, 79, 80, 81
Katju, N. N., 120, 148, 149
Kaul, Lt.-Gen. Brij Mohan, 156–158, 163–173 *passim*, 177, 183, 186
Kechilang River, 174
Kennedy, John F., 107
Keskar, B. V., 44
Keylong, 50
Khalatse, 33

Kham, 64
Khamaria, 203
Khampas, 42, 66, 80, 158
Khan, Liaquat Ali, 84
Khan, Field Marshal Mohammad Ayub, 66–70 *passim*, 154, 160, 189, 191
Khan, Sir Mohammad Zafrullah, 26, 35
Khasali, 85, 175
Khinzemane, 67, 175
Khyber, 15, 16
Kibithoo, 100, 175
Kirby, S. Woodburn, 19n.
Kirki, 11, 127
Kitchener, Lord, 10
Kitchener College, 13
Koderi Pass, 81
Koirala, B. P., 58, 59, 79, 80
Koirala, M. P., 57, 58
Komatsu tractors, 128, 136
Korea, 95, 142, 157
Korean Custodian Force, 164
Korean War, 84, 118
Kotli, 33
Krishnamachari, T. T., 181
Krishna Menon, V. K., 77, 133, 186; political appeal of, 5; on re-equipment, 91; on Himalayan defence, 96, 170, 171, 173; on MIG's, 106, 107; initiative on Hunter purchase, 109; preference for British equipment and bias against French, 112; and indigenous defence industries, 133, 134, 139–140; appointment to Defence portfolio, 148, 149–150; dispute with Thimayya, 154–168 *passim*; removal from Defence Ministry and Cabinet, 179–180; Nehru's assessment of, 180–181; views on Indian nuclear weapons, 215
Kulu, 206
Kulu Valley, 50
Kumaon Hills, 50
Kumaramangalam, Lt.-Gen P. S., 157, 158, 164
Kuomintang, 41, 42, 43. *See also* China, Nationalist
Kutch, 86. *See also* Rann of Kutch

Ladakh: initial Indian interest in, 50–51; Aksai Chin road in, 64; Chinese threat to, 66; Chinese intrusions into, 67, 68, 169; General K. M. Cariappa's views on, 69; development schemes in, 72, 73, 206; contingency military planning for, 87, 88, 98, 99; IAF transport commitments to, 111, 115; Indian response to Chinese intrusions in, 169–171, 185; Chinese military posts in, 171; military operations in, 174, 176; Chinese military gains in, 177; Indian military redeployment in, 178; Chinese claims to, 187
Ladakh Valley, 33
Lahore, 13, 34, 37, 98, 189, 190
Lall, J. S., 52
Laos, 110
League of Nations, India as steward of, 21
Leh, 51, 74, 87, 99, 174, 175, 178, 206
Lepchas, 75
Levy Auto Parts of Canada Ltd., 90
Lhasa, 64, 75
Little, D., Inc., 205
Lohit River, 100
Lok Sahayak Sena. *See* National Volunteer Force scheme
London, 23, 131, 132, 173, 182
Longju, 67, 170, 172, 175
Lucknow, 50, 87, 88

McDonnell Aircraft Company, 108, 198
McMahon, Sir A. H., 41
McMahon Line, 41, 47, 49, 64, 67, 88, 173, 182
Macmillan, Sir Harold, 107
Maddox, John, 212
Madhok, Balraj, 69
Madhya Pradesh, 86, 148
Madras, 86, 131, 173, 196
Madrassis, 184
Maharashtra, 181
Mahatab, Dr Harekruchna, 179
Mahendra, King, 79, 80
Mahmud, Dr. (Secretary-General of External Affairs Ministry), 148n.
Mahura, 33
Majithia, S. S., 149
Malaya, 26, 42
Manali, 51, 99, 206
Manchester Guardian, 161, 162
Manekshaw, Lt.-Gen S. H. F. J., 165, 177
Maneri, 101
Mao Tse-tung, 42
Marmagoa, 202
Maschinenfabrik Augsburg–Nurenberg AG, 129

Mazagon Dock Ltd., 135, 136, 201
Menon, V. K. Krishna. See Krishna Menon, V. K.
Mhow, 96
Middle East, 18, 26, 27, 124
Military aid to India, 193–194. *See also* Air Force; Army; Defence: industries; Navy; Strategic roads
Misamari, 87, 175
Mizos, 189. *See also* Tribals
Mokokchung, 74
Mongrol, 32
Montreal Gazette, 149
Moraes, Frank, 167
Mountbatten, Adm. Lord Louis, 117
Mount Blanc, 96
Mt. Everest, 80
Mukerjee, Air Marshall Subroto, appointment of, 103; denies involvement in Thimayya-Menon affair, 155; alleged support of Thimayya action, 159; alleged shift in attitude, 160; subsequent relationship with Thimayya, 163
Muslims, 31, 32, 36n.; exodus from West Bengal, 84; option of officers at partition, 92; representation in Indian Army, 94
Muzaffarabad, 34

Naga Hills District, 71
Naga Hills-Tuensang Frontier Area, 49
Naga Home (Village) Guards, 49
Nagaland: creation of, 72; administration reshuffled in, 72; Interim Body of, 72; troops in, 88; troops withdrawn from, 175; proposed inclusion in Confederation of Himalayan States, 187; IAF logistics support to administration of, 196; Army role in, 211
Nagas: demand self-determination, 3; security forces deployed against, 3, 49, 72, 86, 88, 98; British policy towards, 49; Indian policy towards, 49, 86; attitude towards transfer from British to Indian rule, 49, 189; Army recruitment of, 194
Nagpur, 196
Namgyal, Palden Thondup, 75, 76, 188
Namka Chu River, 99
Nanda, Gulzaril, 192
Naoshera, 33, 34
National Cadet Corps: establishment of, 82; administrative officers in, 93; size of, 97; expansion of, 202
National Congress party. *See* Congress party
National Defence Academy, 57, 93
National Defence College, 146
National Defence Council, 181
National Defence Fund, 178
National Volunteer Force scheme: establishment and possible significance of, 95; numbers trained by, 97; dissolution of, 202
Natu Pass, 53, 87
Navy, 30, 83, 109; size and composition, 4, 116, 122–123; British contingency plans for, 20, 116; Indian plans for, 116–117, 119; operational role, 117; development of, 118–122; Naval Reserve, 122; Naval Volunteer Reserve, 122–123; expansion and re-equipment plans for, 201–202
Nehru, Jawaharlal, 2–6 *passim*, 20, 22, 75, 77, 110, 167, 186, 192; on defence and foreign policy, 22–28 *passim*, 41; on indivisibility of Indian Ocean region, 26–28; on Chinese threat, 43–53 *passim*, 61, 63, 64, 95; trip to Bhutan, 54; trip to Nepal, 55; views on Nepal, 56, 57, 59, 78–81 *passim*; Tibetan policy of, 65–66; views on joint defence, 66, 70; Himalayan policy of, 70–71, 74, 170, 171, 173, 209–210; talks with Liaquat Ali Khan, 84; policy on re-equipment of Army, 89; response to Thimayya proposals for Himalayan defence, 96; Kashmir vacation, 106; talks with Duncan Sandys, 107; naval policy of, 117; on defence industries, 130; attitude towards Defence portfolio, 147, 148, 149; appointment of Menon to Defence, 150; response to Thimayya-Menon dispute, 154–163 *passim*; meeting with Ayub, 160; relationship with Menon, 166; on Chinese attacks, 178; demotion and dismissal of Menon, 179, 180; defence of Menon, 180–181; death of, 191; nuclear policy of, 212
Nepal, 3, 9, 42, 50, 52, 66, 69, 74, 82, 85, 187–188, 207, 209; lends troops to India, 54; India and, 54–60, 78–81, 188; Rana family, 55, 56; Nepali Congress, 55, 56, 81; Indian military personnel

260 INDIA'S QUEST FOR SECURITY

Nepal (continued)
in, 55–58 passim, 188; Royal Army, 56, 57, 58; King Tribhuvan, 56, 58; response to Tibetan developments, 55, 188; Indian economic aid to, 57–58, 79, 81; first Five Year Plan, 57, 59; United States–India–Nepal road project, 57–58; relations with Soviet Union, 59; relations with China, 59–60, 79–81, 188; Nepalese community in Sikkim, 75; King Mahendra, 79–81
Netherlands, 123
New China News Agency, 182
News Chronicle, 161
New Times (Moscow), 64
New York Times, 185
Niagzu, 169
Nicholson Committee, 11
Nicobar Islands, 202, 215
Nissan Motor Company, 90, 130, 136
Nonalignment, rationale for, 39–41
Noon, Penderal, 26
North American Aviation, 109
North and North-Eastern Border Defence Committee, 46
North Bengal, 188. See also Bengal
North-Eastern Frontier Agency: Chinese threat to, 41–42; administration of, 46, 71; Subansiri Frontier Division, 47; Abor and Mishmi Hills district, 47; Indian policy towards, 47–49; security measures in, 48n., 67, 72, 87–88, 98, 99–100, 196; Chinese claims to, 64; entry of Dalai Lama and Tibetan refugees into, 66; Kameng Frontier Division, 66, 99, 172, 176, 177; Longju incident, 67; General Cariappa's proposals to eject Chinese from, 69; Lohit Frontier Division, 72, 100, 175, 177; development of, 73–74, 206; Indian military assessment of Chinese threat to, 87, 170; IAF support capabilities in, 111, 115; 'forward policy' in, 172–174, 185; Sino-Indian conflict in, 174–175, 177; Army's performance in, 183, 184; defence problem of, 213
North Korea, 84. See also Korea
North Sikkim highway, 74, 206
Nowgong, 13, 93

Olangchung, 188
Operation Amar I, 157
Ordnance. See Defence: industries

Ordnance Factories Reorganization Committee, 128

Pakistan, 5, 6, 26, 31, 32, 34, 61, 71; United States military aid to, 5, 106, 109, 110; Army, 33, 34, 82, 82n., 189, 190; and Kashmir conflict, 33–34; as viewed by Indian defence planners, 35–41 passim, 61, 68, 69, 70, 83–88 passim, 98, 102, 114, 123, 124, 153, 167, 176; and joint defence with India, 68, 69, 70, 184; relations with Nepal, 71, 79–80, 81, 188; share of armed forces acquired at partition, 83n., 103n., 116n.; military officers opting for at partition, 92; Air Force, 102n., 106, 109, 110, 114n., 190, 198; Navy, 116n., 124n., 190; Army coup d'etat in, 141; as viewed by Indian Army officers, 152
Pakyang, 74
Palak, 34
Palam, 108
Pamir Boundary Agreement, 10
Panch sheel, 40, 44, 59, 62, 66, 80, 110, 208
Pangdatshang, Topgay, 42
Pangkangting, 174
Pangong Lake, 67, 171, 174
Panikkar, K. M., 20, 43
Pant, Pandit G. B., 161, 162
Panvel, 205, 206
Paranjpe, Maj.-Gen. Y. S., 147
Paro, 74
Parry, Vice Adm. W. E., 117, 118, 119
Patel, H. M., 83n., 144, 145, 148
Patel, Sardar Vallabhbhai, 2n.
Pathankot, 33
Pathans. See Tribals: North-West Frontier
Patil, S. K., 149
Patterson, George, 81
Pay Code, 143
Payyanur, 22
Peking Review, 171
Persia, 9, 10, 22
Persian Gulf, 38; sheikhdoms of, 9
Peshawar, 69, 98
Phuntsholing, 74
Pillai, Sir N. R., 2
Pioneer, 44
Pioneer Corps, 84
Pizey, Adm. Sir Mark, 119
Planning Commission, 72, 75, 78, 193

INDEX 261

Polem, 101
Police, 46, 97, 142
Poonch, 33, 34, 189; Muslims of, 36n.
Port Blair, 202
Portugal, 181
Praga Tools, 203
Praja Pareshad Party, 58
Prasad, Rajendra, 60, 83, 162
Prasad, Tanka, 58
Premier Automobiles, 129
Press Trust of India (PTI), 154, 161
Prince of Wales Royal Indian Military College, 12
Public Accounts Committee, 144, 197
Public Law 480, 78n., 140
Public Works Development Organization (PWDO), 49
Punakha, 77
Punjab, 33–37 passim, 49, 50, 68, 137, 144, 177, 206; border districts established in, 71; development schemes in, 72–73, 86, 88, 98, 114, 176, 195, 213. See also East Punjab
Punjab Force, 85, 89, 98. See also Army
Punjab Security of the State Act, 71

Quetta, 37

Radhakrishnan, Dr S. S., 180, 200
Radio Nepal, 81
Radio Peking, 178
Raghuramaiah, K., 181
Rajagopalachari, C. S., 35
Rajasthan, 36, 37, 86, 98, 213
Rajendrasinjhi, Gen. M., 129
Rajputs, 94
Ranald, Capt. H. C., 117n.
Ranchi, 88, 175
Rangiya, 175
Rann of Kutch, 189
Rao, V. R. P., 181
Rashtriya Swayamsevak Singh. See National Volunteer Force scheme
Rawalpindi, 33, 37, 98, 190
Reddy, O. Pulla, 181
Regmi, D. R., 59
Reid, Escott, 6n.
Renmin Ribao, 172
Reserve Bank of India, 54
Rezang La, 176
Rolls-Royce Company, 132, 205
Rome-Berlin Axis, 14
Rosenthal, A. M., 185
Round Table (London), 212

Royal Air Force: creation of, 11; re-establishment of, 12; size and composition of, 102; transfer of aircraft, 107; carries emergency military aid to India, 182
Royal Australian Air Force, 111n.
Royal Indian Air Force, 102, 103. See also Air Force
Royal Indian Marine, 12
Royal Indian Navy, 116, 122. See also Navy
Royal Military College, 12
Royal Navy, 16; and defence of India, 10; inability to provide fleet aircraft to Indian Navy, 118; as source of aircraft carriers, 118; warships acquired by India from, 119, 120; cooperation in development of IN, 122, 123, 211; loan of submarine by, 202; former East Indies squadron of, 211
Royal Nepal Army. See Nepal: Royal Army
Russia (Czarist), 10, 11, 13. See also Soviet Union

Sadiya, 73
Sainik schools, 93
Sainwala, 50
Sandhurst, 12, 156
Sandys, Duncan, 107
Sasar Brangsa Pass, 176
Savantvadi, 100–101
Science Research and Development Organization, 127
SEATO (Southeast Asia Treaty Organization), 38, 69
Sechang Lake, 174
Secunderabad, 86, 203
Security Force, 63
Security Intelligence Services, 48
Se La, 176, 177, 183
Sen, Lt.-Gen. L. P., 130, 164, 186
Sentula, 54
Shahjahanpur, 11
Shastri, Lal Bahadur, 191
Shillong, 196
Shipbuilding, 18. See also Defence: industries
Shipki Pass, 62–63
Sholapur, 32
Shrinagesh, Gen. S. M., 71
Shyok Valley, 87
Sialkot, 37, 189, 190
Siam, 9, 14

Sicily, 18
Sikhs, 32, 94, 147, 149, 152
Sikkim, 3, 54, 66, 68, 69, 87, 98, 174, 177, 209; as part of British 'inner ring', 9; Chinese threat to 'liberate', 42; development plan, 52; India's relations with, 52-53, 74-76, 188-189; road construction in, 73-74; Indian military contingency planning for, 88; militia, 99; Indian troop deployment in, 99, 175; Chinese proposal for inclusion in Confederation of Himalayan States, 187
Sikkimese Subjects' Regulation legislation, 75n.
Siliguri, 87, 99
Simla, 41, 47, 50
Sind, 190
Singapore, 123, 211
Singh, Maj.-Gen. Atma, 33
Singh, B. K. P., 179
Singh, C. P. N., 58
Singh, Lt.-Gen. Daulat, 164
Singh, Air Vice-Marshal Harjinder, 108, 136n.
Singh, Dr K. I., 56, 60
Singh, Maj.-Gen. Kalwant, 32
Singh, Lt.-Gen. Mohinder, 164
Singh, Raghunath, 179
Singh, Maj.-Gen. Sardanand, 181
Singh, Sardar Baldev, 31, 35, 84, 102, 128, 147, 148
Singh, Maj.-Gen. Umrao, 173n.
Soman, Vice Adm. B. S., 122
South Africa, 181
Southeast Asia, 18, 19, 24-27 passim, 38, 83, 110, 155, 214, 215
Southern Asia, 27. See also Asia; Asian Federation
South Korea, 84. See also Korea; Korean Custodian Force; Korean War
Soviet bloc, 214; submarines, 117, 211
Soviet Union, 13-41 passim; Indian interest in and purchases of Soviet aircraft, 104-113 passim, 134, 138, 167, 196; attitude on Indo-Pakistan conflict, 190; as source of military aid, 194; purchase of light tanks from, 195; MIG project, 199-200; offer of frigates by, 201; rumoured collaboration in tank project, 203; possible response to Indian nuclear weapons programme, 216
Spanggur, 67, 171, 176

Srinagar, 32, 33, 51, 99, 206
State Forces, 82, 84, 142
Statesman, The (New Delhi), 154, 161
Strategic roads, 48-54 passim, 57-58, 72-78 passim, 206-207
Suez, 19, 211
Survey of India, 78
Sweden, 201

Tank, Dr. Kurt, 133
Tashigang, 74
Tashkent, 190, 191
Tata, J. R. D., 204
Tata Iron and Steel Company, 128
Tawang, 47, 87, 88, 98, 99, 173, 175
Tawang Chu River, 176
TELCO, 129
Territorial Army: creation, 82-83; size and composition, 97; role during emergency, 176; reorganization, 202
Territorial Army (Amendment) Bill, 83
Tezpur, 49, 87, 88, 99, 173, 177, 180, 183
Thag La Ridge, 172, 173, 186
Thankot, 57
Thapar, Lt.-Gen. P. N., 164, 177, 186
Thimayya, Gen. K. S., 33, 96, 172; dispute with Menon, 154-155, 158-163
Thorat, Lt.-Gen. S. P. P., 164
Thought (New Delhi), 5
Tibet, 42, 43, 49, 50, 65, 74, 184, 195; Chinese entry into, 5, 38, 47, 54, 84, 95; as part of British India's 'outer ring', 9; Chinese view of Indian treaty rights in, 41; Tibetan view of McMahon Line, 41; Chinese policies towards, 42, 110; Indian view of Chinese policies in, 43, 44, 61, 65, 209-210; Sino-Indian agreement on, 44; revolt in, 64, 65, 76, 78, 158, 171; Indian response to revolt, 65-66; refugees from, 66, 76, 78, 81; Chinese restrictions on Indians in, 67; Chinese infrastructure in, 113, 115, 217; British response to Chinese policies in, 209
Tilak, B. G., 21
Time and Tide (London), 61
Times of India (New Delhi), 44, 173
Times, The (London), 155, 212
Tinker, Hugh, 166-167n., 210
Tiruchirapalli, 205
Tithwal, 34

INDEX 263

Transport, Ministry of, 46, 48
Tribals, 9, 11, 33–40 *passim*, 98, 208, 213; in Kashmir, 3; in Nagaland, 3; on North-West Frontier, 10–16 *passim*, 21–25 *passim*, 32; tribal levies on North-West Frontier, 17n., 25n.
Trivedi, C. L., 150n.
Trombay nuclear reactor, 216
Tshombe, Moishe, 4
Tuensang area, 71. *See also* Naga Hills–Tuensang Frontier Area
Tungabhadra River, 32
Turkey, 22
Tyagi, Mahavir, 148, 151, 179

United Arab Republic, 204
United Kingdom. *See* Britain
United Nations, 3, 34, 43, 44, 113, 160, 162; observers from, 34; Security Council, 34, 156; General Assembly, 150; Repatriation Commission, 157; UNEF, 158; ceasefire in Kashmir sponsored by, 190
United States, 23, 24, 26, 73, 106, 107; as source of military equipment for India, 17, 90, 91; as source of aircraft for IAF, 102–105 *passim*, 110, 111, 112, 198–200; Indian technical delegation tour of, 105; Indian interest in missiles from, 105–106; Congress, 106–107; State Department, 106, 108, 199; relations with Pakistan, 109, 110, 213; economic aid to India, 112; naval role in Indian Ocean, 123; mutual aid funds, 134n.; Army Air Force, 137; grain shipments to India, 140; Indian military views on, 152–153; military aid to India, 182, 196, 214; Export-Import Bank, 199; response to Indian naval requests, 201; as source of aid for HF-24 project, 205; provides ammunition factory to India, 206; as source of nuclear guarantee for India, 215
Upshi, 206
Uri, 33, 189
Uttar Pradesh, 49–50, 68, 148, 195, 206; border districts in, 71, 72

Varangaon, 205
Vartak (Tusker), 73
Vellodi, M. K., 148
Venderuthy, 120
Verma, Lt.-Gen. S. D., 164
Vickers–Armstrong, 90, 130, 203
Viet Nam, 110
Vijay, Operation, 100
Vizakhapatnam, 202

Walong, 100, 175, 176, 183
War Office, British, 13
Warrant of Precedence, 143
Wat Thana, 14
Waziristan, 15
West Pakistan. *See* Pakistan
World War I: India in, 11–12; Congress attitude following, 22
World War II, 29, 30, 41; demobilization of Army personnel following, 85, 93; organizational changes introduced during, 94; salvage yards from, 102; officers recruited during, 151; British offer of submarine dating from, 202; responsibilities of Army before, 211

Yatung, 54
Yugoslavia, 123

Zinkin, Taya, 166n.
Ziro, 48, 49
Zoji La Pass, 33, 51

MAPS

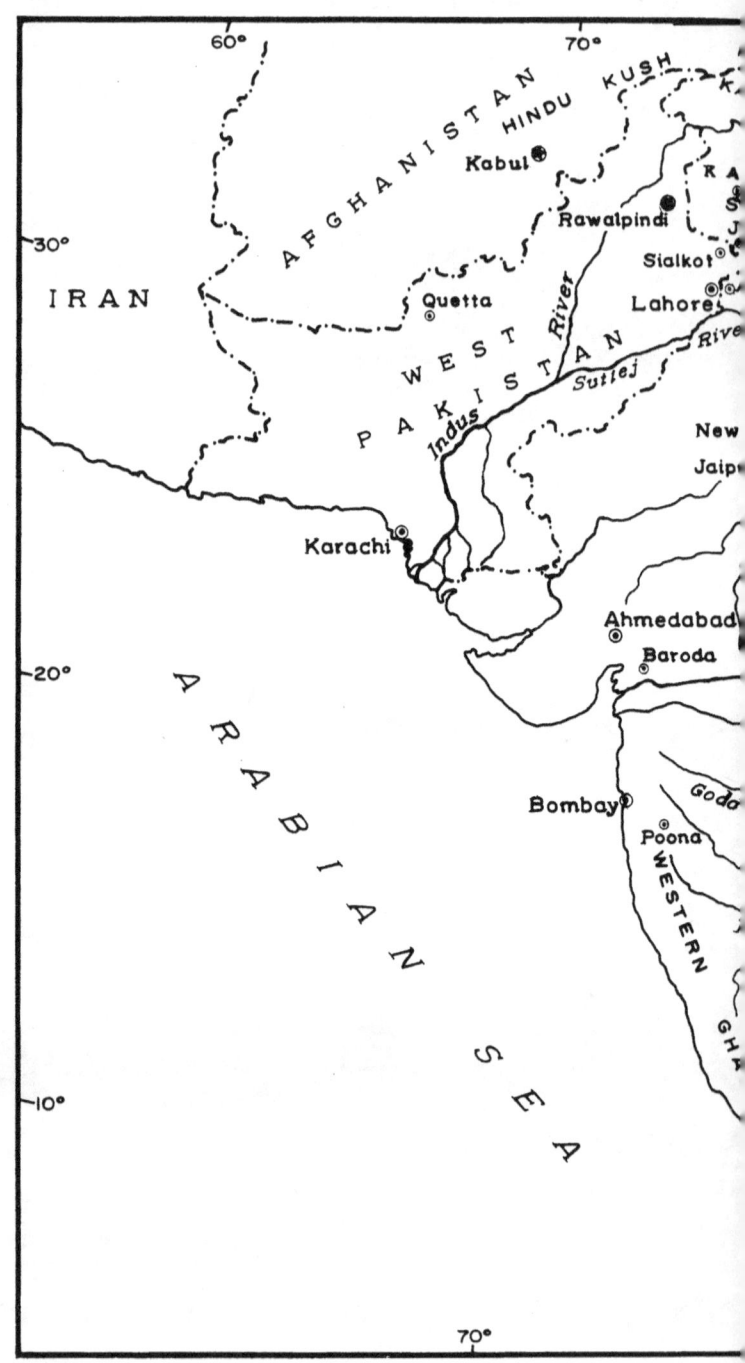

Map 1. India.

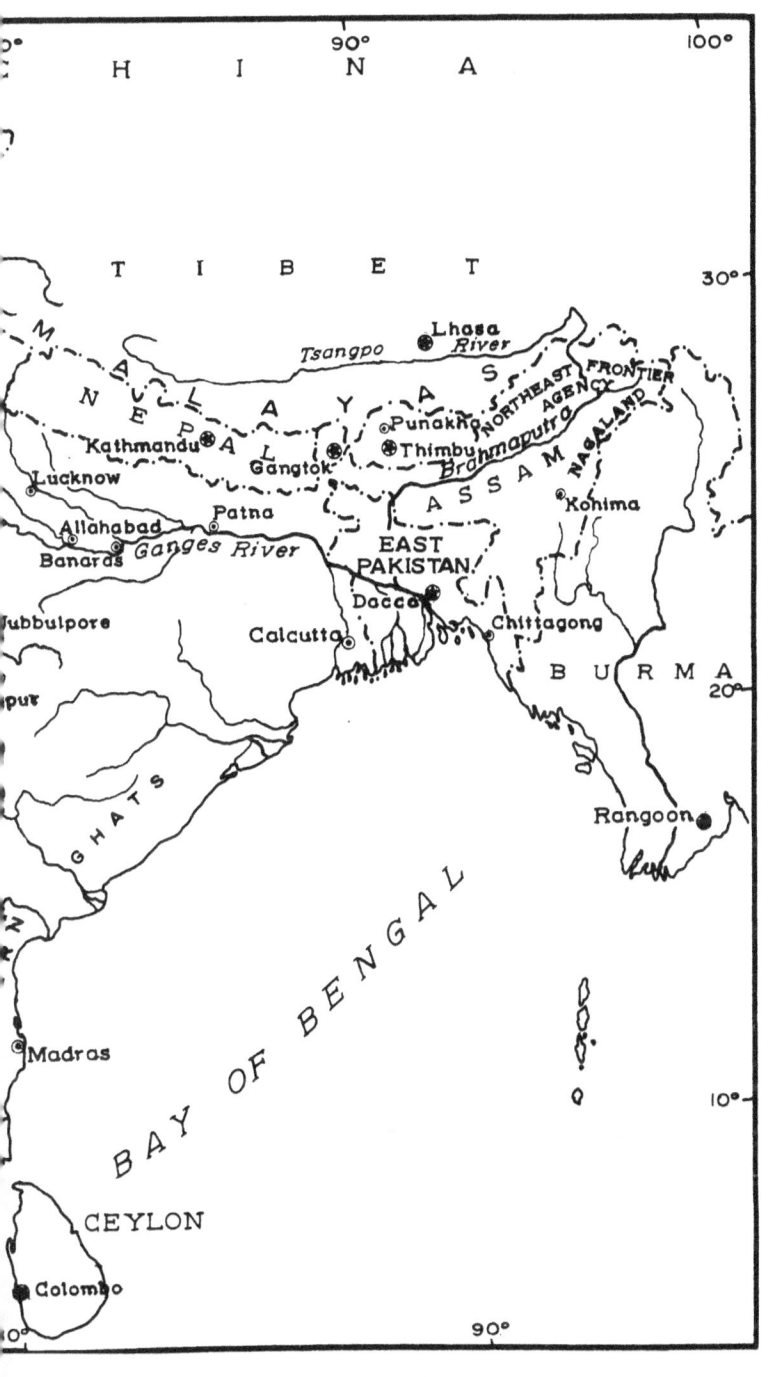

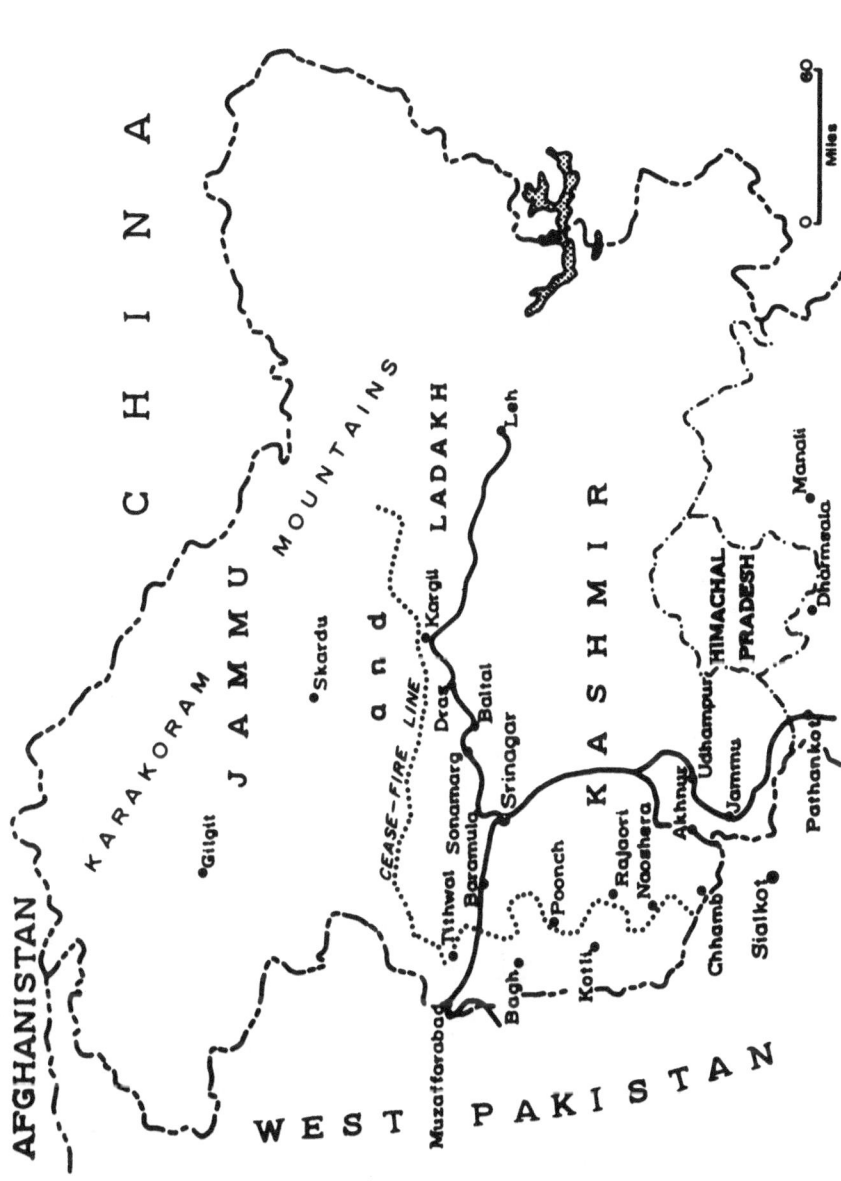

Map 2. Jammu and Kashmir.

Map 3. The Indo-Chinese boundary, 1950-51. For enlargement of eastern sector, see map 6. (Redrawn from 1960 Survey of India map, published by the Ministry of External Affairs)

Map 4. Alleged Chinese border violations, 1955-62. (Compiled from *White Papers: Notes, Memoranda, and Letters Exchanged Between the Governments of India and China, 1954-1963* [New Delhi: Ministry of External Affairs], nos. I-VIII)

1. Bara Hoti
2. Damzan
3. Nelang
4. Shipki La
5. Walong
6. Khurnak Fort
7. Aksai Chin area
8. Lohit Frontier Division
9. Sangcha Malla
10. Lapthal
11. Western Pangong Lake
12. Khinzemane
13. Longju
14. Kongka La
15. Taktsang Gompa
16. Jelep La
17. Hot Springs
18. Chushul
19. Chemokarpola
20. Niagzu
21. Dambur Guru
22. Point 78°12' E. 35°19' N.
23. Roi Village
24. Chip Chap
25. Sumdo
26. Spanggur
27. Road from point 78°35' E. 35°33" N. to 78°8' E., 34°33' N.
28. Point 78°15' E., 35°15'30" N.
29. Galwan Valley
30. Chip Chap, Chang Chenmo and Pangong regions
31. Thag La Ridge
32. Dhola region

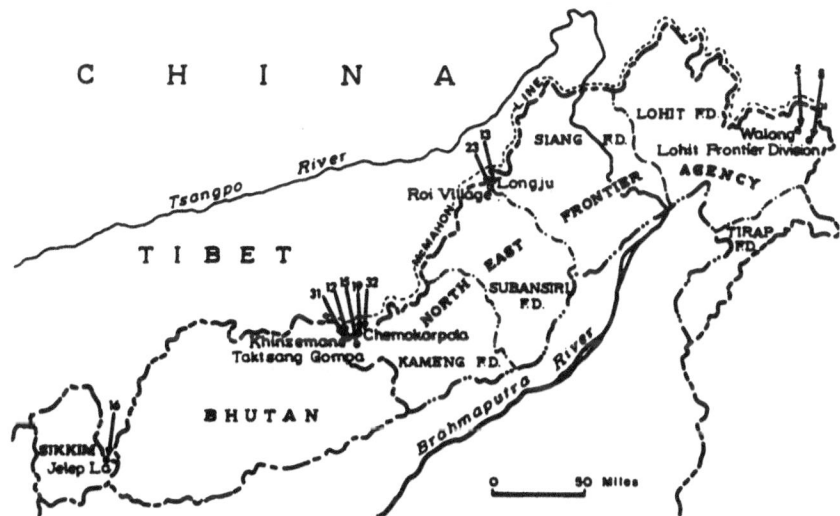

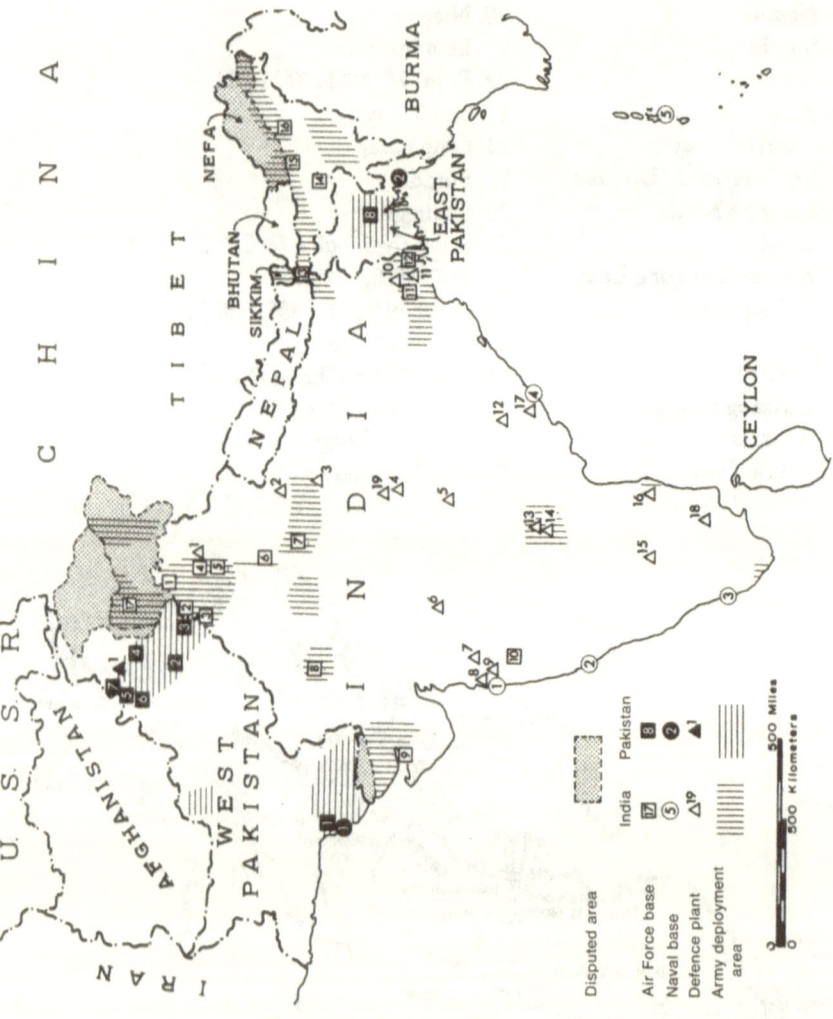

MAP 5. Indian and Pakistani military dispositions and defence plants, 1965.

INDIA

Air Force Bases

1. Pathankot
2. Amritsar
3. Ferozepore
4. Chandigarh
5. Ambala
6. New Delhi
7. Agra
8. Jodhpur
9. Jamnagar
10. Poona
11. Kharagpur
12. Kalaikunda
13. Baghdogra
14. Shillong
15. Tezpur
16. Jorhat
17. Madras

Naval Bases

1. Bombay
2. Marmagoa (proposed)
3. Cochin
4. Visakhapatnam (proposed)
5. Port Blair (proposed)

Defence Plants

1. Chandigarh
2. Shahjahanpur
3. Kanpur
4. Jubbulpore
5. Bhandara
6. Varangaon
7. Nasik
8. Kirki
9. Bombay
10. Ishapore
11. Calcutta
12. Koraput
13. Secunderabad
14. Hyderabad
15. Bangalore
16. Avadi
17. Visakhapatnam
18. Tiruchirapalli
19. Khamaria

other sites

Ambajahari (in Maharashtra state)
Aruvankadu (in Madras)
Ambarnath (in Bombay state)
Muradnagar (in Uttar Pradesh)

PAKISTAN

Air Force Bases

1. Karachi
2. Sargodha
3. Lahore
4. Rawalpindi
5. Peshawar
6. Kohat
7. Risalpur
8. Dacca

Naval Bases

1. Karachi
2. Chittagong

Defence Plants

1. Wah

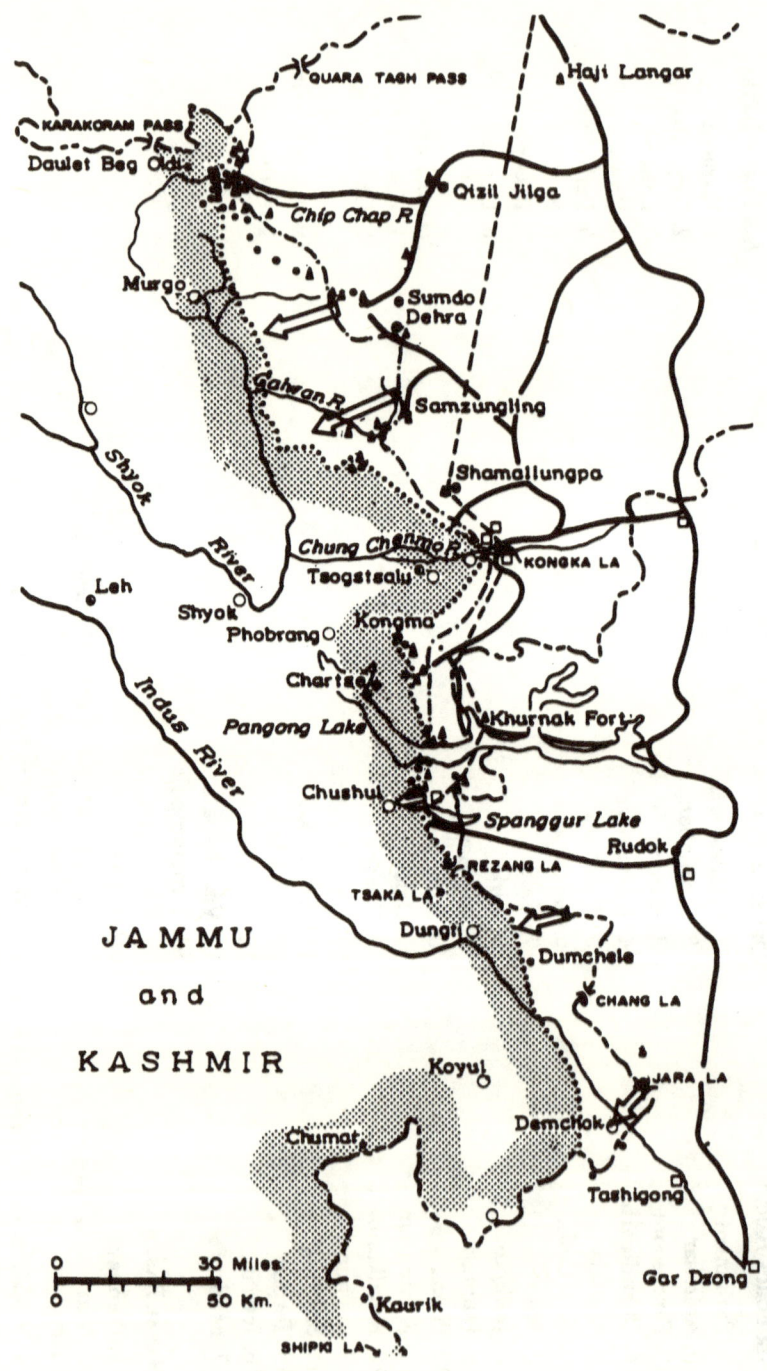

MAP 6. The Indo-Chinese conflict, 1962. (Compiled from official Indian and Chinese maps)

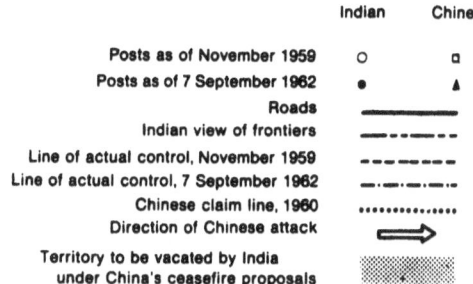
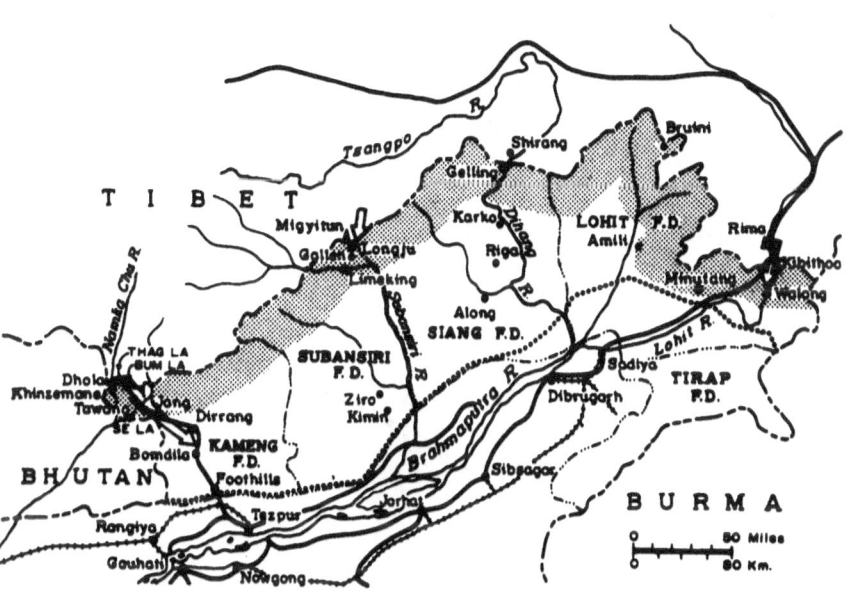

MAP 7. The Indo-Pakistan conflict, 1965.

www.ingramcontent.com/pod-product-compliance
Lightning Source LLC
Chambersburg PA
CBHW021655230426
43668CB00008B/632